SOUTH-NORTH DIALOGUES ON DEMOCRACY, DEVELOPMENT AND SUSTAINABILITY

This book shows how bringing together experts from the Global South and the Global North can help us to understand and combat global economic, political, and social inequalities. For too long, the world's problems have been viewed through the narrow conceptual lenses of the Global North. This book lays the groundwork for a new approach – a truly global approach to political economy.

We are currently facing multiple and overlapping international crises. The current economic crisis, characterized by deepening inequalities, is closely intertwined with intensifying geopolitical rivalries and the environmental crisis. The dialogues in this book aim to move beyond the Eurocentric tradition and bring voices from the Global South to the forefront of the debate. Covering 11 key themes drawn from the United Nations' Agenda 2030, the book conceptualizes democracy, development, and sustainability not only as strategies, but also as values that are integrated into the same – and continuously changing – analytical process.

This book will be of great interest to students, researchers, and experts in international relations, global development, and international political economy, and to anyone looking for new perspectives on pernicious problems.

Cristina Fróes de Borja Reis is Assistant Professor of the Bachelor of Economics at the UFABC, currently the director of the Innovation office at the Federal University of ABC (UFABC/ Brazil), and counselor at the Regional Council of the Economists – Sao Paulo State, Brazil. She was the former coordinator of NEEDDS/UFABC, which organized the dialogues presented in this book. She completed her BA in Economics from the University of São Paulo (USP, 2003),

Master's degree (2008) and PhD (2013) in Economics of Industry and Technology from the Federal University of Rio de Janeiro (UFRJ).

Tatiana Berringer is Assistant Professor of the Bachelor of International Relations at the UFABC and vice-coordinator of NEEDDS/UFABC. She completed her BA in International Relations at Universidade Estadual Paulista (UNESP, 2007), Master's degree and PhD in Political Science at Unicamp. She is author of the book *Brazilian Bourgeoisie and Foreign Policy* (2023).

Rethinking Development

Rethinking Development offers accessible and thought-provoking overviews of contemporary topics in international development and aid. Providing original empirical and analytical insights, the books in this series push thinking in new directions by challenging current conceptualizations and developing new ones.

This is a dynamic and inspiring series for all those engaged with today's debates surrounding development issues, whether they be students, scholars, policy makers, and practitioners internationally. These interdisciplinary books provide an invaluable resource for discussion in advanced undergraduate and postgraduate courses in development studies as well as in anthropology, economics, politics, geography, media studies, and sociology.

COVID-19 and Foreign Aid
Nationalism and Global Development in a New World Order
Edited by Viktor Jakupec, Max Kelly and Michael de Percy

Critical Approaches to Heritage for Development
Edited by Charlotte Cross and John Giblin

Disability and International Development, 2nd edition
A Guide for Students and Practitioners
David Cobley

Researching Development NGOs
Global and Grassroots Perspectives
Edited by Susannah Pickering-Saqqa

South-North Dialogues on Democracy, Development and Sustainability
Edited by Cristina Fróes de Borja Reis and Tatiana Berringer

For more information about this series, please visit: www.routledge.com/Rethinking-Development/book-series/RDVPT

SOUTH-NORTH DIALOGUES ON DEMOCRACY, DEVELOPMENT AND SUSTAINABILITY

Edited by
Cristina Fróes de Borja Reis and Tatiana Berringer

Routledge
Taylor & Francis Group
LONDON AND NEW YORK

Designed cover image: Mariana Zanetti

First published 2023
by Routledge
4 Park Square, Milton Park, Abingdon, Oxon OX14 4RN

and by Routledge
605 Third Avenue, New York, NY 10158

Routledge is an imprint of the Taylor & Francis Group, an informa business

British Library Cataloguing-in-Publication Data
A catalogue record for this book is available from the British Library

Library of Congress Cataloging-in-Publication Data
Names: Fróes de Borja Reis, Cristina, editor. | Berringer, Tatiana, editor.
Title: South-North dialogues on democracy, development and sustainability / edited by Cristina Fróes de Borja Reis and Tatiana Berringer.
Description: New York, NY : Routledge, 2023. |
Series: Rethinking development | Includes bibliographical references and index.
Identifiers: LCCN 2022057684 (print) | LCCN 2022057685 (ebook) |
ISBN 9781032470443 (hardback) | ISBN 9781032470436 (paperback) |
ISBN 9781003384366 (ebook)
Subjects: LCSH: Economic development. | Economic development Developing countries. | Developing countries—Economic policy—21 century. | Sustainable development—Developing countries. | International relations. | Democracy.
Classification: LCC HD82 .S69 2023 (print) | LCC HD82 (ebook) |
DDC 339.5—dc23/eng/20230206
LC record available at https://lccn.loc.gov/2022057684
LC ebook record available at https://lccn.loc.gov/2022057685

ISBN: 978-1-032-47044-3 (hbk)
ISBN: 978-1-032-47043-6 pbk)
ISBN: 978-1-003-38436-6 (ebk)

DOI: 10.4324/9781003384366

Typeset in Bembo
by codeMantra

CONTENTS

FIGURES

CONTRIBUTORS

Authors/Researchers from NEEDDS/UFABC:

Rodolfo Aguiar is Master's candidate in World Political Economy at UFABC. He completed his Bachelor's degrees in Economic Sciences and in Sciences and Humanities, both at UFABC. Technical Court Clerk at the Court of Justice of the State of São Paulo. He has experience in the field of Economics, with emphasis on Development and Sustainability, working mainly on the following topics: sustainability, development, capitalism, accumulation, and hegemony.

Fernanda Graziella Cardoso is Professor of the Bachelor of Economics at the UFABC, current pro-rector of graduation of UFABC. She completed her BA in Economics from USP (2005), Master's degree in Economics of Industry and Technology from UFRJ (2008), and PhD in Development Economics from the USP (2012). Her research areas include Socioeconomic Development, Brazilian Economic History, and History of Economic Thought.

Tatiana Berringer is Professor of the Bachelor of International Relations at the UFABC, vice-coordinator of NEEDDS/UFABC. She completed her BA in International Relations from the Universidade Estadual Paulista (UNESP, 2007), Master's degree and PhD in Political Science from the Unicamp. She is adjunct Member of the group "Neoliberalism and Class Relations in Brazil", related to the Center for Marxist Studies (Cemarx) and the Group of Studies and Research for Alternatives in International Relations (GARI/UNESP). She is member of the Editorial Committee of *Revista Crítica Marxista* and of the Editorial Board of *Revista Interação*.

Vanessa Empinotti is Professor of Rural Planning and Policy at the UFABC, member of the Laboratory of Territorial Justice – LabJuta at the UFABC, and coordinator of the research group on Political Ecology, Planning and Territory. She completed her BS in Agronomy from the Federal University of Paraná (UFPR), Master's degree in Soil Science from the Federal University of Rio Grande do Sul (UFRGS) and PhD in Geography, with specialization in Sustainable Development from the University of Colorado at Boulder, USA. Her research areas include socio-environmental governance, focusing on water insecurity, rural-urban relations, and territorial planning from the perspective of Political Ecology.

Arilson da Silva Favareto is Professor of the Bachelor of Territorial Planning/UFABC. He completed his BA in Social Sciences from the Pontifical Catholic University of Campinas (PUCC, 1992), Master's degree in Sociology from the State University of Campinas (Unicamp, 2001), and PhD in Environmental Science from the University of São Paulo (USP, 2006). He is Visiting Professor at the École des Hautes Études en Sciences Sociales (EHESS/Paris, 2002/2003), the Facultad Latinoamericana de Ciencias Sociales (FLACSO, Ecuador), and the University of Caldas (Colombia). He has performed several consultancy and research projects funded by multilateral and/or foreign institutions such as the International Development Research Centre (Canada), the United Nations Development Programme, the Institute of Development Studies (United Kingdom), and the Inter-American Institute for Agricultural Cooperation.

Ramatis Jacino is Professor of the Bachelor of Economics at the UFABC, member of the Center of African and Afro-Brazilian Studies/UFABC. He completed his Master's degree (2007) and PhD (2013) in Economic History from the USP. He is currently a postdoctoral fellow at the Center for Social Studies, University of Coimbra. He has experience in the field of History, with emphasis in Brazilian History, working mainly on the following topics: blacks, labor market, abolition, black population, exclusion, work and racism.

Leonardo Freire de Mello is Professor of the Bachelor of Territorial Planning and of the Graduate Program in Planning and Territorial Management at the UFABC. He completed his BS in Agronomy from the Federal University of Lavras (1992), BA in Public Administration from the João Pinheiro Foundation (1997), Master's degree in Civil Engineering Environmental Planning from Unicamp (2003), and PhD in Demography from Unicamp (2007). His research areas include Planning, Environment and Demography, with emphasis on the population-environment interface, the population-environment-consumption complex, and the human dimensions of global environmental change.

Sara Aparecida de Paula is Doctoral candidate in World Political Economy at UFABC. She completed her Master's in World Political Economy at UFABC, graduated in the Interdisciplinary Bachelor of Sciences and Humanities and in Bachelor of International Relations, both at UFABC. She is part of the study group Paradox – Anthropocene and Happiness and of the Environment and Climate Working Group of the Observatory of Foreign Policy and International Insertion of Brazil. She is co-founder and member of the Editorial Board of the Journal ÎANDÉ – Sciences and Humanities of the Federal University of ABC, member of IUSSP – International Union for the Scientific Study of Population. She works mainly on the following topics: demographic dynamics, migration, population and environment, consumption, territory and border, Anthropocene.

Claudio Penteado is Professor of the Graduate Program in Human and Social Sciences at UFABC. He completed his BA in Social Sciences from the University of São Paulo (1997), Master's degree (2001) and PhD (2005) in Social Sciences from the Pontifical Catholic University of São Paulo. He has experience in Political Science, with emphasis on Internet and Politics, working mainly on the following research areas: Internet, democracy, blogs, public policies, political marketing, cyberactivism, and digital culture. He is researcher at the Center for Postgraduate Studies in Social Sciences at PUCSP (NEAMP) and at the Laboratory of Free Technologies at UFABC (LabLivre).

Marcio Pochmann is retired, full-Professor of the Institute of Economics/Unicamp and currently a Senior Visiting Professor at NEEDDS/UFABC. He completed his BA in Economic Sciences from the Federal University of Rio Grande do Sul (1984), Master's degree in Political Science from the Federal District Higher Education Association, and PhD in Economics from the Unicamp (1993). He was president of the Perseu Abramo Foundation from 2012 to 2020, president of the IPEA from 2007 to 2012, and Sao Paulo Mayor's secretary from 2001 to 2004. He has experience in Social and Labor Economics, working mainly on the following research areas: development, public policies, and labor relations.

Cristina Fróes de Borja Reis is Professor of the Bachelor of Economics at the UFABC, current coordinator of NEEDDS/UFABC, and counselor at the Regional Council of the Economists – Sao Paulo State, Brazil. She completed her BA in Economics from the University of São Paulo (USP, 2003), Master's degree (2008) and PhD (2013) in Economics of Industry and Technology from the Federal University of Rio de Janeiro (UFRJ). She was awarded a two-year post-doctoral fellowship at the International Post-Doc Initiative of the Technische Universitat Berlin/Marie Curie Actions (2017/2020). Her research areas include global value chains, development, public investment, productive structure, and international trade.

Gabriel Almeida Antunes Rossini is Professor and coordinator of the Bachelor of Economics at the Federal University of ABC (UFABC). He completed his

MSc (2009) and PhD (2015) in Economics at the Unicamp. He coordinated the NEEDDS-UFABC between 2019 and 2021. He is the leader of the Political Economy and Economic History Research Group (GPEPHE/UFABC). He is a researcher of the INCT Observatory of Metropoles São Paulo. His research areas include Political Economy, Economic History, and Economic Development.

Giorgio Romano Schutte is Professor of the Bachelor of International Relations at the UFABC. He completed his BA and Master's degree in International Relations from the University of Amsterdam (1987), PhD in Sociology from the USP (2003), and postdoctoral studies at the National Chengchi University, Taiwan (2020). He was Planning and Research Technician and Coordinator of the International Policy Studies at the Institute for Applied Economic Research (IPEA). His research areas include globalization, public policies, trade unionism, multinational companies, productive restructuring, and integration.

Luciana Travassos is Professor of the Bachelor of Territorial Planning and the Bachelor of Sciences and Humanities at UFABC. She completed her BA in Architecture and Urbanism from USP (1999), Master's degree (2005) and PhD (2010) in Environmental Science from USP. She was an advisor to the Sao Paulo Mayor's Secretariat of Urban Development, Professor at the School of Architecture and Urbanism/USP, Mauá Institute of Technology and FIAM/FAAM University Center, and Researcher at the Laboratory of Urbanism of the Metropolis, LUME-FAUUSP. She has experience in the area of Urban and Regional Planning, with emphasis on environmental issues of the urban environment, working mainly on the following themes: urban drainage, urban environmental planning, public policies, urban environment, and environmental sustainability.

Guest-authors from research centers abroad:

Susana Beatriz Adamo is Research scientist at the Center for International Earth Science Information Network (The Earth Institute, Columbia University) and Adjunct Assistant Professor in the Undergraduate Program in Sustainable Development in the same university. She is Co-coordinator of the Population-Environment Research Network (PERN), member of the Climate Change Working Group of the Group on Earth Observations-GEO, and former member of the Scientific Advisory Committee of IAI (Inter American Institute for Global Change Research). Her research areas include environmental migration and displacement, social vulnerability and environmental change, dynamics of internal migration in developing countries, and all aspects of data integration related to demography and environment links, particularly global and regional georeferenced population databases. She completed her BS in Geography from the University of Buenos Aires, MS in Population Studies from FLACSO-Mexico, and PhD in Demography/Sociology from the University of Texas at Austin.

Carolina Cristina Alves is Joan Robinson Research Fellow in Heterodox Economics at Girton College, University of Cambridge, UK, co-founder of Diversifying and Decolonising Economics D-Econ, and editor of the Developing Economics blog. She sits on the Rebuilding Macroeconomics Advisory Board (RM Advisory Council), the Progressive Economy Forum Council (PEF) and Positive Money. She completed her BA in Economics at the Unicamp, Master's degree in Sociology from Unicamp (2007), and PhD in Economics from SOAS University of London (2017). She is a member of the Cambridge Social Ontology Group (CSOG) and the Alternative Approaches to Economics Research Group at the University of Cambridge.

Andreas Bieler is Professor of Political Economy and Fellow of the Centre for the Study of Social and Global Justice at the University of Nottingham, UK. He completed his MA (Econ) in European Politics and Policy, Department of Government, University of Manchester/UK (Distinction), and PhD in Politics and International Studies, University of Warwick/UK. He was awarded a one-year research fellowship at the Helsinki Collegium for Advanced Studies (2019/2020). His general expertise is in the area of International Relations/International Political Economy theories and the analysis of European integration as well as resistance to neo-liberal globalization with a particular emphasis on the possible role of trade unions and labor movements understood in a broad sense.

Eva Campos-Dominguez is Professor of Modern, Contemporary and American History, Journalism, Journalism and Audiovisual Communication and Advertising at the Faculty of Philosophy and Letters, University of Valladolid, Spain. She completed her PhD from the Complutense University of Madrid, Extraordinary Doctoral Award and is Associate Professor of Journalism at the University of Valladolid (Spain). She has participated in different publicly funded research projects on Internet politics and is the author of several publications on cyberdemocracy such as La ciberdemocracia en el Congreso de los Diputados (2011) or Deliberative Digital Democracy (2012). Her research areas include political communication on the Internet, with special interest in recent years in the open communication of government and parliament.

Patrick Caron is Vice President for International Affairs, University of Montpellier, France. He is veterinary doctor and completed his PhD in Development Geography. He is a specialist of farming systems and territorial dynamics, with a special focus on livestock farming. He joined CIRAD in 1988 where he was Director-General for research and strategy from 2010 to 2016, after serving as scientific director for the "Territories, Environment and People" Department of CIRAD (2001–2004) and as "Environments and Societies" Department director from 2007 to 2010. He is member of many institutional and inter-institutional bodies. In particular, he chairs the Scientific Council of AgroParisTech and is member of the French National Council for Development and International Solidarity. In 2015, he chaired the Organizing committee of the Global Science Conference on Climate Smart Agriculture (Montpellier, France), in 2016 of the international conference Agrichains and sustainable development, and in 2017 the international conference on Living Territories. He has been appointed as Chair of the High Level Panel of Experts (HLPE) of the Committee on World Food Security (CFS) in November 2015 and once again in November 2017 (until 2019).

Hilde Heynen is Professor of Architectural Theory at the University of Leuven, Belgium. She studied architecture and philosophy at the University of Leuven, where she also received her PhD. She was Paul Getty post-doctoral fellow, research fellow at the Radcliffe Institute (Harvard University), and held visiting positions at MIT (Cambridge, MA), at the AA-school (London), RMIT (Melbourne), and Harvard. Her work was supported by grants from the Research Foundation Flanders, the Research Council of the University of Leuven, the Netherlands Architecture Fund, the Graham Foundation, and the Radcliffe Institute of Advanced Studies. Her research focuses on issues of modernity, modernism, and gender in architecture. More recently, she engaged with the intersection between architecture and gender studies.

Ingrid Harvold Kvangraven is Lecturer in International Development at King's College, London. She completed her PhD in Economics from The New School and MSc in Development Studies from the London School of Economics. She previously worked as Lecturer at the University of York's Department of Politics. She is founder and editor of the blog Developing Economics, founder and steering group member of Diversifying and Decolonising Economics (D-Econ), coordinator of the Association for Heterodox Economics. Her research areas include the role of finance in development, structural features of underdevelopment, the political economy of development, and critically assessing the economics field.

Guilherme Riccioppo Magacho is Researcher at the Agence Française de Développement Government of France. He completed his BA in Economics from the USP (2008), Master's degree in Economic Theory from Unicamp (2012), and PhD in Territorial Economics from the University of Cambridge (2016). He was Visiting Professor at the Federal University of ABC. He is Associate Researcher at the Cambridge Centre for Economic and Public Policy (CCEPP), University of Cambridge, and at the New Developmentalist Center, Fundação Getúlio Vargas, and Coordinator of the INET-YSI Keynesian Working Group. He has experience in Economics, with emphasis on economic growth and development, fiscal policy, open macroeconomics, productive insertion, input-output analysis, structural change, regional and urban economics, and technological innovations.

Vijay Prashad is Executive-director of Tricontinental: Institute for Social Research and the Chief Editor of LeftWord Books. He was the George and Martha Kellner Chair in South Asian History and Professor of International Studies at Trinity College in Hartford, CT from 1996 to 2017. In 2013–2014, he was the Edward Said Chair at the American University of Beirut and has been a Senior Fellow of the Issam Fares Institute for Public Policy and International Affairs in Beirut. Prashad is a journalist, the Chief Correspondent for Globetrotter – a project of the Independent Media Institute. He is a columnist for Frontline and writes regularly for *The Hindu* and *BirGun*. He has reported from around the world for the Indian media. In 2015, Prashad joined as the Chief Editor of the New Delhi-based publisher LeftWord Books. He is also an advisory board member of the US Campaign for the Academic and Cultural Boycott of Israel, part of the global Boycott, Divestment and Sanctions (BDS) movement.

Alfredo Saad-Filho is Professor of Political Economy and International Development in the Department of International Development. Previously, he was Professor of Political Economy at SOAS University of London; Chair of the SOAS Department of Development Studies (2006–2010); Head of SOAS Doctoral School (2018-19); and Senior Economic Affairs Officer at the United Nations Conference on Trade and Development (2011–2012). He was awarded the Lifetime Achievement Medal from the Federal University of Goiás, Brazil in 2014 and the SOAS Director's Teaching Prize in 2016. He has degrees in Economics from the University of Brasília (Brazil) and SOAS University of London and has taught in universities and research institutions in Brazil, Canada, Germany, Italy, Japan, Mozambique, Switzerland, and the UK. His research areas include political economy of development, industrial policy, neoliberalism, democracy, alternative economic policies, Latin American political and economic development, inflation and stabilization, and labor theory of value.

Yaffa Truelove is Professor of Geography at the University of Colorado Boulder. She completed her PhD from the University of Cambridge in 2015. Her research interests include the connections between urban landscapes and socio-political processes in cities of the Global South. In particular, she examines water and its infrastructures as a lens for analyzing social and material relations in cities as well as differing regimes and institutions of everyday urban governance. Her prior research has predominately focused on Indian cities, contributing to theorizations of urban and feminist political ecologies, southern and comparative urbanism, and "actually existing" modalities of urban water governance in postcolonial cities. Her recent work includes a collaborative intra-urban comparison of precarious infrastructures in the cities of Mumbai, Delhi, and Cape Town as well as a project examining infrastructural violence and the everyday politics of water disruption in India's capital city, Delhi.

PREFACE

Learning from the Global South in the search for alternatives

Andreas Bieler and Marcio Pochmann

We are currently facing multiple, overlapping global crises. Ongoing economic crises characterized by deepening inequalities are closely interlinked with intensifying geo-political rivalries and an environmental crisis, which is threatening the very survival of humanity. Hence, this book is a highly timely and urgently needed contribution, reflecting on the potential lessons we can learn through interactions between scholars from the Global South and Global North. For too long, scholarship has been dominated by Eurocentrism exploring global phenomena through the narrow conceptual lenses of the Global North (see, for example, Nowak 2021). This book is an attempt to go beyond this tradition and bring voices from the Global South to the forefront of debate.

The nature of global crises implies that people in both the Global South and North are being affected. As the chapter by Travassos and Heynen makes clear, rising inequality in cities is a key challenge experienced everywhere, often fragmented along ethnic, racial, and gender lines. These country internal inequalities, however, go hand in hand with a continuation of inequality between Global South and Global North, in which the poverty of the former is based on the increasing wealth of the latter. Countries in the Global South remain locked in a position of increasing under-development in the words of dependency theory or relations of uneven and combined development from an alternative Marxist perspective. As Rossini and Magacho outline in this volume, Brazil currently experiences a process of reprimarization of its exports, after the opening-up of its economy during the 1990s resulted in a decline in industrial production in a process of "non-creative" destruction. The promises of industrial upgrading as a result of the establishment of global value chains (GVCs) under the direction of transnational corporations (TNCs) turned out to be hollow across the Global South, as countries have remained stuck in the lower, labor-intensive end of GVCs (see Reis and Kvangraven in this book).

Faced with Northern, generally US-dominated imperialism, countries in the Global South have the possibility of two diverging courses of action according to Schutte and Prashad in this book. Either they work on establishing multipolarity providing space for a potential alternative as for example Brazil during the presidencies of Lula or they pursue a subordinate-ally model similar to India under the leadership of Modi. In our view, however, this hope for multipolarity as a way out of crises is rather doubtful. Of course, Latin America more than any other continent has experienced the full force of US imperialism. Nevertheless, is Jacino right with their argument in this book that the imperialist US is the greatest danger to the survival of humanity and, therefore, needs to be confronted head-on?

The BRICS countries are often referred to as the potential basis for such a multipolarity. Under closer scrutiny, however, it is rather unclear whether they can really fulfill this role as a basis for progressive alternatives. South Africa's economy is weak and it has always been questioned whether it should even be considered a part of this group of emerging economies. India as such has not really operated as an alternative pole and its internal, massive inequalities raise doubts whether it can ever be. Brazil's reprimarization of exports, covered in this volume, indicates its problems, while the war in Ukraine demonstrates that Russia's military power has been exaggerated, while its economy based to a large extent on the export of fossil fuels and dominated by a few superrich oligarchs was always of no more than secondary rate. China remains a potential alternative pole, and its economic growth rates over recent decades have been impressive indeed, as have been the various projects linked to its Belt and Road Initiative. However, economic growth has very much relied on foreign direct investment and cheap labor at the lower end of GVCs. The country's break-through into capital intensive production lines is anything but assured (King 2019, 2021). Considering its human rights record and the maltreatment of Uyghurs raise doubts that even if it provides an alternative pole, whether this pole can be the basis for a progressive way forward in the interest of working people.

Hopes for progressive alternatives in the Global South are often centered around projects of state-led development. Nevertheless, Ben Selwyn has clearly demonstrated that not only market-led development occurs at the expense of the interests of working people. State-led development models too have been based on the extreme exploitation of labor.

> Admiration for and advocacy of constructing strong, bureaucratically autonomous states that are able to rationally and effectively generate and allocate resources cannot hide the fact that these states are involved in overseeing and reproducing highly exploitative labour regimes where workers are regarded as fuel for the accumulation of capital.
>
> *(Selwyn 2014: 52)*

Moreover, state-led alternative development in the Global South is still within core capitalist parameters. As Rossini and Magacho argue in this book, development should be pushed through a process of productive transformation based on collective capabilities and the creation of good-quality jobs and sustainable structural change. The aftermath of the pandemic with calls for a re-orientation of industrial production to the domestic level may offer new opportunities in this respect, they argue. However, development through increasing industrial production is not only in line with a Eurocentric, capitalist definition of development. It also disregards the increasing challenges of the environmental crisis, discussed in detail by de Mello, Adamo, and de Paula in this book.

When it comes to tackling the environmental crisis, here too the state is often referred to as the key actor in overcoming it. Green New Deals under state direction with a focus on green growth and the creation of new, high quality green jobs are developed as a response to climate change in both the Global South and North. Nevertheless, as Hickel and Kallis (2020) make clear, there is a fundamental contradiction in these proposals. On one hand, capitalism is structurally dependent on continuing economic growth. On the other, "growth in GDP ultimately cannot plausibly be decoupled from growth in material and energy use, demonstrating categorically that GDP growth cannot be sustained indefinitely" (Hickel and Kallis 2020: 475). Moreover, while there are signs that GDP can be decoupled from carbon emissions over time, it is highly doubtful whether this will be fast enough to stay within the Paris agreement of limiting global warming to 1.5 or 2 degree Celsius. In fact, rather than addressing climate change, capitalism continues to rely on increasing access to what Jason Moore (2015) calls "cheap natures" in its relentless search for higher levels of economic profit.

In short, relying on a strong state within our existing capitalist political-economic system can neither successfully address the problems of development and increasing inequality, nor does it provide a way forward in tackling the environmental crisis. Equally, a focus on new technologies will not provide an easy, quick fix to our current crises. As Empinotti and Truelove discuss in relation to access to water in this book, existing inequalities are often the result of past colonial structures and require therefore wider social transformations than simply the application of new technologies. Perhaps it is time to move towards a project of degrowth, which combines continuing growth in developing countries of the Global South with degrowth in industrialized countries in the Global North? Importantly, degrowth does not mean economic recession. "Degrowth calls for a different kind of economy altogether: an economy that does not require growth in the first place, and which can deliver justice and well-being even while throughput declines" (Hickel 2021: 1108).

In moving ahead, the focus should perhaps be placed on what Selwyn (2014) calls labor-centered development, i.e. development which is at the benefit of working people. As Reis and Kvangraven point out in this volume, solutions to the crises of our time must be built from the bottom up. Considering that there is a convergence between core and peripheral countries around neo-liberal economic policies, struggles associated with identity politics need to become part of more general struggles to avoid a fragmentation of the left (see Saad Filho and Berringer in this volume). Bottom-up solutions must be based on broad alliances covering the internal relations of class, gender, sexuality, and race bringing together resistance in the workplace with struggles in the wider sphere of social reproduction and against environmental destruction (Bieler 2021: 11–21). The way forward, as Jacino argues in this book, has to be around a pact in defense of non-white and peripheral youth, who are faced with the most severe forms of violence, in which economic exploitation is inter-related with racial forms of oppression. Green New Deals must be anti-colonial rather than within existing capitalist structures of inequality (Ajl 2021). And there are projects, experiments in the Global South, from which people in the Global North can learn. Whether it is the settlements of the Brazilian Landless Workers Movement (MST) and its struggles for social and economic justice or movements around food sovereignty in South Africa (Satgar 2013), people are developing concrete alternatives to capitalism in the here and now. Importantly, as Favareto and Caron make clear in this volume, transforming the way of how we produce food – such as in projects of food sovereignty – can also address problems related to poverty, health, biodiversity, and climate change.

In the context of the first quarter of the 21st century, the set of contributions from authors gathered in this book offers the reader an expanded perspective on national possibilities in the midst of global difficulties. While TNCs operate in the world market, national states continue to operate in their aforementioned territorial spaces. The scarce and fragile presence of global public authority compromises the provision of solutions consistent with the contemporary challenges of inequality, poverty, and the climate crisis.

References

Ajl, Max (ed.). *A People's Green New Deal.* London: Pluto Press, 2021.

Bieler, Andreas. *Fighting for Water: Resisting Privatization in Europe.* London: Zed Books, 2021.

Hickel, Jason. What Does Degrowth Mean? A Few Points of Clarification, *Globalizations*, Vol.18/7: 1105–1111, 2021.

Hickel, Jason and Giorgos Kallis. Is Green Growth Possible? *New Political Economy*, Vol.25/4: 469–486, 2020.

King, Sam. Why China Cannot Win a Trade War against the USA, *Rupture Magazine*, 2019; available at https://rupturemagazine.org/2019/08/04/why-china-cannot-win-a-trade-war-against-the-usa%E2%80%A8-samuel-t-king/; accessed 10/09/2020.

King, Sam. *Imperialism and the Development Myth: How Rich Countries Dominate in the Twenty-First Century.* Manchester: Manchester University Press, 2021.

Moore, Jason W. *Capitalism in the Web of Life: Ecology and the Accumulation of Capital.* London: Verso. Read Chapter 1, 2015.

Nowak, Jörg. From Industrial Relations Research to Global Labour Studies: Moving Labour Research beyond Eurocentrism, *Globalizations*, Vol.18/8: 1335–1348, 2021.

Satgar, Vishwas. Challenging the Globalised Agro-Food Complex: Farming Cooperatives and the Emerging Solidarity Economy Alternative in South Africa, In Jeff Shantz and Jose Brendan Macdonald (eds.) *Beyond Capitalism: Building Democratic Alternatives for Today and the Future.* New York: Continuum Press, 177–190, 2013.

Selwyn, Ben. *The Global Development Crisis.* Cambridge: Polity Press, 2014.

INTRODUCTION

Cristina Fróes de Borja Reis and Tatiana Berringer

Talking about change, since the 2008 crisis, Industry 4.0, the new financial and technological paradigm of production, commercialization, consumption, and 3R (reduce, recycle, reuse), is promoting major transformations worldwide (Fiori, 2009; Chesnais, 2016; Chomsky et al., 2020). Under Industry 4.0, development, democracy, and sustainability become even more conflicting concerns, projects and practices for Nation-States. Although there are attempts to understand these processes co-jointly, non-Eurocentric interdisciplinary approaches (Amin, 2010; De Souza Santos and Paula, 2014) remain an epistemological challenge for international researchers committed to transformative thinking for reducing asymmetries. Such progress is necessary because the capitalist accumulation has internationally and domestically been renewed through authoritarian political swerves, environmental degradation, and class, gender, and racial segregation (Foster et al., 2010; Fraser, 2017; Mbembe, 2017; Brown, 2019).

The Covid-19 pandemic may have accelerated those transformations (UNCTAD, 2020), deepening domestic and international political, economic, and social contradictions, in which inter-state and inter-business rivalries are heightened (Keohane & Nye, 1970; Strange, 1970; Cox, 1977; Gilpin, 1987), as well as intersectional class struggles (Davis, 1981; Crenshaw, 1990). At the core of these rivalries, there is the hegemonic dispute between the United States and the Chinese state, as well as the competition in the vanguard technological sectors – such as pharmaceutical products, medical and hospital instruments, electronic equipment, and information technology and telecommunication services (Schutte, 2020; Mazzucato, 2021; Reis & Guedes, 2021). Yet, the strengthening of conservative ideologies, with the rise of far-right and/or neo-fascist governments and movements, is significantly impacting dependent social formations on the periphery of the system – either by increasing inequalities, by the crumbling of

DOI: 10.4324/9781003384366-1

democratic institutions and civil rights, by the control and exploitation of natural resources and strategic spaces, and especially by their patriarchal and racist characters (Fine & Saad, 2017; Boito 2018; Almeida, 2019; Berringer & Reis, 2021).

These movements have been analyzed by the International Political Economy (IPE) since the 1970s which brought together studies of international relations, political science, economics, sociology, history, and other sciences that were working apart in the same research object: the relationship between states and companies – their conflicts, rivalries, complementarities and overlapping on the international system. The main question, then, was whether or not there was a crisis of the United States' hegemony. The best sellers of IPE manuals or handbooks reflect the predominance of studies from the United States and from Europe. For example, the important manual from Routledge, entitled "International Political Economy as a global conversation", edited by Mark Blyth (2009), is largely centered on studies from the American and British perspectives, even when analyzing Asia and other countries, too. Another important manual, organized by Benjamin Cohen (2008), is also Eurocentric, though it contains more critical Marxist approaches.

This was a discomfort for us, not only because of the vast and meaningful intellectual production from other regions such as Latin America, e.g. the developmentalist and dependency theories, decolonial and revolutionary studies at that time, but also because of later contributions born precisely in the field of IPE. Particularly and briefly, in Brazil, for instance, there are many studies on IPE from the Brazilian Society of Political Economy, as well as in the Brazilian Association of International Relations. In 2008, respected thinkers such as Maria da Conceição Tavares and José Luis Fiori, created the graduate program of IPE at the Federal University of Rio de Janeiro. Ten years later, the graduate program of World Political Economy (WPE) was launched at UFABC with many members from NEEDDS.

That is not simply a concern of saying here "Look, these authors from the South need to be heard". The real challenges are structural, associated to the hierarchical positions in the production of knowledge and in the academic circuits worldwide. Positions derived from power and capital situations of their states and firms that will drive their investments on science, technology, and innovation. So, it is not something necessarily typical of one or another research field. But, we claim that our field deserves special attention because the absence of plural perspectives has devastating effects on the IPE *praxis*, furthering uneven distribution between countries, markets, classes and intersectional groups of people. Hence, considering that there are several contributions from the South to think on development, democracy, and sustainability from the 1970s and later, the second major aim of this book is to find more room for international dialogue breaking the ice for structural and institutional change.

For accomplishing this aim, we had as advantage our academic networks and experience of interdisciplinary studies at the Center of Strategic Studies on Democracy, Development and Sustainability at the Federal University of ABC

(NEEDDS/UFABC) in Brazil. The researchers from NEEDDS combine different themes and backgrounds, with a convergent critical perception of the WPE – as we prefer to name this scientific field, for differentiating our plural approaches from the Eurocentric IPE approaches. In fact, WPE ends up as a broad area of contemporary social sciences that seeks to understand the logic and dynamics of the world-system (Wallerstein, 2004; Dos Santos, 2015). Then, this book is the outcome of virtual dialogues[1] from the beginning of the pandemic to broaden the conversation and the understanding of the global transformations in motion, doing truly interdisciplinary and non-Eurocentric studies on development, democracy, and sustainability.

From an intellectual point of view, our inspiration is the Southern criticism of the Eurocentrism, related to where the main IPE reference works are placed and produced. And our contribution here is to apply, to systematize, to cover critical WPE perspectives. By doing so, we show that there is something beyond, in the sense of overcoming the prior junction of international relations and economics fields, combining geography and sociology and other sciences to look better at the territorial and cultural dimensions. This enables us to analyze intersectional conflicts, such as race and gender issues. Though many references in the North are also focused on understanding the issues of race and gender as part of the capital accumulation processes and inter-states struggles, we think that WPE have succeeded in showing how racism, sexism, and machismo are related to the center-periphery dependency, combining local and global categories of analysis.

So, now that we are in a very crucial moment in world history, when the pandemic is making the capitalist contradictions and inequalities more pronounced, we have the chance to strengthen WPE approaches that value lives of oppressed people and nature. Provoked by this context, we took the challenge of structuring these dialogues with internal consistency. That is why we defined four guiding questions for the conversations on multiple subjects. They are the following: (1) what are the main productive and technological transformations underway today for the next decades?; (2) how do the interstate disputes and the environmental challenges manifest?; (3) what are the distributional consequences, including from the intersectional point of view (ethno-racial, gender, geographic, locational)?; (4) How do we alleviate/fight these distributional asymmetries? The last question is important due to the commitment with proposing solutions, too. Solutions that have a popular character, that come from the people, that have adherence and strengthen democracy, that protect nature. Solutions that not solely relegate to the State a transformative role without discussing the State itself, the power coalitions supporting him, and how to improve the participation of oppressed people in power coalitions leading the State. The 11 chapters of this book are dialogues about democracy, development and sustainability, on different themes related to the Agenda 2030. They form a consistent group of analytical categories for WPE studies to define and to interpret the inter-connections between our core three concepts. All chapters address the SDGs 5 (gender equality), 10 (reduced inequalities), and 13 (climate action) because of their structures based on the 4 questions just mentioned.

Starting with the political analysts, whose perspectives are worried with issues related to SDGs 16 and 17, on the institutions for peace and global partnership, the first dialogue between Giorgio Romano Schutte (PhD in Sociology, associate professor at UFABC, researcher in NEEDDS) and Vijay Prashad from the Tricontinental Institute for Social Research (India) is on geopolitics and war. Though their conversation was before the war in Ukraine, they were already emphasizing the importance of keeping war as an important analytical category to understand the world system, mentioning examples that impact the health and well-being (SDG 3) and the energy (SDG 7) sectors. Next, Tatiana Berringer (PhD in Political Science, assistant professor at UFABC, researcher in NEEDDS) and Professor Alfredo Saad-Filho (PhD in Economics) from King's College analyze neoliberalism, democracy, and authoritarian regimes, proposing some space for resistance, too, especially looking at the labor side (SDG 8 on decent work and economic growth). In the third dialogue, Claudio Penteado (PhD in Social Science, associate professor at UFABC, researcher in NEEDDS) with associate professor Eva Campos-Dominguez (PhD in Journalism), from the University of Valladolid in Spain, dialogue on the internet and its dangers to democracy. Their examples shed light on educational challenges (SDG 4), too. Chapter 4 has Luciana Travassos (PhD in Environmental Science, assistant professor at UFABC, researcher in NEEDDS), with Professor Hilde Heynen (PhD in Architecture) from University of Leuven, Belgium, debating on urban development and justice. They raise key dimensions related to SDG 11 (sustainable cities and communities) and SDG 12 (responsible consumption and production (SDG 12).

Then, moving to the dialogues between economists, generally concerned with SDGs 8 (economic growth) and 9 (industry, innovation, and infrastructure), in Chapter 5, Fernanda Cardoso (PhD in Economics, assistant professor at UFABC, researcher in NEEDDS) and Carolina Alves (PhD in Economics) from Cambridge University, UK, remark the contribution of the decolonial perspective to the greatest challenges of development, democracy, and sustainability – providing a deeper theoretical background to achieve no poverty (SDG 1) and zero hunger (SDG 2). In Chapter 6, Professor Cristina Reis (PhD in Economics, researcher in NEEDDS) and assistant professor Ingrid Harold Kvangraven (PhD in Economics) from the King's College, UK, talk on global value chains' hierarchies led by transnational corporations – providing structural basis to think on sectorial development, as in the case of pharmaceutical (SDG 3) and energy sector (SDG 7). In Chapter 7, Gabriel Rossini (PhD in Economics, assistant professor at UFABC, researcher in NEEDDS) and Guilherme Magacho (PhD in Economics) working at the French Agency for Development, consider the possibilities of natural resources-based development. Their conversation covers issues related to SDG 2 and 12.

Next, we have the environmental and social experts, particularly concerned with SDGs 6 (clear water and sanitation), 14 (life below water), and 15 (life on land). In Chapter 8, Leonardo Mello (PhD in Demography, assistant professor at UFABC, researcher in NEEDDS), Sara Aparecida de Paula (Master in World Political Economy, UFABC) and associate professor Susana Adamo (PhD in Demography and Sociology), from the International Center for Earth Sciences and Information Networks, Columbia, USA, critically analyze the global environmental crisis. Then, in Chapter 9 we have Arilson Favareto (PhD in Environmental Science, associate professor at UFABC, researcher in NEEDS) dialoguing with Professor Patrick Caron (PhD in Development Geography) from the University of Montpellier, France, about agri-food systems – directly related to SDG 2 and 12. In Chapter 10, Vanessa Empinotti (PhD in Geography, assistant professor at UFABC, researcher in NEEDDS) and assistant professor Yaffa Truelove (PhD in Geography), working at the University of Colorado, USA, make a conversation on embodied political ecologies of water, gender, and inequalities in urban spaces in India and Brazil, targeting SDGs 6 and 11. Finally, Ramatis Jacino (PhD in Economic History, assistant professor at UFABC, researcher at NEEDDS) discusses about racial conflicts emerged with the transformations during the Covid-19 pandemic and its related inequalities jeopardizing the non-white youth – bringing elements influencing SDGs 3, 4, and 8. His insights show that a class approach to understand racial relations is upmost not only for fighting inequalities in Brazil but also worldwide – what forces us to remember that there is no SDG on race.

In the final remarks, we show how the dialogues were able to deeply analyze their topics based on WPE non-Eurocentric approaches, allowing us to conceptualize democracy, development and sustainability in a single analytical process able to enrich the flawed framework of SDGs. Because their arguments are grounded in historical and theoretical analyses, they highlighted what are the main contradictions and the struggles emerging from the current concrete situations, presenting alternatives for the progressive and democratic forces to understand the moment, and based on this, to reinvent ourselves. We mean by "to reinvent ourselves" not only to fight for equality and justice, but also to reflect on the political, economic, social, and environmental paths; its limits, forgetfulness, priorities, and how to incorporate these learnings in the next steps. The challenges for the leftwing movements are many, but the starting point is to not fall into division. We have to make the diagnosis, the plan, and the action for change in an integrated way. There are no segmented and prior struggles. We won't be able to solve the environmental issues without solving the issues of race, gender, and class, as the entire imperialist structure of the WPE must be put in check. Because the international contradictions of the capitalist system of accumulation are also nationalized, the South-North dialogues are appropriate and stimulating means for finding new alternatives.

To wrap-up, this book registers this methodological path. During the conversations and, afterwards, when writing together the chapters, we authors were getting freer and more comfortable for exchanging ideas in a very critical way. Moreover, all the researchers who participated on this project took the same decision: to talk, to listen, to share, to elaborate together so many insightful thoughts. We hope that whoever reads the book not only learns more on democracy, development and sustainability issues of the WPE, but also spreads this way to do science, which seeks to reduce inequalities and also the distances between us.

We thank all people who collaborated in this project, especially Carla Abrão and Rodolfo Aguiar from NEEDDS, the research rectory at UFABC, the School of Parliament of Sao Paulo Municipal Camara, and Routledge.

Note

1 The so-called South-North Dialogues on development, democracy and sustainability was a cycle of online videos recorded in 2021, and publicized by the Parliament School of the Municipal Chamber of Sao Paulo. Official website: https://www.saopaulo.sp.leg.br/escoladoparlamento/cursos/cursos-anteriores/cursos-realizados-em-2021/dialogos-sul-norte-em-democracia-desenvolvimento-e-sustentabilidade/. Official video playlist: https://youtube.com/playlist?list=PL7WmlcfNQHf45SDppeUrDKg-UCyAPM_Fw

References

Almeida, Silvio. *Racismo estrutural.* São Paulo: Pólen Produção Editorial LTDA, 2019.

Amin, Samir. *Eurocentrism.* New York: Monthly Review Press, 2010.

Berringer, Tatiana; Reis, Cristina F. B. Inserção externa decadente e estrutura produtiva dependente. In: *O Brasil Pós-Recessão das origens da crise às perspectivas e desafios futuros.* 1 ed. Santo André: Edufabc, Vol 1, pp. 173–186, 2021.

Blyth, M. *Routledge Handbook of International Political Economy (IPE).* Abingdon: Routledge, 2009.

Boito, Armando. *Reforma e crise política no Brasil.* Campinas: Editora da Unicamp. São Paulo: Editora da Unesp, 2018.

Brown, Wendy. *Nas ruínas do neoliberalismo: a ascensão da política antidemocrática no ocidente.* São Paulo: Politeia, 2019.

Chesnais, François. *Finance capital today: Corporations and banks in the lasting global slump.* Boston, MA: Brill, 2016.

Chomsky, N.; Pollin, R.; Polychroniou, C. J. *Climate crisis and the global green new deal: The political economy of saving the planet.* London/New York: Verso, 2020.

Cohen, Benjamin. (2008) *International Political Economy: an intellectual history.* Princeton and Oxford: Oxford University Press.

Cox, Robert W. Labor and hegemony. *International Organization,* 31(3), 385–424, 1977.

Crenshaw, Kimberle. Mapping the margins: Intersectionality, identity politics, and violence against women of color. *Stanford Law Review,* 43, 1241, 1990.

Davis, Angela. *Mulheres, Raça e Classe.* São Paulo: Boitempo, 2016 [1981].

De Sousa Santos, Boaventura; Meneses, Maria Paula. *Epistemologias do sul.* Cortez Editora, 2014.

Dos Santos, T. *A Teoria da Dependência: Balanço e Perspectivas.* Rio de Janeiro: Insular, 2015.

Fine, Ben; Saad-Filho, Alfredo. Thirteen things you need to know about neoliberalism. *Critical Sociology,* 43(4–5), 685–706, 2017.

Fiori, Jose Luís. O Poder Global e a Nova Geopolítica das Nações. *CyE* Año I N° 2, 2009.
Foster, J.B. The Financialization of accumulation. *Monthly Review*, 62(5), 2010.
Fraser, Nancy. From progressive neoliberalism to trump – and beyond. *American Affairs*, 1(4), Winter, 2017.
Gilpin, Robert. *The political economy of international relations*. Princeton, NJ: Princeton University Press, 1987.
Keohane, Robert O.; Nye, Joseph S. Power and interdependence revisited. *International Organization*, 41(4), 725–753, 1987.
Mazzucato, Mariana. *Mission economy: A moonshot guide to changing capitalism*. London: Allen Land, 2021.
Mbembe, Achille. *Critique of black reason*. Durham, NC: Duke University Press, 2017.
ONU. Organização das Nações Unidas. *Objetivos Sustentáveis do Milênio,* Agenda 2030. Disponível em: https://brasil.un.org/pt-br/sdgs
Reis, Cristina F. B.; Pinto, Jose Paulo G. Center–periphery relationships of pharmaceutical value chains: A critical analysis based on goods and knowledge trade flows. *Review of Political Economy*, 34(1), 124–145, 2021.
Schutte, Giorgio R. *Oásis para o Capital–Solo Fértil para a "Corrida De Ouro": A Dinâmica dos Investimentos Produtivos Chineses no Brasil*. Editora Appris, 2020.
Sengupta, Mitu. Transformational change or tenuous wish list?: A critique of SDG 1 ('End poverty in all its forms everywhere'). *Social Alternatives*, 37(1), 12–17, 2018.
Stewart, Frances. Changing perspectives on inequality and development. *Studies in Comparative International Development*, 51(1), 60–80, 2016.
Strange, Susan. International economics and international relations: A case of mutual neglect. *International Affairs*, April, 46(2), 304–315, 1970.
UNCTAD. *World investment report 2020: International production beyond the pandemic*. New York: United Nations Conference on Trade and Development, 2020.

1

GEOPOLITICS AND POLITICAL ECONOMY IN THE 21ST CENTURY

Giorgio Romano Schutte and Vijay Prashad

First of all, this dialogue is part of the project "North-South" and, in fact, we are playing a little bit with the idea because taking our case: Giorgio was raised in the North and did his PhD in the South, where he works now for so many years. Prashad is from the South but he has done his PhD in the North. So, the first thing we were wondering is whether it still makes sense to talk about the North and South divide. Of course, it's not exactly geographical, that was never the idea. The idea is that there is a clear divide of two worlds with two different dynamics. And that overcome the idea of a Third World, because there is no Soviet Union anymore, which was the Second World.

What remains is the North-South divide, but some will argue that it is more fragmented, that there are some countries or some regions in the South that already have climbed up to the North. While in the North, parts of population are in very poor conditions, there is hunger in parts of the US, for example. Does it make sense?

The first statement is that imperialism is alive and well. The concept of imperialism allows us to understand some specific features of the world. We don't hold to this concept because of the nostalgia from the past.

For instance, the growing debt crisis, 34 countries in 2020 spent more money servicing the debt than spending on their own healthcare in the middle of the pandemic. Thirty-four countries paid more money to international bond holders than taking care of their own population (Jensen, 2021). How can we explain this? These countries went to the Paris Group, the London Group – Paris Group is the public creditors, London Group is the private creditors – and they said: "please, give us a suspension in debt payment, debt servicing...please, give us a recount on our debt, cut the level of our debt" ... and so on nothing doing, you have to pay your debt servicing. And the bondholders all are basically based in north-Atlantic States where Paris and London groups have its constituency.

DOI: 10.4324/9781003384366-2

Then, 34 countries will basically drain exchanges rather than paying healthcare. How can we explain this? The concept of imperialism might be very useful.

What are the main productive, technological and financial transformations in process?

The quest of development is not the level of industrial capacity. That's an illusion. One can say, "well, look, I come to Brazil, we go to the South...we look at the whole factories where Lula used to work...and we'll see it around São Paulo there is all these industrial developments. Brazil is a developed country". Is that really the case? We don't think so...because in the way capitalism has advanced, initially, industry was the heartland of capital. Then, capital reorganizes industrial production, breaks up factories along commodity chains and it becomes clear that the firm or the actual site of production is not the element key for the power of capital any longer; the power of capital is manifest not in this factory or that factory but along the entire commodity chain, but dominating the chain through near monopoly conditions over intellectual property and finance. So, the center allowed other countries to industrialize because their companies can take advantage of lower labor costs and so on. But somebody else is controlling something else. Let's put on the table five areas of control which defines 21st-century Imperialism.

The first is basically control of science and technology. Certain countries dominate science and technology. This control leads to rivalry among the highly industrialized countries and a firm policy to prevent newcomers from entry into certain high-tech sectors. This is also the key area of conflict between the West and China. In fact, China is developing autonomous capacity in Science and Tech, thus, contesting a key source of northern power (Wübbeke at al., 2016).

Second, northern power controls large parts of the global financial system. There are at least two elements to this – the dollar-Wall Street-IMF complex, around which is shaped the large parts of the global trade and development agenda, and the SWIFT system of money transfer. The US Treasury Department plays an outsize role in shaping the policy of both. That is the reason why it is so easy for the US to sanction a country, since US sanctions cuts countries out of the dollar-Wall Street-IMF complex and the SWIFT system. Currently, thirty countries are under unilateral US sanctions (Cohen, 2018).

Third, control mechanism: access to resources. Take the example of cobalt, a strategic raw material for electronic devices and batteries, among other uses. The Democratic Republic of Congo (DRC) is the biggest producer of cobalt, which is bought by a handful of major companies. One of them is called Glencore, a Swiss company that sends the Congo's cobalt to factories in China – essentially controlled by the North. The access to resources is funded through mining companies that are based in Canada, Switzerland, Australia, the US, or the UK. Sixty percent of the world's mining companies are registered in Canada, Canada is

They shouldn't interfere, but an extremely important and corrosive dispute has been created that has paralyzed the left in Scotland, for example.

The left has to be able to meet the challenges. Now, it's very easy to issue that kind of opinion generically. When you come to talk to the people that are involved in these conflicts everything has an explanation, and things revolve around events, revolve around an individual, somehow we have to be able to transcend this and make identity struggles aspects of a more general struggle. Instead of being exclusionary struggles, the politics of exclusion is a neoliberal politics, and it can end up neutralizing and destroying the unity that is necessary to make a systemic change. You can't win a dispute with neoliberalism if you don't propose general alliances. To defeat an extremely powerful system of accumulation with the institutional support it has, we cannot divide ourselves into a thousand small movements. That is the problem with small movements, they end up being acceptance movements: Please accept me as I am! This is a conservative movement; this is a movement to ask for the favor of the dominant politics. It is not going to solve problems; much less be transformative. Not at all. You have to embed the understanding of these specific struggles within the more general transformative process. But it is difficult to do this in practice, and today this is not the ethic. It has been more about engaging in those specific struggles to the exclusion of others. One more challenge to plant.

I see that there is a great deal of convergence within the left. Distinct analyses, slightly, but a civilized coexistence, more profound, is the overcoming of petty and small understandings and of the smallness of reasoning and the smallness of politics. It is necessary to think big, I think that everyone is thinking big, yes, by understanding the depth and the enormity of the challenges that lie ahead of us. This gives hope!

Notes

1 Saad-Filho, Alfredo and Deborah Johnston. Neoliberalism: A Critical Reader. London Pluton Press 2004; Saad-Filho, Alfredo and Fine, Ben. Thirteen Things You Need to Know About Neoliberalism, *Critical Sociology* 43 (4–5) 2017, pp.685–706. Translated into Chinese and published in *Political Economy Review* 8 (5) 2017, pp.200–217; Neoliberalism: A Marxist Analysis, *Revista do NIEP* 3 (4) 2015, pp.58–73 (in Portuguese).

2 Saad-Filho, Alfredo; Cahill, D. Neoliberalism since the Crisis, introduction to a special issue of Critical Sociology 43 (4–5) 2017, pp.611–614; Saad-Filho, Alfredo. On the Crisis of Neoliberal Capitalism: A Discussion with D. Kotz, A. Saad Filho, A. M. Flores, D. Plihon and A. Lechevalier, *Actuel Marx* 51, 2012, pp.12–26 (in French).

3 Saad-Filho, Alfredo and Alison Ayers. Democracy Against Neoliberalism: Paradoxes, Limitations, Transcendence, *Critical Sociology* 41 (4–5), 2015, pp.597–618; Saad-Filho, Alfredo. *The Rise and Rise of Authoritarian Neoliberalism*, Alternativy (in Russian, forthcoming, 2020).

4 Saad-Filho, Alfredo. Capitalism and Anti-Capitalism: Challenges and Opportunities after September 11, *Revista da Sociedade Brasileira de Economia Política* 11, December 2002, pp.103–124.

major player in access to resources (Garside, 2020). Governments are overthrown when they try to prevent access to resources.

Fourth, the control over weaponry. There are certain countries that dominate the arms trade. Certain countries have a much larger military footprint than others. They can bomb you if you misbehave. They can refuse to sell you arms to defend yourself.

And the fifth that define imperialism is control over communications. CNN, for instance, can so quickly dominate the news cycle. We see that in terms of what happened in Libya in 2011. It was not the Libyan media defining what was the events happening in Libya, it was a newspaper in Saudi Arabia which defined it for CNN. Not only the Libyan did not define their own reality, but the Saudis were telling the US how to do it.

There is a kind of hierarchy, in our understanding, among these control mechanisms. Among the five control mechanisms, the focus needs to be on science and technology. Why? because, taking the example of cobalt, what are companies doing? They see that it is becoming difficult to have control over cobalt due to the political situation in the DRC. What happens then? They are looking for technologies to make the same batteries without cobalt. So, even when you think that the cobalt producers have maybe some negotiation power, this might not be true when the producers want to exercise it. You can substitute cobalt. But you cannot easily substitute technology, since the key technologies of our times are under intellectual property rules that benefit the near monopoly corporations. Even the military and communications and financial circuits are reliant upon intellectual property claims made by near monopoly firms, which is why science and technology are key.

But also, there is the idea of imperialism in the North-South divide. To stay with Brazil and India. These are two very large countries, but they do not have full financial, neither technological sovereignty. The scale of the country has some impact on the ability to have informational sovereignty, because it's big enough, there are enough people there, there is a way you can connect and support a media ecosystem that doesn't require external sources and so on. Even there, we find vulnerabilities.

We can give another example of this. Whether we are in India or in Brazil, we will be following the minutiae of the US election campaign: "will Trump win? will Biden win?" This becomes global news. In Kerala, a state of 35 million people, the left was recently re-elected. Most of left people around the globe don't have any clue about that. When Lula case came up first, Prashad tried to write about this in the Indian media and the editor first look and say "who is gonna read this story?". Second, the case itself is bafflingly incomprehensible, we don't understand what this case means. But, the audience in India has a clue of anything about the US Supreme Court, what's happening in California and so on. In the South, one can talk much more about the US, than we can talk about the places where we are currently based. That is how this thing of North-South reproduces itself. This level of imbalance is part of the way the North-South divide reproduce itself.

Now, countries like Brazil and India have resources, have a certain degree of technological and knowledge...what is lacking? An important question is: is Brazil not climbing the ladder because of the imperialist structure of the world that says "no, Brazil, you cannot rise" or is it not rising because there is a ruling class which gets profits out of that structure and is it not interested in guiding Brazil to an independence? This complex relations between the internal and international power structures needs careful analysis to identify the potential political liberation strategies.

Inter-state disputes and environmental challenges

The concepts of unipolarity and multipolarity might be important to understand the complexity of current world affairs. Imperialism on the political terrain, because imperialism is about economics, politics, society, culture. It is about all these things, but if you just slice out in political terrain, imperialism manifests itself through the drive for unipolarity. The US and its key allies operate to define the behavior of other countries in a kind of top-down way. So, the US through the IMF, for instance, will show up in a country and say, "this is all you have to do, if you don't do this, we will penalize you, we will sanction you, we will overthrow you, we will coup you". That's unipolarity. India and Brazil, again particularly these two countries, had an opportunity about 20 years ago to entering through a different dynamic.

There were two paths to India and Brazil in the year 2000. In the first case, the political project was to explore a national democratic path. That was exactly the path that Brazil did go on when President Luiz Inacio Lula da Silva came to office. He drove a hard agenda to diminish suffering for the Brazilian people. So, let's try to end hunger, let's try to improve education, including high education, building institutions, for instance, UFABC. Let's produce a kind of direction not only about food and education. Let's improve the health structure. Brazil has a new super health structure. But that path requires a kind of international order. And, thus, Brazil got involved first with India and South Africa in IBSA, and then in BRICS. This is a genuine project of multipolarity (Garcia, 2010). Let's create an alternative pole, where we create South-South collaboration, where we try to get a better deal for us, selling soy to China let's say, let's get good resources in. That is one path, that was available to Brazil, but it required that the Brazilian to be cognizant of the importance of a national democratic agenda, which included erasing hunger, better healthcare. That is how we have to understand the relationship between Lula's domestic policy and BRICS. These are not two detached things. There is an integral relationship: the national democratic, the domestic agenda leads to this kind of multipolarity.

The second path is what we called a "subordinated-ally approach". This is the path taken by India, for instance, under president Narendra Modi in India, and Brazil, under Temer and Bolsonaro. They governed essentially on this subordinated-ally posture, where they say "look, we are not going to bother with the national democratic agenda, we don't care that people are starving in our country, the health system is being privatized, we don't care about all it", "Our main thing is if we hitch our wagon to the United States, that's how we will arise". We will become, essentially, what Ruy Mauro Marini (1977) was saying decades ago, a kind of subimperial formation. Although we don't actually agree with taking Marini's ideas to the present, because Marini was writing about a completely different era, but just using it metaphorically, there is a subordinated-ally approach according to which we will remain with the unipolar system. This means abandoning the national democratic agenda. The center will allow Brazilian and Indian companies abroad and accept the presence of Brazilian and Indian oligarchies. It's a stupid word to use oligarchy, but enables the understanding of the point, the people on the big mining companies domestically (and Brazil has big companies in mining), we let them flourish. At the same time, if people are hungry, they are hungry.

So, there are the two path approaches. Therefore, when we look at India and Brazil and so on, it is not path dependency. There is no necessity that we should go on this direction. It depends on which class dominates the state in the country. Certainly, if more liberal fractions of the bourgeoisie, maybe other classes, working class and peasantry dominate the state, then you could develop a truly national democratic agenda. And this would require multipolarity, because you can't do a national democratic process in a unipolar system. I believe it's a contradiction, the unipolar system does not allow it, imperialism prevents some outcomes to take place.

Now, going to the North, where there is what people are calling a kind of revolution...the Bidenomics, just looking at the US itself and not its external policies. Regarding the US government support to trade union organizations, the new government really comes forward on it, it was not only a rhetoric, there is a law to worker unions to organize. On the race issue, he clearly has a strong stance and all his fiscal policies, trillions to create cohesion in the US society and that confused the left, because the left is not up about making imperialism or its foreign policy more friendly. Not at all. This can be a way to rejuvenate US capitalism. The US understood that the only way to keep this regime is to reinvent itself, to invest in science and technology, and the State has to do it because the companies will not make investments; in the past what was good for General Motors was good for US, but now not anymore. US companies invest in China, attracted by its huge market and technological dynamism. So, we are in a moment where the State has to intervene to the benefit of the capitalism as a whole, even if it means going against specific interests in the short term. (Schutte, 2021). But, it means also the need to come up with a kind of New Deal between the working classes, black communities, women, they really have a chance to move forward. In the US, there is also the contradiction between the promise of a more workers friendly capitalism and migration. When Biden shouts "jobs, jobs, jobs!", millions of people who are hungry in Central America and all-over South America, are incentivized to take the route to the North.

Some people are underestimating the importance of this new agenda. There is no movement to socialism, not at all. It is a new way to organize or modernize US capitalism, independent of the difficulties Biden is facing to implement his offensive.

One can break this idea into two things. One is the political side: the unions, the question of Black Lives Matter and so on. And on the other the massive stimulus, which Biden could not pass, because they are different things. Maybe related, but different things. So, what was the proximity reason for the protest cycle in 2020? Was it once more the killing of a black man in Minneapolis, George Floyd who was suffocated to death on the street? In the US three people are killed every day by the police, thousands of people killed a year by the police. It's extraordinary, this has not changed. The *New York Times* has a website on it. Three people killed a day by the police, it's extraordinary! It's the highest per capita rate in the world. Watch videos on social media of Los Angeles, where the police just randomly fire and beat people, pretty vicious events, the exact reason for the cycle of protests last year and periodically the cycles before… death of Eric Garner, Michael Brown, and others have not resulted in major change. So that's the first thing to put there, in terms of actual reforms of policing. There's been no move by Biden administration. It is important to say that because that is the proximity issue, the rate of police killing is not going down.

The issue of union support and so on is interesting. It is true that compared to Europe's pandemic stimulus, the Biden administration and even the Trump administration produced considerable stimulus payments. But let's understand why this is the case. The first thing to recognize is that in the US (and now, we are comparing to Europe), almost every social service is privatized. Europe does not need such a substantial stimulus check. In most countries, healthcare is funded through small fees on the social wage. In most countries, there are very good social benefits packages for unemployed. Germany has a very generous package on that. So, in these countries there is no need to increase stimulus spending to people because they have welfare states. In the US, there was no social welfare state. Everything people need to survive the pandemic have to come on the stimulus bill and that's why the stimulus bill is so much greater than in Europe. To take these two as examples. It does not mean that Biden is more generous than Merkel, it is just that Biden had to write a bigger check because people don't have public services.

Regarding the second part, the Monthly Review has a tradition to look to American political economy reframing things as the old soviet economists' business cycles, the Kondratiev waves, where there is a business cycle swimming up, swimming down, up, down, and so. On the Monthly review tradition, and Sweezy (2018) did this first analysis on his book on the theory of monopolies, they point that the US sees a secular decline in per capita social spending. So, from a certain period the decline starts, then comes a depression and then comes what Monthly Review calls salvage spending. Then, the government reacts on the spending to salvage from a period of crisis, plus they use that spending for compensate purposes because there is no market compensate cyclical mechanisms in US economy. They have done everything in the last 50 years into the monetary policy handle, where you increase money supply, you decrease money supply…then, how to encourage economic activity? Increase money supply, put more dollars into the system…that's monetary policy. In terms of fiscal policy, budget policy has very little room. The mechanism is given, because you have balanced budgets amendment, because of the lever of fiscal policy been stuck, there is this social spending decline.

Then comes a crisis… housing crises, pandemic crises and now at the time we see suddenly the salvage spending. So, there are two things happening with stimulus: one is salvage spending and the other is the spending compared to Europe, on social services. From this perspective what Biden tries to do is by itself no nothing new.

But Bidenomics is a totally different scale. However, for the last maybe 60 years, the US government hadn't a good infrastructure spending bill. The last major state sponsor of infrastructure was made by Eisenhower. For 60 years there's not been a comprehensible infrastructure bill and things are in bad shape. Things are in bad shape, bridges are collapsing, there is a lot of repair work to be done, to maintain things. Infrastructure really needs to be overvaulted, including digital infrastructure. There are larger parts in US with no broad band of internet. This is no longer a luxury; this is a human right. People need good internet in a pandemic, children need to study from home, people have to work from home. So, part of the other scale spending is going towards infrastructure spending footage has no regular spending trench in the budget. Since the 1950s, every decade had low infrastructure spending.

And that's bring us to the issue of China. Every time Biden is trying to sell his ideas, to get support, he talks about three C's: Covid, Climate and China. Then he puts the three B's as the answer: Build Back Better. And China is exactly about technology. Because if the US does not invest now, there is the idea that China will go forward and lead the new industrial-technological revolution. In fact, part of what Biden is doing looks like coping a long-term technology investment plan that China is doing, and Europe by now as well. For many years, industrial policies were seen as bad policies. This changed completely. The US feels that, otherwise, China will surpass them. Because, as we have said, before: it is about technology and control. And Biden is really clear on this. It is about who controls technology.

Where does it leave us? Is there a new Cold War? Has the perspective of a multipolar world gone? It is just China, US and the rest? How far it will go? Some people say there is no Cold War, because in the economics dimension the companies are interrelated. That's true, because US companies do not move out from China's very attractive market. There can be proxy wars. Biden says openly, several times, as longer as he is in presidency, China will not be the main player. And he has a very aggressive foreign policy linking up with Japan, with Australia, with India, with Europe, now he goes down to South America, Colombia, etc.

First, there is a Cold War that was not declared last year or last month. It has been going for the last two decades. The US is trying to control developments in Eurasia. Henry Kissinger's book "On China" (2011), for instance, was part of a dialogue in the US security establishment on how to control Eurasia. Kissinger argues in favor of friendship with China, like they did in the 1970s, and make them a US ally against Russia. Other people in Washington are saying: "no, be friends with Russia and we have to go ahead against China". This has been going through the thinking of Washington for 20 years.

In the end, the US turned up the heat against both China and Russia, driving these two former adversaries closer together. Obama's policy in Syria and Ukraine threatened Russian interests, since these countries hosted Russia's two warm water ports in Tartus (Syria) and Sebastopol (Crimea). The US knew what it was doing. This was not accidental. It deliberately poked at Russia. Putin's response was to defend the sovereignty of Russia and Russian interests, so Russia intervened in Crimea in 2014 and in Syria in 2015, both times using its military might outside its borders, something we have not seen since the USSR collapsed. Putin gained popularity in his country because of his policy to uphold Russian interests and sovereignty. This is a turn-around from the 1990s, during which President Boris Yeltsin (1991–1999) humiliated the country, with Yeltsin – drunk – begging for US approval in public. Putin renewed a sense of aristocratic dignity for the Russian people.

There was a miscalculation on the US side. They kept looking for vulnerabilities, they used the language of human rights, trying to accuse Russia of human rights violations. But this was incoherent. When Russia conducted a brutal war in Chechnya, it was defended in the West as part of the War on Terror. Nobody cared then. So, in this period, when the West talks about human rights, it makes no impact inside Russia.

On the other side of Eurasia, the West miscalculated with China. They thought that they could find a Gorbachev of the Communist Party of China (CPC), to dismantle the state from within. But they failed. There is simply no Gorbachev. The CPC learnt its lessons carefully. The CPC has 95 million members. It has many strands of opinion within the party. Currently, the left is in charge, with Xi Jinping as the standard-bearer. There is little possibility of an internal collapse led by the CPC. Other factors might be there, but not a repeat of what happened in the USSR.

China is very aware of its history. But the Chinese actually made their bet. They bet on science, unique amongst the Third World country. It's easy for Germans, the French and others to say "China steal things...". They don't steal it, they put conditions on the entry of foreign firms in the late 1980s and early 1990s. And it is also not "forced technology transfer" as the West likes to put it, but the outcome of negotiations. In 1990, the South Commission, led by Julius Nyerere, said, "you have to learn from the Chinese". What they meant was not from Chinese culture per se, but from the path set by the Chinese, including how they negotiated with the capitalist firms. You are a German company? You want to come to Shenzen and use our healthy, intelligent workers? Well, then you have to show us how you do thing, transfer the technology and transfer the science. They were not only allowing the foreign firms to use Shenzen as a way to merely take, but also as a way for China to get important developments. In India, Sri Lanka, other places we just said: "please come here, here is the land, here is the labor; take it over". We never asked for transfer of technology; the Chinese did. They were asking companies, "show us how you make...solar panels". And then China becomes the leader in solar panel manufacturing. It's because they included it in the agreements they made. Then comes the great Chinese economic development. That is a reality. There was industrial espionage, too. But it's part of capitalist competition, a normal thing. That was not invented by China. China also made strong connections with Russia, which is very significant phenomenon.

This new cold war is a real thing. The "HMS Queen Elizabeth", as we speak today, is sailing across the Strait of Malacca, to conduct so-called freedom of navigation exercises in the Taiwan Strait. They join US, German, Japanese, Australian warships going around Chinese waters. Tensions are rising around Taiwan. All of this is dangerous. You can't settle disputes in this way. People's patriotism rises and then they refuse to back down. They are cornering the people. No solution to these problems is going to come from threats. Yes, you can win a military confrontation and solve it, but that's not a real negotiation.

The second point is that the emergence after 2013 of the New Silk Road or the Belt and Road Initiative (BRI) has put on the table for countries an alternative to the World Bank and the IMF. The BRI is not socialism, but it is an alternative to the IMF-led debt trap development. A country like Zambia is now able to play both sides off against each other, and get a good deal for itself. The BRI poses a challenge to the IMF path, not because one is socialist and the other is capitalist but because it gives developing countries a choice. The problem is that many developing countries do not have a well-articulated national development project, which means that they are not always in the best position to make a choice between the BRI and the IMF. What is the national project of a country? Do they have such a project? Will they be able to get the best option on the table? That's a new opening for our countries.

The real issue is that these are two development opportunities. Countries should be allowed to trade with each other. And the other point is, about whether with the arrival of China multipolarity this would still be possible. Of course, it would. In fact, more than ever. Because if China emerges as a major pole in relation to the Western pole, this allows other people to organize regionally. Over the past decade, the South American regional project – through ALBA and UNASUR – has held its own, but has not been able to advance largely because of the US sanctions policy. Now, with the arrival of the BRI in the hemisphere (Argentina signing on as an indicator of its arrival), it is likely that the regional project can be resurrected.

It is still very early, and wrong to write the obituary of multipolarity. These things happen in zigzags. The fact that we have China and next to it these countries in the South, show that they have an alternative. They don't have to obey Washington, because they can make a deal there and if it doesn't work out, they can turn to China. And this is very clear also for African countries.

However, if this tension is growing, the US will intervene, especially in Latin America. They cannot allow something like the balance of power with China in South America, and they cannot accept a regional power that is friendly to China. So, there will be more and more pressure. One can predict that there will be more tension between the US and China, more pressure on Latin America to keep it in the US backyard, which has been reinvented by Trump. But Biden is going in exactly the same direction, because this is part of the general idea, of reinforcing the US responses to the new global environment. And that would make it more difficult for Latin America to invent its own smaller regional pole. But that is the challenge.

There is an opportunity, the only way forward. But the region shouldn't get too anxious about being forced to choose sides, because the relationship between China and Latin America is not about South-South. Nor does China represent a new imperialism. It is a developing country, but it is a new center. It is not a peripheral region; it is not the South. But it offers a new perspective to geoeconomics and geopolitics, which can allow other developing countries to advance.

Now, if we analyze, for example, and it is crucial that the Chinese said, "okay foreign companies, you can come, you can exploit our market, our labor, but you have to invest in technologies and you have to operate within a strategic national development framework". Brazil could have done that. In some points it even did a little bit because it has a huge market, like India etc. Other countries maybe not so much. But the question is: let's suppose governments in South America try to implement these policies, then they will apply also to Chinese companies. Because now the Chinese are there too. And that is fine, but they should create technology centers and reinforce R&D in the region. And we don't want to just export soy, iron, and oil to China, and then hear, "oh, it's a wonderful relationship, because we complement each other". That is not the win-win relation South America should be satisfied with.

What are the distributional consequences, including from an intersectional point of view?

First, it is important to put the view that the Chinese have made it clear that they do not want a dispute. They use the phrase "win-win". Now, the point is that they are not using aggressive language, saying "we want to take down the United States". They express a desire to cooperate. But they also want to fight back when they are pressured. This is important, it means that they are no longer going to take everything lying down, but we don't see them saying "we are in a dispute with the United States". They are saying that the US is imposing a dispute. Like the example of El Salvador. El Salvador wanted to build a port on the Pacific coast and they made a deal with a Chinese company. When the president of El Salvador was in Beijing, he flew back with a stopover in Tokyo. In Tokyo, the prime minister was Shinzō Abe told him, "Discard the deal with the Chinese. The Americans told me to tell you that". He arrives back in El Salvador and discards the deal with the Chinese, and then the US comes with their "American box project". And they do this public-private partnership, which is a worse deal for El Salvador, by the way. But that is imposed on El Salvador. Many say that the coup against Abel was imposed because he was too close to the Chinese. (Kyodo, 2019)

How do you make sure that people can resist being dragged into this so-called cold war in South America and other developing countries? The answer is two-fold. First, each country should have its own national project. What is your national strategic project? Most countries don't have one anymore. They have stopped thinking in these terms. What is your five-year project? Your ten-year project? What sectors do we want to develop? Do we want to just look for high commodity prices or do we want to process these commodities? Do we want to trade for something else, high technology or something else? What else can we do? You need to develop this, but you also need to develop regional projects. It is very important for all areas of the world to have regional projects. Why? China is a region. China is not a country; it is a continent. The US is a region. With Canada, it is a giant domestic market, it is a huge country. And it is not the same in South America. You need regional complementarities.

Only if you have a sense of yourself, can you impose yourself on others. If you don't know who you are, you will accept what you are being told about yourself. In developing countries, in general, to be very frank, we don't know who we are. And when the Americans come and tell us "oh, you are that", you say "well, maybe I am". Or when the Chinese come and say "you are soybean exporters". Yes, we are soybean exporters! No, what are you? What are you capable of becoming?

What do you want, what is your own history? In political economy and international relations, we need to emphasize more: What is the national project? What is the regional project? We cannot spend our lives saying that the Americans are doing this to us, the Chinese are doing this, the Europeans are doing this. What do we want to do for ourselves? Right. So, we need leadership and strong social organizations. And to have at least part of the ruling classes following engaged in a national program.

But what about India? In the early 1980s, when we started studying international relations, a lot of people talked about Japan and nobody talked about China. Now, people talk about China and nobody talks about India. Some say that India will be the China of the future. But it seems that there is something missing in India, this strong national development strategy. So why is that? Because what we see is that now the BRICS has become almost insignificant.

And a lot of people think that Brazil did this because of Bolsonaro, but it has a lot to do with India. India has accepted this policy of containment to China for years, it would rather work with Australia and Japan, than engage more with China. Although, of course, economic relations are moving in another direction. What are India's prospects after Modi, who will not be there for his lifetime? There is no guarantee that Modi, or his party, will not be there for quite some time yet. But the first thing to say is that after India became independent in 1947, China won its War of Liberation in 1949. Those are two interesting parts. In the Mao Era, the Chinese did some things that were fundamental.

Without land reform, you couldn't do what China did. That meant, in rural areas, creating democratic institutional structures to improve health, nutrition, education, adult literacy, in a broad sense. Improving culture. This was as a function of aggressive land reform and overthrowing the culture of the landlords. In India, there was nothing like that (Dasgupta, 2016). Then in the 1980s, 1990s, 2000s, and so on, in China, the differences narrowed between the literate and the non-literate, between the hungry and the able-bodied, and between the healthy and the unhealthy. Now inequality increases, that is another problem. But you have seen many problems disappear. In India you don't see that. The average Indian worker is less literate than the Chinese, less healthy, less nourished, and therefore more prone to disease. This meant that India's fundamental base is not as strong as China's. In India, you have a highly educated middle class. One of our key languages is English due to our colonial history. This enables our middle class workforce to better integrate into Anglo-American circuits of capital accumulation. This is also India's downfall, because it means that a lot of Indian workers have gone to work for American and European companies. Whereas China has built up its own capacity.

Do you know what China's greatest "wall" is? Mandarin. It is a great wall. In the Mandarin-speaking world, people don't speak English. Mandarin is the main language. Their whole internet system is in Mandarin, they have their own internet, their own social media: "wechat, weibo". They are all their own systems, and that is the function of the "great wall of Mandarin". It's a real thing. India has many vulnerabilities. It may be easier to integrate, because of English, but there is less physical strength in the people, because land reform has not been done. It's a fundamentally undemocratic thing, not to do land reform. And furthermore, it has not developed its internal technology. It is totally dependent on buying technology from outside.

However, in India, like in Brazil there has been some important development, for several reasons. First, the pent-up demand: 50 years of a relatively closed economy. Second, the massive export of varied resources. India is brimming with resources. Iron ore, coal, whatever, a lot of things. But there is also Indian industry. Which doesn't sell to the West alone, but sells to Africa, sells to Southeast Asia, among others. India has not moved up the ladder and continues to produce for these so-called secondary markets. India has a pharmaceutical industry that produces 60% of the world's syringes, but this is a low value-added sector.

Syringes are in the low value-added sector, what has value is the contents of the syringe. And that is patented by Western companies. India is vulnerable, trapped in a submissive relationship, it's trapped in this middle-income place, because it can't take its great scientific breakthroughs, and convert them into domestic technological breakthroughs. Take a silly example: India has decided, as part of the Chinese containment strategy, to ban Chinese apps from Indian smartphones. Done. The joke was that the Chinese had no app to ban. Chinese cell phones don't have any Indian apps, because there are almost no apps from India. And that is the difference. India is still producing middle-income commodities; it can't go to the next level. It needs a robust economy that has high-yield commodities, that has a high value-added sector. It needs some mid-level stuff, intermediate products. It needs some primary goods. It needs a complex economy to build on, but no, India needs to import a lot of high value-added goods, and so it's going to stay in this mid-level sector of profitability. This is very similar to the situation in other middle-income countries, like Brazil.

How to alleviate distributive asymmetries, based on popular solutions and state action?

But under Modi, India is moving closer to the US within this conflict with China, at least that's how it looks from the outside, and how ingrained is that in the society? Huge protests by Indian farmers have occurred in 2020 and 2021 forcing to Modi government to make concessions. At some point can we imagine that this is translating into some kind of a new independence movement or will it take more time and maybe we can't expect a new "Southern Voice" of India in the short term? This alone would take a lot of explaining, but it is true that tens of thousands of Indian farmers remained garrisoned in Delhi. Millions of workers went on strike on November 29, 2020. 250 million workers went on strike. That's incredible, but translating all this into electoral gain is a very complicated question. In these democracies, in India, Brazil, among many others, the power of money dominates. The power of the media dominates. The power to shape the narrative dominates. In Bengal, there were 1 million people from the left at a rally, but they did not win a single seat in next elections. Little things happen, but who controls the *whatsapp* groups? Look at the Brazilian presidential election in 2018. They painted Haddad in a way where he couldn't get out of the little box he was stuck in. They said he was going to teach children about sex and turn them into homosexuals. This is the way politics is done now, by fear and things like that.

Democracy can assimilate hate and fear much more easily than it can assimilate love. And that's the problem for the left. We go in there saying that we need to take care of each other. We haven't figured out how to make love an integral part of the democratic public space.

Hate we know how it works. Just go out and shout some hate speech and a crowd will gather to beat him up. Now, to go out in public and talk about love and good feelings, it feels good, but it doesn't captivate people enough to run to the ballot box. Somehow, we have seen it since the Nazi period, after all the Nazis won elections. Anyway, we have seen how hate is not incompatible with democracy. And we have a hard time understanding that. And there are, of course, examples of hope reviving people. Of course, there are examples of that. Hope becomes a material force.

But it is much more difficult to make hope into a material force, than it is to make hate. This is an important reflection as well, which brings us to the importance of the "Tricontinental" networks and contacts. The Tricontinental Institute for Social Research is only part of a network of social movements and political organizations. They are in a network called the International People's Assembly. And we are part of this network. Over the years, we have realized how neglected this joint work between movements and intellectuals has been in intellectual practice. That is why Tricontinental is very encouraging. We try to build some bridges. One of them is precisely between movements and intellectuals, whether academic or of any kind. That is an exciting bridge, and not because of a single meeting or an event, but to actually develop a process together.

The second bridge is to develop a relationship between these kinds of activities in India, in South Africa, and in Brazil. There are huge epistemological gaps between, for example, how intellectual activity in Brazil takes shape and how intellectual activity in India takes shape. It is not language, the structure is different. Even the terms. In Brazil how we talk a lot about articulation, methodology. It is impossible, really, because we need to learn not the work, but the context of it. When we talk about articulation, it can be translated as a relationship. But the most significant thing that we are learning on this journey is how we are dealing with the fact that the Story sometimes seems blocked, and sometimes it seems to move as well. And how when history seems blocked, what do we focus our attention on? What do we look at? How are our research objects derived from the movement of History, rather than from gaps in the literature? I remember being in undergrad and the professor asking "what are the gaps in the literature?" Understand them. Go and fill in the gaps. It's an approach to fill the gaps.

References

Cohen, Benjamin. *Currency Statecraft: Monetary Rivalry and Geopolitical Ambition.* Chicago: University of Chicago Press, 2018.

Dasgupta, Chirashree. *State and Capital in Independent India.* Jawaharlal Nehru University. Cambridge: Cambridge University Press, 2016.

Garcia, Marco Aurélio. O lugar do Brasil no Mundo. A Política Externa em um momento de transição. In: Sader, Emir e Garcia, Marco Aurélio (Orgs). *Brasil entre o passado e o futuro.* São Paulo: Editora Fundação Perseu Abramo: Boitempo, 2010.

Garside, Marco Aurélio. Canadian Mining Industry. Statistics & Facts. Statista, New York, Nov. 2020. https://www.statista.com/topics/3067/canada-s-mining-industry/#dossierKeyfigures. Accessed January 15, 2022.

Jensen, Lars. *Sovereign Debt Vulnerabilities in Developing Economies Which Countries Are Vulnerable and How Much Debt Is at Risk?* United Nations Development Programme (UNDP), New York, 2021.

Kissinger, Henry. *On China.* London/New York: Penguin Books, 2011.

Kyodo. Japan pressed El Salvador to Prevent Chinese Influence Over Port. *The Japan Times,* Dec., 30, 2019. https://www.japantimes.co.jp/news/2019/12/30/national/politics-diplomacy/japan-pressed-el-salvador-prevent-beijing-influence-port

Marini, Ruy Mauro. La acumulación capitalista mundial y el subimperialismo. *Cuadernos Políticos*, n. 12, abr./jun. 1977.

Schutte, Giorgio Romano. The Challenge to US Hegemony and the "Gilpin Dilemma". *Revista Brasileira de Política Internacional,* Vol 64 (1), 2021.

South Commission. *The Challenge to the South.* Oxford University Press, 1990.

Sweezy, Paul. *Theory of Capital Development.* Monthly Review Press, 2018.

Wübbeke, Jost; Meissner, Mirjam; Zenglein, Max J.; Ives, Jaqueline; Conrad, Björn. *Made in China 2025.* The making of a high-tech superpower and consequences for industrial countries. Mercator Institute for China Studies (Merics), dezembro, 2016.

2

NEOLIBERALISM, DEMOCRACY, AUTHORITARIANISM AND RESISTANCE

Alfredo Saad-Filho and Tatiana Berringer

This chapter presents our dialogue on neoliberalism, democracy, authoritarianism and the role of the left today. Saad presents a refined definition of neoliberalism, the 2008 crisis and the deepening with the Covid-19 pandemic, as he does in detail in his articles and books. The richness of details and the precision of concepts that the Brazilian researcher, who has been working in London for more than three decades, presents us with is crowned by the vision about the role of the left, the combination of struggles against neoliberalism, against authoritarianism, and against all kinds of oppression and exploitation (race, class, and gender). The hope in another possible future appears at the end of the conversation and shows that it is not just a desire of an intellectual to bring good conclusions, there is a basis and a political and theoretical engagement for the referred points. We start, therefore, from the definition of neoliberalism and the crisis in this arrangement, a phase of development of capitalism, to understand the crisis of democracy and the emergence of authoritarian and/or fascist movements and governments. Since we are dialoguing with a senior professor, with a very consolidated publication, we indicate in the footnotes of each section of the text (and at the end of the chapter), the professor's books and articles in which the issues are more carefully treated. Let us begin.

Neoliberalism: a definition[1]

Neoliberalism is part of the existence of capitalism as a mode of production, but like any mode of production, capitalism is defined on a very generic and abstract level. Capitalism is defined by property, labor, and exploitative relations. This includes a very large number of historical moments, of circumstances in each country, and of arrangements that change over time. Then, the idea of looking at

DOI: 10.4324/9781003384366-3

the periodization of capitalism and the local arrangements of capitalism aims to make this analysis more concrete, turning the analysis of modes of production, which is quite abstract, into an operational analysis in the sense of explaining contemporary phenomena both in the domain of economics and of politics.

One notes, for example, the evolution of capitalism in the last 200 years of industrial capitalism after the Industrial Revolution, there is a phase, which everybody generally agrees on, of Victorian liberal competitive capitalism, which goes more or less up to World War I. Then there is a phase after World War II associated with Keynesianism, which involves the arrangement of the social democracies in the advanced economy countries, and with different forms of developmentalism in the countries of what we now call the Global South. In the early 1980s there is a new configuration of capitalism as neoliberalism, a phenomenon common to several countries. Neoliberalism as an arrangement, phase, constitution, mode of existence of capitalism that has points in common in different experiences, be they almost prehistoric in Chile after the military coup of 1973, but more typically in the United Kingdom from 1976 onwards, in the United States from 1978 onwards, spreading to the Global North, and to the Global South after the foreign debt crisis.

Neoliberalism is marked by four points:

1 a set of state policies: policies of privatization, policies of dismantling the welfare state, policies of individual accountability instead of universal social policies, for example.
2 an ideological discourse involving ideas of "free enterprise" and "competition", and democracy. Neoliberalism is associated with a specific type of democracy.
3 financialization, is the most important aspect that directs and guides these transformations of capitalism. It is the domination of economic activity, and the control over social reproduction by what Marx called "interest-bearing" capital, and what is commonly called, without much loss of content, financial capital. It is the logic of finance over the accumulation process in the different countries. The dominance of finance over public policy and the dominance of finance over people's subjectivity. On how people position themselves in the world, they position themselves by maximizing gains, they position themselves by making investments in themselves, this is the logic of financial capital that characterizes this moment, this arrangement, this phase of global capitalism.
4 the productive restructuring. The integration of the work processes of products stopped being manufactured in their entirety within specific economies and started being internationalized, within the production process itself, not only in the consumption process. You produce something here and buy the coffee produced in Brazil and consumed around the world. It is no longer about that. It is about the internationalization of the production of manufactured goods, with the design being done in one country,

with the intellectual property possibly being the company based in a third country, with part of the product being manufactured in different continents, and with the final assembly of the product in a specific location for international distribution. It turns out that Southeast Asia, for various reasons, has become the center of this assembly process, but, the capture of the profits remains centered in the advanced economy country, in particular, the United States.

The 2008 crisis and the Covid-19 pandemic[2]

In 2007/2008 there was a very serious crisis within neoliberalism as a result of the accumulation strategies that were being used up to that point domestically in the United States as a great example. It was the accumulation strategy based on a relatively small public deficit, and a very large household debt, in a circumstance of stagnant wages. Real wages in the United States peaked in 1973, then did not grow. It was a major destructuring of labor markets and a change in labor processes associated with, in general terms, deindustrialization in advanced economy countries like the United States in particular, but also in the United Kingdom and in several other countries.

This model collapsed in 2007. The capitalist economies had been losing dynamism for more than 50 years, and the rate of economic growth declined around the world, and particularly in the advanced economy countries, the OECD countries. This is a phenomenon that was not reversed with neoliberalism, and it got worse after 2007, when we entered the period that neoliberal, neoclassical economists themselves (economists of the dominant school both at the level of theory and in political practice, at the level of government), began to talk about a great stagnation, the second great stagnation. The first one would have been at the end of the 19th century. This second one would be linked to the fact that no economy had the dynamism to pull the global economy: the United States did not have the capacity to do this, Western Europe completely stagnated, Japan stagnated, and China, which is still a developing country, does not have the capacity to do this.

The global economy was paralyzed by lack of an engine. This situation has continued over time. The GDP growth rate has fallen in the advanced economy countries and in several developing countries. The pandemic hit the global economy, and this causes an immediate economic catastrophe. It was a sudden economic contraction. The economic crisis was then accentuated, due to an external event: the pandemic. To the extent that you can deal with the pandemic, you can return to a higher level of economic activity. The question is whether they are going to maintain the economic recovery, whether they are now going to have another engine of growth that is going to keep neoliberalism running at the higher level of activity. There is no evidence that this is going to happen. The Biden plan to spend a lot of US resources on a transition to a green economy, with spending on infrastructure, is an attempt to address this issue of economic stagnation. But the plan is a bit of a quagmire at the moment, and it is not clear that President Biden is going to be able to reactivate his idea. This is all at the level of ideas, we will see if neoliberalism recovers, but the expectation is pessimistic. The capacity exists. But the economic challenge today is a political and social challenge, which is the problem of the environmental crisis. If global capitalism at this moment of neoliberal capitalism, with all the deficiencies it has, is not able to face this challenge that could give it economic dynamics, there is no way out. Neoliberal capitalism has so far shown neither the awareness nor the capacity to face these challenges. Despite the urgency of the problem, there are political deadlocks, economic deadlocks, and social deadlocks that neoliberalism itself has created. It may have created an impasse that leads to an economic and social, and therefore political, catastrophe.

The crisis in neoliberalism and the crisis in democracy[3]

The crisis of neoliberalism would be a crisis of the functioning of this stage of capitalism, a deep, structural crisis. The crisis of neoliberalism affects the system of accumulation, but does not necessarily lead to transformations. The crisis of neoliberalism is linked to the fact that there is no alternative, there is no social movement, there is no political alliance that proposes concrete alternatives, that challenges the form of economic and social reproduction associated with neoliberalism.

For, as, neoliberalism spread around the world, it gradually consolidated a form of political functioning. Neoliberalism emerged in various forms. It initially emerged through military coup in Chile, Uruguay, and Argentina during the 1970s. It was a local solution to a problem contained at the level of international political economy. It was geographically contained. And it spread through the election of democratic governments, which impose institutional and constitutional changes, which entrench neoliberal institutions within the structure of legal, economic, and social functioning of countries. This form of institutionalization of neoliberalism continued around the world (in advanced and developing countries, and after the fall of the Soviet Union, in the Eastern bloc countries) with structural adjustment programs, economic policy changes, and ideological and legal changes. Neoliberalism was consolidated around a specific institutionality: neoliberal institutionality.

And it also gained ideological space. It became the common sense of our period, competition becomes a good thing, people have to be competitive, competition is everything, it's a freedom of choice. These neoliberal clichés became unquestionable truths, this kind of thing is not even debated and, at the same time, the ways in which neoliberalism works in favor of it are ingrained within the institutionality. The policies of inflation targeting and Central Bank independence, which are precisely to maintain the hegemony of the financial sector and place these key institutions to guarantee the value of financial assets (and which guarantee the influence of financial interests in the reproduction of economies and society), do not enter the political debate. So, there is no point in people being dissatisfied or one political party or another trying to challenge neoliberalism, because it is institutionalized many times within the text of the Constitution, making it very difficult to make any change. State institutions are committed to neoliberalism.

In general, all over the world, neoliberalism has become institutionalized, and, with this, it becomes entrenched. As it becomes entrenched, it excludes the proposal and the possibility of alternatives from the political debate, it impoverishes the domain of politics, it leaves this domain. It impoverishes by excluding economic matters from consideration, from divergence between political parties. The party cannot diverge significantly from economic policies. It can diverge like this, at the margin. So the electoral game already in the 1990s, continuing in the 2000s, the electoral game in a large number of influential countries becomes a dispute between neoliberal factions, between political parties offering neoliberal programs with differences at the margin and not much because it could not, because institutionality does not allow it, because there is no way you can rock the boat. It is more because institutionality is very fragile, because you need political alliances in order to govern. The example of Brazil is during the PT government, whether they wanted to or not, the PT governments realized that it was not possible to do what they wanted to do, that it would be a lot of work trying to shake the hegemony of neoliberalism in Brazil. So, let's do other things: let's do social programs, let's do Bolsa Familia and other programs trying to tackle neoliberalism by the edges, but within stricter limits so as not to create too much turbulence. It turned out not to be possible, for other reasons. But that was a widespread phenomenon.

Neoliberalism impoverishes democracy, and in doing so, at the same time that it restructures the production process, that depresses wages, worsens employment conditions around the world, increases competition and the penalty for failure at a time when the entire production process is being restructured, new technologies are being introduced, creating economic losers in various countries, particularly in the large central economies that have lost a large part of their manufacturing sector is that it has been exported to China, exported to Southeast Asia and in other regions of the world.

The developing countries that have lost the possibility to develop, have lost the capacity to industrialize, except for localized cases. If there are a large number of economic losers around the world who have no voice, there is no way that their interests can be reflected politically through structures of representation, the political parties have become very weak, the institutionality has become very rigid, the unions have lost the capacity to represent, and they have lost power to the nationalist movements around the world. Nationalist governments lost power. The left-wing governments associated with national independence movements lost space, disappeared completely. The large number of people who had a certain contestation, dissatisfaction with neoliberalism, lost the capacity to express this politically.

A situation of turbulence has been created in the political base of a large number of countries that has no solution within neoliberalism, because neoliberalism is not able to reach these people, and this process of corrosion of political representation has continued over many years since the economic crisis that began in 2008. The solution of neoliberalism was: let's save the financial sector. Whatever the cost. It was a huge fiscal cost. Then we are going to charge the poorest people, somebody is going to have to pay that fiscal bill. We are going to charge the poorest people, further dismantling the welfare state, squeezing wages, making working conditions worse, making people's living conditions worse. It was an absolutely regressive solution. And this created political instability, because the number of dissatisfied people tends to grow with an absolute lack of representation for the interests of these people.

Neoliberalism then created political dysfunctionality at the same time, and because of it having political hegemony, and ideological hegemony in a large number of countries. This is a very unstable situation that was eventually resolved through the emergence of independent and authoritarian leaderships in a large number of these countries. The alternative leaderships were stifled at the very bottom and were left out. What was left were these right-wing leaders, associated with neoliberalism, with big names with recognition in the political system that were not going to shake up the functioning of neoliberalism, but who appeared as people independent of the entrenched interests. They appeared as people who could directly represent the interests of the economic losers, they appeared as people who were not corrupt. Corruption became very much associated as a routine operation of neoliberalism, then people appeared who had the intellectual capacity to supposedly fight it. Businessmen, with experience and the capacity to represent those interests that were not being represented within the neoliberal system. These people emerged as leaders in a number of countries, for example, Donald Trump in the United States, Erdogan in Turkey, Modi in India, etc. Bolsonaro in Brazil is an extremely weak leadership, a political leader with very important deficiencies at all levels, assumed a little by chance and a little by desperate search of various sectors within Brazil for an alternative to the left. He is a person who has the capacity to cause damage, absolutely immense. Not only to institutionality, he is all the time trying to sabotage the functioning of democracy, but also people's lives, to the extent that he sabotages the response of public policies to the coronavirus pandemic.

The dysfunctionality is gigantic, as we have seen in Brazil, in the United States, in the United Kingdom, in Turkey, in India, and a number of other countries. It is a reflection of the basic dysfunctionality of neoliberalism: political dysfunctionality, and an economy that doesn't work either. It doesn't work because it doesn't understand the needs of the people, so the crisis is serious and the rise of these authoritarian, spectacular leaders doesn't solve either the economic crisis or the political crisis, on the contrary, it destabilizes even more.

There is a concrete risk of this process leading to the emergence of new forms of fascism, not the fascism of the 20s and 30s of the last century, but it will be the neoliberal fascism, it will be the fascism of now or that doesn't need to be based on such large street militias, with exceptions in the case of Brazil. It doesn't need that. It's going to be a fascism based on social media, fascism based on interception of communication, it's going to be a fascism based on a different kind of terror, but with a similar character to the traditional fascisms, of elite, of division, regime that raises nationalist slogans. Politics of confrontation, of exclusion, policies of creating enemies in succession, etc. This would be a very serious fate, very sad for Brazil and for the world. It is necessary to find alternatives. The political function of the left at this moment is to look for options that allow us to neutralize this danger.

In the recent period, the case of Chile shows that the institutional apparatus prevents the change of economic policy. It shows that an immense sacrifice is required, gigantic mobilizations, often sacrificing lives, to be able to discuss the constitutional text, to be able to discuss the basic arrangement of the functioning of society. An extremely important victory that happened in Chile has a transforming potential at the international level of gigantic importance. Let's see if this potential can be harnessed.

Authoritarianisms: in the North and in the South

One peculiarity of neoliberalism is that for the first time in human history, there is a convergence of economic policies. Previously, until the 1970s, there was clearly one type of economic policy for the central countries, and another type of economic policy that was completely different for colonial or peripheral countries. In the neoliberal period, these policies converged around privatization, and the dismantling of the welfare state, which was very distinct in each country. The whole political apparatus of neoliberalism converged on this, and created distinct challenges. You don't apply similar policies in different circumstances, they are different challenges.

The response in the form of the emergence of spectacular political leaders has important similarities in several countries: in Italy, the United States, Brazil, India, and the Philippines. But it is not a universal phenomenon. Part of the social scientist's job is to locate the common elements that characterize this phase, this moment, and what drives the succession of events we are experiencing. This convergence of challenges and, in some cases, of responses, is due precisely to the reorganization of the international economy that occurred during the neoliberal period; to the extent that you reorganize you create distinct problems. Problems of deindustrialization in the United States, but also in Brazil. Problems of economic growth in South Africa, but also in Russia; problems of internal divisions in society that then allow unscrupulous political leaderships to exploit, as in Turkey, as in India. Then, divisions are created of the native people against the immigrants in any advanced economic country, that this necessarily slips into racism. Nationalism is always a weapon available to the government to disarm the opposition. And this is also as part of a common discourse that has become increasingly sharper, more aggressive in recent years. To the extent that the government loses the capacity to create economic dynamism, to create social integration and political integration based on improving the living conditions of the majority of the people. It loses the capacity and loses the interest to do this. They then slip into building unity and building their political support in more negative ways, and this is extremely destructive to the collectivity of these countries.

India is a particularly dramatic example. To the extent that the political leadership exercises deeply and decisively its potential to create divisions among the people who live there, to create differences of identity, and to exploit those differences in other countries as well. In the United States, the Trump administration made deliberate attempts to create divisions with Mexico, and with immigrants from Central America. This is an extremely corrosive thing, and one that cannot be accepted. It is very difficult to resist this easy discourse of nationalism and racism. But it is a very important mission for people who want to build more integrated societies, more solidary societies, which are the only forms of sociability, to allow us to accumulate the necessary forces to not only confront the pandemic. Countries with less political divisions did better in the pandemic period. But to be able to build unity, essential to face the problem of climate change, and to build technologically advanced societies that also have decent living conditions for the overwhelming majority of their population. This we are not even close to achieving.

The struggle against neoliberalism and authoritarianism[4]

The struggles that aggregate are those to improve people's living conditions, for job stability, for improved working conditions, for economic policies that build the economic and social base, that supports people building infrastructure, public transportation, public goods in general, health, education, etc. Obviously, these are things that add up. Thus, the potential is there. You have to build on this, so that you can realize this potential of the struggles that can integrate this confrontation against neoliberalism.

Just as neoliberalism is an internationalized system of accumulation, the struggle against neoliberalism must also be international. These have always been challenges for the left, which have been faced in different ways over time. This unity is very important. There are some advantages today, pandemics aside, international travel has become easier, social media has advanced a lot, so it's perfectly possible to interact more internationally, and that strangeness that there was in the past with people based in different places in the world, that has diminished a lot. But on the other hand, methods of intercepting communications have also evolved a lot. The repressive apparatus of the state has become much more sophisticated, the response of the left to this challenge can only be around building the unity of building the mass movement. The left cannot fall into conspiracy politics, into small group politics. The strength of the left has always been and will continue to be the strength of the masses. The strength of numbers, the strength of honest and open confrontation against state policies, saying clearly: we are here because of this. Come with us! We must try to aggregate as much as possible.

There is no secret in this struggle. One has to be careful in the case of some countries in particular, as in the case of Egypt, the Philippines, and Brazil. One has to be careful about personal security, because the state is deeply infiltrated, militias committed to the violent politics of extermination. This has to be faced on the basis of democratic struggles: the struggle for life, the struggle for the right to express political opinion, and the respect for civil rights. Society has to go out for these fundamental values of civilization and defend them. And governments that do not align themselves with those values have to be removed from power. So, again, another challenge that is posed in a very strong way today. Unfortunately, the struggle is very difficult, very hard.

The struggles against capitalism, racism and patriarchy

Today, particularly among younger people, there is a very strong identification with specific causes and with sectional movements, whether it's feminism, or the gay movement, and so on. Identity politics, in general, is fundamental to liberating people so that they can realize their potential, and to oppose specific forms of oppression and exploitation of inequality that are completely incurable. These struggles need to be built on a more general unity, on the basis of seeking alliances, on the basis of aggregating and not dividing. And this is not a political question, it doesn't have a theoretical background problem practically. It is a question of the political practice of the people involved with these movements. Obviously, there is no difficulty in dedicating oneself to a movement x, whatever it may be. A movement of denunciation and liberation of affirmation of certain values. It would be constructive to attract alliance, to work together with other movements as well so that this x movement is recognized as one aspect of a more generalized liberation process. To make clear that the systemic links between these specific inequalities are embedded within the more global functioning of society. So why does this specific struggle exist? Why does this kind of inequality exist? How does it reproduce itself, how does it insert itself within other struggles that we have to have as well? The trap that the left fails to understand, and to act in the most constructive way.

You often see very strong divisions because of political differences that become entrenched within movements and can end up paralyzing those movements. The Scottish independence movement, for example, in the recent period has become very divided because of the position of different factions or different groups within that movement with regard to the rights of transgender people. In principle, these are two struggles that have nothing directly to do with each other.

References

Saad-Filho, Alfredo. Capitalism and Anti-Capitalism: Challenges and Opportunities after September 11, *Revista da Sociedade Brasileira de Economia Política* 11, December 2002, pp.103–124.

Saad-Filho, Alfredo. Crisis in Neoliberalism or Crisis of Neoliberalism?, *Crítica e Sociedade* 1 (3), 2011, pp.6–19 (in Portuguese), http://www.seer.ufu.br/index.php/criticasociedade/article/view/14547/8275

Saad-Filho, Alfredo. On the Crisis of Neoliberal Capitalism: A Discussion with D. Kotz, A. Saad Filho, A. M. Flores, D. Plihon and A. Lechevalier, *Actuel Marx* 51, 2012, pp.12–26 (in French).

Saad-Filho, Alfredo. Neoliberalism: A Marxist Analysis, *Revista do NIEP* 3 (4), 2015, pp.58–73 (in Portuguese).

Saad-Filho, Alfredo. Cahill, D'Neoliberalism since the Crisis', introduction to a special issue of *Critical Sociology* 43 (4–5), 2017, pp.611–614.

Saad-Filho, Alfredo. *The Rise and Rise of Authoritarian Neoliberalism*, Alternativy (in Russian, forthcoming, 2020).

Saad-Filho, Alfredo and Ayers, Alison. Democracy Against Neoliberalism: Paradoxes, Limitations, Transcendence, *Critical Sociology* 41 (4–5), 2015, pp.597–618.

Saad-Filho, Alfredo and Fine, Ben. Thirteen Things You Need to Know About Neoliberalism, *Critical Sociology* 43 (4–5), pp.685–706, 2017. Translated into Chinese and published in *Political Economy Review* 8 (5), 2017, pp.200–217.

Saad-Filho, Alfredo and Johnston, Deborah. *Neoliberalism: A Critical Reader.* London Pluton Press 2004.

3

INTERNET AND THE RISKS TO DEMOCRACY

Claudio Penteado and Eva Campos-Dominguez

The rapid expansion of Information and Communication Technologies (ICTs), especially the Internet, has brought numerous transformations to human practices, incorporating important changes to the economy, sociability, culture, and politics. The development of digital technologies and the world communication network has enabled the consolidation of global financial capitalism and new business models controlled by large technology companies, the so-called Big Techs (Google, Apple, Facebook, Amazon, and Microsoft) (Morozov, 2018). In the political field, the increase of connection by smartphones has transformed social Internet networks into important channels of political information, human sociability, and political mobilization, as shown by the events of Los Indignados in Spain in 2011, the Journeys in June 2013 in Brazil, and other mass mobilization events of protests articulated by the use of social media (Castells, 2015). Social media has also become central to electoral processes and the formation of public opinion, changing the traditional logic of political communication (Chadwick, 2019).

After the optimism about the possibilities of expanding citizen participation and greater transparency of political processes through the use of ICTs in the construction of a cyberdemocracy (Lemos & Lévy, 2010), the development of the Internet through a process of platforming the society (Van Dijck et al., 2018) has generated a series of problems associated with the increase in online conflicts expressed in the form of affective polarization (Iyengar et al., 2019), informational disorder processes influencing electoral results (Benkler et al., 2018), rise of populism (Gerbaudo, 2018) and authoritarian politicians (Levitsky & Ziblatt, 2018) that put them at risk liberal democracy (Castells, 2018). This chapter aims to present our reflections on the risks of the Internet for democracy, based on our studies in the area of Internet and Politics, a Spanish researcher in the field of Communication and a Brazilian researcher in the field of Political Science.

DOI: 10.4324/9781003384366-4

The debate on the risks of the Internet to democracy is part of the context influenced by two crises (the 2008 global financial crisis and the crisis of political institutions) and two social change processes (digitalization of society and platformization of society). The effects of the 2008 global financial crisis (unemployment, homelessness, environmental problems, etc.) put in check several ideas of neoliberalism and financial globalization (Duménil & Lévy, 2011) and increase of inequality (Piketty, 2015). The crisis of political institutions is linked to a process of distrust in traditional representation models, driven by neoliberal values (Brown, 2019), information disorder with spread of disinformation that have affected the electoral process in several countries (Wardle & Derakhshan, 2017) and the crisis of democracy itself and its regulatory devices (Przeworski, 2019).

The process of digitization of society is characterized by the intensive and daily use of digital technologies in various human practices (Lupton, 2014), creating new forms of sociability mediated by Internet communication channels (Keenan & Shiri, 2009). The other process of social change is associated with the emergence of digital platforms as private socio-technical infrastructures of concentration of the flow of information that had impacted on social, cultural, economic, and political activities and practices, in the process known as the platform of society (Van Dijck et al., 2018).

In this context of crises and social changes, from the perspective of a researcher from the global south and a researcher from Europe, the chapter discusses the risks of the Internet for democracy, based on four questions that structured the South–North Dialogues on Democracy, Development, and Sustainability project: (1) the main transformations (technological and business model) in the communication system in the Internet era; (2) how the environmental theme manifests itself in the new digital communication ecosystem in Spain and Brazil; (3) what are the consequences for democracy of the transformation of the communication ecosystem; and (4) how to ensure the formation of a more democratic and inclusive communication system.

What are the main transformations (technological and business model) in the communication system in the Internet era?

The transformations in the communication system in the Internet age are not only technical, also involve transformations in the social relations, producing new sociabilities and subjectivities, in the cultural field with an emerging and pulsating digital culture of remixing, collaborative practices and "gamification" of society, in the political field, with new dynamics and political strategies that migrate to digital platforms. All of these transformations are appropriate in new business models and economic practices in the Internet age.

If at the beginning of the Internet expansion, it was not very clear how to "earn money" on cyberspace, it was evidenced in the "Internet Bubble", or in the dot-com crash (Birkinbine, 2020). After two decades, companies in the Information Technology business (the Big Techs) are among the richest in the world, according to Fortune Magazine's 2021 Fortune Global 500 ranking: Amazon (3rd), Apple (6th), Alphabet (21st), Microsoft (33rd), and Facebook (86th), not counting other hardware and software technology and games companies.

Unlike other industries that controlled some stages of production processes, these technologies companies, beyond to concentrating the flow of information on the world wide web, also influence the preliminary stages, through the processing of (personal) data and content produced by the users themselves, using artificial intelligence (AI) and machine learning techniques to create recommendation systems aimed at anticipating users' choices, which impact the information consumption diet, cultural habits, and social practices. And these massive uses of AI, hidden some social, economic, and environmental problems (Crawford, 2021).

The mainstream communication system always played an important role in capitalism in the 19th and 20th centuries, mainly due to the formation of consensus around liberal and more recently neoliberal values (Mullen, 2010; Herman & Chomsky, 2012). The new communication system, organized in distributed information networks, opened space for the emergence of new private communication companies and even other communication formats such as collectives of journalists, personal blogs, cooperative journalism, among other experiences born online. However, despite there being a great variety of information sources formats, in a few years the Big Techs concentrated the informational flow in their platforms (Morozov, 2018), creating a new logic associated with the idea of network power (Castells, 2013), which aggregates the main users and contents of the web.

This model of content aggregation on private platforms enables the development of a new business model based on the processing of personal data and customization of content (and even products) according to profiles created by the platform's algorithms. We changed from a mass communication model in which the contents were aimed at an "average" audience, to a hyper-oriented communication towards personalized profiles by modern digital marketing techniques, targeting content, products, and even the modulation (induction) of the behaviors of the users.

Is it possible to identify the entry of new actors into the public debate on the new ecosystem of digital communication?

The issue of sustainability is a very important topic for NEEDS and also for public debate in Europe (Čavoški, 2020). However, in monitoring surveys of social networks sites (SNS) it is possible to detect that the public debate in Brazil is contaminated by political discussion and disinformation, involving the ideological and affective polarization about supporters of the Bolsonaro government and opposition sectors to the current president's administration, mainly in relation to the environmental issue (Recuero & Soares, 2020).

In the first three years of the Bolsonaro government (2019–2021), Brazil has been registering an increase in fires affecting the Brazilian Amazon and the Pantanal, an increase in deforestation, expansion of the agricultural and livestock frontier and a decrease in environmental inspection. With a critical discourse on existing environmental preservation policies, actors aligned with President Bolsonaro and the then Minister of Environment, Ricardo Salles, adopt a discourse on digital platforms associated with a developmental vision, contrary to a vision of sustainability (Ferrante & Fearnside, 2019).

The Twitter monitoring data, developed by the Amazonometer project, show that a discursive antagonism has formed between environmentalists, NGOs, influencers, journalists (environmental experts), opposition parties, indigenous leaders, and even international personalities (celebrities such as Leonardo de Capri, Lewis Hamilton, and even Korean pop bands) that use their profiles to denounce the concern with Brazilian environmental problems. On the other hand, it is possible to identify an alignment between Bolsonaro supporters (influencers, government allies, digital media, politicians, etc.) and profiles associated with the Brazilian agribusiness sector.

However, the data show us a fragmentation (and antagonism) of the environmentalist discourse articulated in different ways by its defenders, assuming a character of "empty signifier" (as presented in Laclau's theory of discourse), open to different interpretations and mobilizations of meaning in defense of a project to defend the environment and the promotion of sustainability (Brown, 2016). While the profiles of Bolsonaro's supporters and agribusiness are more homogeneous and articulated with each other.

Despite the Brazilian environment process having its specificities, it is not dissociated from a broader process of destruction (or self-destruction?) of the development model of contemporary society as a whole, lack of awareness of a common destiny (Morin & Kern, 2003).

The current information consumption (diet) model, characterized by hyper-segmented content on Internet communication channels, makes it difficult to build a minimum consensus on major issues related to citizenship, especially a global sustainability project. On the one hand, the current digital communication ecosystem has expanded the entry of new actors into the public debate (environmentalists, leaders of traditional peoples, environmental defense collectives, etc.), on the other hand, within a dialectical process, it has created a more fragmented society and disconnected, which hinders the construction of a "planetary citizenship" of a common destiny (Morin & Kern, 2003), capable of building a new model of a more sustainable and fair society.

In a comparative perspective of the digital network's debate in Brazil and Spain, it is possible to identify these patterns of fragmentation and polarized political dispute (ideologically and affectively) around almost all themes, including the environmental one. The rise of politicians associated with the ultra-right (Bolsonarists in Brazil and the Vox party in Spain), the use of robots to spread disinformation and boost profiles, and other computer propaganda techniques (Woolley & Howard, 2017) have strained public debate, creating obstacles to the implementation of more effective agreements and policies for environmental protection and sustainability promotion.

In the optimistic view, the digital platforms also allow the participation of new environment voices on the public debate that didn't have visibility in the traditional system of mass media agenda-setting. One important example is the case of environmental activist Greta Thunberg who, through Internet channels, mobilizes a huge network of environmentalists around the world (Jung et al., 2020).

The new digital communication ecosystem certainly modifies information processes, allowing the entry of new actors (human and non-human, as in the case of chatbots), making the debate more plural and democratic, and at the same time, more cacophonous, with the difficulty of forming a common (and minimal) project of citizenship, as well as contributing to the increase of distrust in the institutions of modernity, causing a process of epistemological crisis (Dahlgren, 2018), which makes it difficult to adopt effective measures to protect the environment, and even in the vaccination process, as we are witnessing in the current Covid-19 pandemic crisis (Sallam, 2021).

However, it is necessary to avoid the risk of "trap" of a conservative discourse in defense of an idealized past, and to emphasize that however much progress has been made in the construction of an agenda associated with the sustainability discourse in the 1990s (ECO-92) and early 2000s (Rio+10), it is important to highlight the traditional model of mass communication. It effectively contributed to environmental destruction and spread a consumerist discourse and lifestyle (Lipovetsky, 2007; Bauman, 2008), which also hampered the formation of an agenda of sustainability and citizenship.

What are the consequences for democracy of the transformation of the communication ecosystem? And what challenges arise for democracy with the popularization of the internet?

The new configuration of the communication ecosystem, guided by the architecture of distributed networks, connectivity and the use of digital technologies made the communication process more democratic, on the one hand, but on the other hand, made it difficult to build consensus around the principles of liberal democracy of the bourgeois public sphere (Rasmussen, 2013).

The epistemic crisis (mentioned above) also has profound impacts on political dynamics, especially with the crisis of confidence in traditional political representation institutions (parties, parliaments, and even the government itself), opening up space for the rise of authoritarian populist leaders (Levitsky & Ziblatt, 2018), systematic use of disinformation processes to influence electoral processes (Benkler et al., 2018) and the radicalization of political polarization processes that have led to a process of social fragmentation, which reverberates on digital platforms (Sunstein, 2017) and in the formation of ideological antagonist niches.

These antagonistic ideological niches use digital technologies to promote a political identity articulated around hate speech, directed in general to stigmatized groups (black population, women, gay population, immigrants, etc.). The "politics of hate" is structured in an efficient communication strategy that seeks to mobilize through emotions (Castells, 2013, 2015). This type of affective polarization configuration does not help to formulate a common vision of the social which respects the differences existing in societies.

Recent studies have shown that emotions are important elements of engagement on digital platforms. Emotions such as indignation, anger, pride expressed by profiles on social media are efficient ways of mobilizing and producing storytelling and affections that influence people's political behavior (Papacharissi, 2015).

In studies carried out in our research groups, it was possible to observe that in Brazil and Spain authoritarian leaders such as Jair Bolsonaro (Brazil) and Santiago Abascal (Spain) are characterized by the use of a discourse that is articulated around the creation of "enemies", mobilizing symbolic elements related to nationalism and conservative values, with criticism and accusations against political institutions (Parliament and Judiciary) and press, which have failed to provide effective answers to social problems that affect the lives of thousands of people around the world, such as unemployment, homelessness, hunger, violence, and social inequality, aggravated by neoliberal fiscal adjustment policies, end up straining the dynamics and stability of liberal democracy.

The liberal democracy is an important institution in the project of modernity in Western societies. The social relationships are based on trust, guaranteed by modern institutions (State, Science, Bourgeois Economy, etc.), allowing for a new social reorganization of people dispersed in space and time that the modernity was built (Giddens, 2013). However, the new communication ecosystem calls into question the trust in these institutions (especially the State and Science), posing important challenges for contemporary democracy, as we can observe in the anti-lockdown and anti-vaccine movements around the world in the context of the pandemic of Covid-19 (Pleyers, 2020).

Emotions in political dynamics and uncertainty regarding trust in the State and in Science stand out as important variables that pose challenges for contemporary democracy. It is important to highlight those emotions themselves are not a problem, on the contrary, they are elements that constitute our human condition (Arendt, 2013), which the liberal democracy project sought to eliminate from politics, in favor of the production of a political central (negation of the political conflict), associated consensus to a managerial discourse of politics, which are aligned with the interests of a hegemonic liberal bourgeoisie (Mouffe, 2005). The challenge here is to transform emotions into elements that help guide people's political behavior so that they can make their choices around different (and alternatives) political projects that compete according to democratic norms, rather than being used to transform opponent politicians into "enemies" who need to be eliminated, whose existence cannot be tolerated.

Despite causing doubt and insecurity, uncertainty is not a problem for democracy either. Uncertainty is the basis of scientific and human knowledge (Morin, 2002) which seeks to answer the doubts and challenges that surround humanity. The "certainties" can cause dogmatism problems and contribute to the creation of authoritarian knowledge systems. In the political field, uncertainty is also an important element for producing political alternatives, creating an open system to adapt to the transformations and for the practice of dissent in plural and heterogeneous societies (Rancière, 2011).

Within the new digital communication ecosystem, the challenges that arise for democracy are associated with the democratic incorporation of emotions and uncertainty in political processes. In the paradigm of mass communication, emotions were turned into a marketing tool for manipulating public opinion around a neoliberal consensus (which does not accept being questioned) that excludes and stigmatizes political identities and any questioning of hegemonic models and the status quo.

Understanding the ambivalence of the Internet and democracy is necessary for building a common project for global citizenship within democratic societies. Digital technologies enable new forms of domination/exploitation, dissemination of disinformation discourse and surveillance and control devices, as well as alternative ways of practices and political struggles, the incorporation of participatory political innovations and tensions of power mechanisms (Chadwick, 2019). This ambivalence is today an enormous challenge for democracy (and to researchers) in order to avoid technological "solutionism" or conservative and authoritarian responses.

How to promote and ensure a more democratic and inclusive communication system?

The tensions and challenges that the Internet incorporates to democracy involve the discussion of the creation of a more democratic and inclusive communication system. This is a system in which everyone can have access to connection, free information, freedom to speak and be heard without necessarily being controlled (or artificially driven) by the platform's algorithms. Companies that operate these platforms need to be more transparent (especially regarding the operation of their algorithms and the use of people's personal data) and the States need to create an urgent public regulation. This regulation is in order to ensure that citizens know how these devices work (explainability of the algorithms) and that if there is any irregularity, it is possible to hold the people and companies involved accountable, as in the case of Cambridge Analýtyca and Facebook.

It is not possible to separate the democratic from the inclusive and perhaps this false dichotomy is the "great trap" of Liberal Democracy. It was concerned with the discourse of formal democracy, aimed at the development of formal guarantees of individual and political rights, but in practice this democracy proved to be little inclusive for a large portion of the population that cannot enjoy these rights, as they do not have material conditions minimum to guarantee a dignified existence.

The same phenomenon happens on the Internet. Today, with the popularization of smartphones and Internet social media, many people have access to information. But this information is not necessarily leading people to have a better life and access to knowledge. On the contrary, studies have shown that Internet social networks have influenced electoral political processes (Castells, 2018), the operating mechanisms of platforms profit from conflicts and dissemination of disinformation (Benkler et al., 2018) and also from the precariousness of labor relations mediated by applications (Van Dijck et al., 2018). Thus, it is necessary to think of mechanisms for public regulation (non-state) of platforms, with controls and forms of public auditing of the use of robots and AI, which guarantee not only the connection, but a more democratic and inclusive use.

It is important to highlight that ICTs go beyond digital platforms controlled by Big Techs. They also allow the development of innovations in the repertoires of social movements and political agents of experiences in promoting citizen participation through collaborative practices, collaboration networks, and free technologies (free software, creative commons licenses, etc.). However, in general these experiences are very fragmented and have a local reach (Araújo et al., 2021; Lynch, 2021), and fail to promote a more democratic and inclusive use of digital technologies beyond specific collective actions and projects.

The construction of a democratic and inclusive society requires the recovery of a common project of global citizenship, in which digital technologies can help society, from a citizen perspective (non-state and non-commercial), answer questions such as: What is information for us? What can we do with this information? What information do technology companies have about people and what do they do with it? How to become less dependent on digital technologies? How to use these technologies to promote a more dignified life and a less unjust society socially, politically, economically, and culturally?

Finally, it is necessary to think about how to break with the "machine servitude" of neoliberal logic (Lazzarato, 2014), in which the practicality of digital technologies imprisons us in digital "golden cages", highly individualized from Californian ideology (Barbrook & Cameron, 1996), and to recover a participatory and collaborative digital culture, present at the origin of the Internet (Castells, 1996; Lèvy, 1997; Jenkins, 2006; Shirky, 2009), also for having moments of disconnection.

Final considerations

In this final section, we would like to highlight the ambivalence of the Internet, particularly remarking the concentration of information flows on the platforms of large technology corporations, contrary to the principle of networked distributed communication, as opposed to the massive model of broadcast communication. Another highlight is the politicization of the environmental debate, influenced by a climate of affective polarization in Internet social networks. However, researchers observe an important movement of new actors into the public debate, guided by the fragmentation of discourses and the strong influence of emotions. This configuration brings new challenges to democracy, such as the spread of misinformation influencing political processes, the emergence of authoritarian politicians (in Brazil and Spain), and the increasing crisis of political institutions. Finally, the conversation posits that the great challenge for democracies is to think about the use of technologies to have more time to think, create, cooperate, and even more time to be disconnected and less exposed to the neoliberal practices of human life digitalization.

References

Araújo, Rafael de Paula Aguiar; Penteado, Claudio Luis de Camargo; Santos, Marcelo Burgos Pimentel dos. Political participation and Citizen Innovation Laboratories: the study of CitiLab and MediaLab Prado in Spain. *Cadernos Metrópole*, 23: 1193–1212, 2021.

Arendt, Hannah. *The human condition*. University of Chicago Press, 2013.

Barbrook, Richard; Cameron, Andy. The Californian ideology. *Science as Culture*, 6.1: 44–72, 1996.

Bauman, Zygmunt. *Vida para consumo: a transformação das pessoas em mercadoria*. Editora Schwarcz-Companhia das Letras, 2008.

Benkler, Yochai, Faris, Robert; Roberts, Hal. *Network propaganda: Manipulation, disinformation, and radicalization in American politics*. Oxford University Press, 2018.

Birkinbine, Benjamin J. Political economy of peer production. *The Handbook of Peer Production*. John Wiley & Sons, 33–43, 2020.

Brown, Trent. Sustainability as empty signifier: Its rise, fall, and radical potential. *Antipode*, 48.1: 115–133, 2016.

Brown, Wendy. *In the ruins of neoliberalism*. Columbia University Press, 2019.

Castells, Manuel. Rupture: *The crisis of liberal democracy*. John Wiley & Sons, 2018.

Castells, Manuel. *Networks of outrage and hope: Social movements in the Internet age*. John Wiley & Sons, 2015.

Castells, Manuel. *Communication power*. OUP Oxford, 2013.

Castells, Manuel. *The information age: Economy, society and culture* (3 volumes). Blackwell, Oxford, 1996, 1997: 1998.

Čavoški, Aleksandra. An ambitious and climate-focused Commission agenda for post COVID-19 EU. *Environmental Politics*, 29.6: 1112–1117, 2020.

Chadwick, Andrew. *The new crisis of public communication: Challenges and opportunities for future research on digital media and politics*. Online Civic Culture Center – O3C 2. Loughborough University, 2019.

Crawford, Kate. The hidden costs of AI. *New Scientist*, 249.3327: 46–49, 2021.

Dahlgren, Peter. Media, knowledge and trust: The deepening epistemic crisis of democracy. *Javnost-The Public: Journal of the European Institute for Communication and Culture*, 25.1–2: 20–27, 2018.

Duménil, Gérard; Lévy, Dominique. *The crisis of neoliberalism*. Harvard University Press, 2011.

Ferrante, Lucas; Fearnside, Philip M. Brazil's new president and 'ruralists' threaten Amazonia's environment, traditional peoples and the global climate. *Environmental Conservation*, 46.4: 261–263, 2019.
Gerbaudo, Paolo. Social media and populism: an elective affinity? *Media, Culture & Society*, 40(5): 745–753, 2018.
Giddens, Anthony. *The consequences of modernity*. John Wiley & Sons, 2013.
Herman, Edward; Chomsky, Noam. 17 a propaganda model. *Media and Cultural Studies: Keyworks*, 204, 2012.
Iyengar, Shanto; Lelkes, Yphtach; Levendusky, Matthew; Malhotra, Neil; Westwood, Sean J. The origins and consequences of affective polarization in the United States. *Annual Review of Political Science*, 22: 129–146, 2019.
Jenkins, Henry. *Convergence culture*. New York university press, 2006.
Jung, Jieun; Petkanic, Peter; Nan, Dongyan; Kim, Jang Hyan. (2020). When a girl awakened the world: A user and social message analysis of Greta Thunberg. *Sustainability*, 12.7: 2707.
Keenan, Andrew; Shiri, Ali. (2009). *Sociability and social interaction on social networking websites*. Library review.
Lazzarato, M. *Signos, máquinas, subjetividades*. São Paulo, SP: Edições Sesc São Paulo & N-1 edições, 2014.
Lemos, André; Lévy, Pierre. *O futuro da internet: em direção a uma ciberdemocracia planetária*. São Paulo: Paulus, 2010.
Levitsky, Steven; Ziblatt, Daniel. *How democracies die*. Broadway Books, 2018.
Lévy, Pierre. *Cyberculture: rapport au conseil de l'Europe*. Odile Jacob, 1997.
Lipovetsky, Gilles. *A felicidade paradoxal: ensaios sobre a sociedade de hiperconsumo*. Trad. Maria Lúcia Machado. São Paulo: Companhia das Letras, 2007.
Lupton, Deborah. *Digital sociology*. Routledge, 2014.
Lynch, Casey R. Contesting digital futures: Urban politics, alternative economies, and the movement for technological sovereignty in Barcelona. *Antipode*, 52.3: 660–680, 2020.
Morin, Edgar. *Terra-Pátria*/ Edgar Morin e Anne-Brigitte Kern / traduzido do francês por Paulo Azevedo Neves da Silva. – Porto Alegre: Sulina, 2003.
Morin, Edgar. *Seven complex lessons in education for the future*. UNESCO, 2002.
Morozov, E. *Big tech*. Ubu Editora, 2018.
Mouffe, Chantal. *The return of the political*. Verso, 2005.
Mullen, Andrew. Twenty years on: The second-order prediction of the Herman-Chomsky propaganda model. *Media, Culture & Society*, 32.4: 673–690, 2010.
Papacharissi, Zizi. *Affective publics: Sentiment, technology, and politics*. Oxford University Press, 2015.
Pleyers, Geoffrey. The pandemic is a battlefield. Social movements in the COVID-19 lockdown. *Journal of Civil Society*, 16.4: 295–312, 2020.
Piketty, Thomas. *The economics of inequality*. Harvard University Press, 2015.
Przeworski, A. *Crises of democracy*. Cambridge University Press, 2019.
Rancière, Jacques. Democracies against democracy. *Democracy in What State*, 76–81, 2011.
Rasmussen, Terje. Internet-based media, Europe and the political public sphere. *Media, Culture & Society*, 35.1: 97–104, 2013.
Recuero, Raquel; Soares, Felipe Bonow. Desinformação e Meio Ambiente. *Journal of Digital Media & Interaction*, 3.8: 64–80, 2020.
Sallam, Malik. COVID-19 vaccine hesitancy worldwide: A concise systematic review of vaccine acceptance rates. *Vaccines*, 9.2, 160, 2021. https://doi.org/10.3390/vaccines9020160

Sunstein, Cass R. # *republic*. Princeton University Press, 2017.
Van Dijck, José; Poell, Thomas; De Waal, Martijn. *The platform society: Public values in a connective world*. Oxford University Press, 2018.
Wardle, Claire; Derakhshan, Hossein. *Information disorder: Toward an interdisciplinary framework for research and policy making*. Council of Europe, 27, 2017.
Woolley, Samuel C.; Howard, Philip. *Computational propaganda worldwide: Executive summary*, 2017.

4

URBAN DEVELOPMENT AND JUSTICE

Luciana Travassos and Hilde Heynen

This essay was written based on a conversation between the two authors about urban development and justice. It was conducted around four main questions: (1) What are the main productive, technological and financial transformations that are ongoing? (2) How do interstate disputes and environmental challenges manifest? (3) What are the distributional consequences, including from an intersectional point of view? (4) How to alleviate distributive asymmetries, based on popular solutions and state action?

Although the theoretical approaches are not cited directly throughout the text, the authors base their understanding of urban development processes, their unequal impacts and their challenges on two theories, that of environmental justice and the ethics of care.

The environmental justice concept has been used for at least a couple of decades, inaugurating a broad field of knowledge that discusses together the concepts of justice and several environment-related concepts, such as sustainability, transition, ecology and others (see e.g. Sze 2018). The distribution of goods and prejudices and also the impacts that this distribution has on the flourishing of individuals and communities, as put by Schlosberg (2009), is essential to the debate of urban development, regarding distribution, recognition, participation and capabilities. The ethical debates advance to the notion of care, as proposed by Carol Gilligan (1982) and further elaborated by Joan Tronto (1993). They hold that moral behaviors center on the value of interpersonal care, where human beings should assess their own and one another's actions against questions that relate to relationships of caring and fostering. Ecofeminists have enlarged this framework to also include caring vis-à-vis non-human actors, such as land or water (Gaard 2015).

It is important to point out that we are talking about urban development: we are not just talking about the cities but also about the surrounding areas that are

DOI: 10.4324/9781003384366-5

involved in the transformation of the territory, configured by urban sprawl. Also, we highlight that the empirical approach was taken considering Belgium and the State of São Paulo, in Brazil, with their connections with other scales and levels of governance.

The dialogue went through some key issues that characterize the current debates on urban modernization and its limits and challenges in the context of climate change and the resurgence of inequality and poverty. The essay is divided into four topics: Energy transition, transportation system and urban patterns of sprawl; Impacts of urban sprawl on environment and disasters; Green new deal and carbon regulation; and Multidimensional inequalities.

Energy transition, transportation system and urban patterns of sprawl

What seems globally one of the most important issues to address in terms of technological and productive transformations related to urban development is energy transition: how we are going to make sure that our urban systems but also our transportation systems can be further developed relying upon energy sources that are carbon neutral.

This transition towards more solar energy, wind energy, water-based energy sources seems to be extremely important. In Europe this takes the form of a pressure to, on the one hand, make sure that our buildings become more energy neutral or even passive buildings (meaning that they would not consume any energy for heating or cooling) – which is very ambitious. On the other hand, it relates to the patterns of mobility. It seems that transportation needs are still growing and there is a huge energy consumption in transportation. The need to reduce carbon emission in transportation is currently addressed by making the shift to electrical cars – that is in Europe now clearly the policy will be rolled out over the next decade. So, in ten years' time there will be many electrical cars on the roads. And also, and that is where our field comes in in terms of urban development, it is very important how the settlement patterns are further growing or possibly shrinking due to these changes.

In a country like Belgium, we have a lot of low-density suburban developments where one needs to rely on cars, where you almost cannot organize public transport because the density is so low. This pattern is very detrimental for this energy transition and for sustainability: it consumes a lot of land and so forth. In Europe, it is very important to address these density issues of how to organize mobility. These are important transformations that are ongoing and that are indeed impacting urban development. There are, of course, other aspects, but the energy transition – trying to avoid further greenhouse gases to be out there in the atmosphere in order to counter the effects of climate change – is one of the main things that is ongoing right now.

In São Paulo, we combine three patterns that seems very detrimental to energy transition, high building density with low population density in central areas and high population density in the peripherical ones, and low building and population density as a regional sprawl pattern to middle class population. The last two with a precarious or absent transportation system.

Also, in Europe there are many different patterns but sprawl definitely is there. In the last two decades, it has been intensifying. In 2016, there has been a report documenting the sprawl in the different European countries (European Environment Agency and Swiss Federal Office for the Environment 2016, 38–46). For example, Belgium and the Netherlands are neighboring countries but the former has a very high level of sprawl whereas the latter does much better in that respect. But in Belgium, for reasons of policy and culture – people have always loved to build themselves a one family home, a low-density pattern, was subsidized by the authorities. Individual families bought a piece of land somewhere in the near or far vicinity of a city and built their one family house there, resulting in a huge level of sprawl. Compared to the United States, which is known by its low urban density, there is historically a difference because Belgium has many towns or small cities, usually at 20–25 kilometers from one another. That is historically determined because that was what people could travel in one day back in the Middle Ages. So, we have these 25-kilometer distances and the space in between these small cities is quasi-filled up by sprawl, presently. So, the old pattern is indeed small cities but the space in between is filling up rapidly.

The change of pattern in Belgium was due to both cultural factors and regulatory issues. Regulation change was in fact in the 1970s, when the land destination plans were made and then they appointed a lot of land for future housing developments. These are still not full but in fact if you look at the pattern, we have too much of that buildable land that is supposedly good for housing. A critical look will now point out that some of that land is in flooding areas, some of that land is on fertile agricultural areas, some of that land is really where we should rather have natural developments and nature reservations, etc. Now the experts –- urban planners, geographers, architects, urbanists – regret very much that 50 years ago, planners have appointed so much land for housing. But now, of course, it is legal and it is very hard to turn the tables and to tell people who own a piece of land, that they cannot build on it. If new restriction rules would apply, the value of the land decreases and in our legal system, the government would have to financially compensate for that loss of value. Practically, this is not doable or at least it is politically unfeasible. Hence, it is very difficult to develop counter strategies.

This point is very important. In Brazil, if a property becomes protected land for whatever reason, the state has no responsibility to pay the rights to the landowner, there is no vested right to use the land. This is something that lessens the pressure on the state when there is a need for change in the land use and occupation legislation. Certainly, this is a huge debate between landowners and the state, which creates pressure to decrease protection or not to adopt more protective criteria.

Differently from Belgium and Europe, in Brazil the ownership of land is a dispute, a central issue to human rights, because we have a lot of large rural and urban landowners, even on the outskirts of cities, so the land right is very concentrated. This characteristic has a very strong implication for the compact city agenda of TOD – transit-oriented development. If it is possible to state that this is an agenda in the public administrations of Brazilian cities, it must be stated that there are many difficulties to actually implement it. So, there is a discourse of the compact city, of transit-oriented development, which would be very good for the homogeneous access of people to the city, but the reality is a double city. We have been able to implement part of the compact city agenda and part of the transit-oriented development agenda for the part of the cities that historically have a lot of amenities, like green areas, sanitation, good mobility and very good infrastructure, to the detriment of the rest of the urban areas, whose transformation requires investments in many sectors and dealing with the issue of securing urbanized land for the poorest people. So, the new urban agenda came for some people in Brazil but not for all.

Even in Belgium, however, there are challenges to the implementation of this agenda. In the 1990s, 25 years ago, we had a very ambitious spatial plan for Flanders which also was about compact cities and protecting the open spaces. The ambition was to have more land for nature and for open space and to have a clearer differentiation between the urban areas and the more rural regions. Then because of these pre-existing land destinations, it was very difficult to implement this policy. It turned out that it is indeed extremely difficult to change the mechanisms that foster sprawl. These mechanisms were not disrupted, so even if the official plan was "we are going for compact cities" the reality was that more and more land was taken up and became built-up area.

Impacts of urban sprawl on environment and disasters

These issues, both in Brazil and in Belgium, are even more serious when we put them together with the environment crisis. Urban sprawl is responsible for an increase in land sealing, which makes the water run off too fast. Although in Belgium there is quite some rainfall yearly, the groundwater levels are dropping because a lot of the rain immediately goes to the sea thanks to sewage systems and rivers that are straightened out. Also, from this point of view it is clear that we have too much built up lands. There are, on the one hand, the good intentions of the planners and the ambitious plans enthusiastically presented by ministers, and there is on the other hand, the difficult process of developing new mechanisms and instruments that would enable the plans to be implemented and that would prohibit further incremental taking up of land for new industry, new houses and new infrastructure. Thus far, it does not work out in a very coherent way.

There are lots of discussions about new projects. A typical example is a project developer who wants to develop new housing in a good location near a railway station (which is beneficial for reasons of mobility, because it fosters the use of trains rather than cars) but, on the other hand, this new housing scheme is located in a flood-prone area, and that is an argument contra this development. Such discussions flare up, but the net result usually is that project developer wins out (because the land destination is housing) and the project gets built even though it is not an adequate move from the point of view of water management and adaptation to climate change. In July 2021, Belgium had very serious flooding events, which were directly related to climate change. In the southern part of the country, a so-called water bomb fell: it was the amount of rain that one usually sees over a two-month period in the space of only 24 hours. Because of the hilly topography with narrow valleys, the effects were very bad, with rising water levels that flooded towns and villages. This was really unexpected, 24 hours of heavy rainfall.

The rivers were bursting and, in some valleys and towns, the water was three or four meters above the highest level they ever knew before. It was very strange but it was also a bit of a wake-up call, but again we are now facing a very tricky discussion about what to do. In some of these areas, the houses were completely destroyed – so it might be a bad idea to reconstruct them, since the future might bring similar floods. At the same time people have been living alongside these riverbanks for hundreds of years. For many people, it feels very strange if now it would be decided not to rebuild their home because this is a flood-prone area. Nobody remembers that ever the waters came that high.

Therefore, it doesn't seem likely that it will be new rules in place, because a lot of property owners are involved, who are eager to get their money from the insurance companies and to reconstruct. In some cases, moreover these were neighborhoods where rather low-income people were living, who do not have the means to immediately figure out alternatives as to where to go and where to find alternative cheap housing. It is a very complicated issue, but the sense of urgency is now more clearly there than it used to be. Still, it is difficult for a mayor, for example, or for a municipality to really prohibit people to rebuild the homes that have been destroyed, whereas who knows in 5 years' time, in 10 years' time, in 20 years' time, the same thing might happen again.

The directive on flood regulation at the European Union, which implies the re-allocation of uses and activities from flood-prone areas just applies for the greater basins and does not consider these specific valleys. Also, these valleys were never designated as flood-prone areas, because before the water level was going up and down maybe one or two meters but not four or five meters. So, this event was really big due to this exceptional rainfall. Usually if we have a lot of rain, it is mild rain, that goes on and can last for days but at a very slow pace. Now, it was torrential rains in a very short time and the streams and the rivers simply could not cope with it. It was not something that people had thought about before. There were forecasts and warnings the last two days before the event, so maybe they could have been better prepared and maybe people took it too easy and thought "well we are Belgium we know what rain is" – well, not this time.

In Brazil, this situation is much more common, we state that the civil defense has to be prepared to alert people and to act on the emergency. these rains affect a lot of residential areas and especially low-income residential areas and to cope with this situation, more than an emergency plan, its necessary to put together urban planning and civil defense planning. In many Brazilian cities it is possible to observe two problems regarding rainfall events: on the one hand the landslides, in areas with little infrastructure, and on the other hand floods and torrent waters in areas with and without infrastructure, in the latter mainly due to historical choices, often based on only a partial understanding of the climate in our regions. The transition to a green infrastructure and the focus on low-income areas is obviously required. Besides that, we have to change the idea that we will be able to halt inundations, we will have to deal with them and prepare the city and citizens to do so.

There is also an interesting governance issue related to this flooding in the summer in Belgium. The country is a federal state, where Flanders in the North and Wallonia in the South are two different regions. The flooding happened in Wallonia but the weather forecast is national (on the federal level) and that means that the weather forecasters can tell us that it will be raining but they cannot use the term flooding, because flood protection is a regional and not a national responsibility. In other words, the rain is a national responsibility, but as of the moment that the rain touches the ground it is another institution's responsibility. According to some people, this was one of the reasons why the municipalities and the civil defense were not that well prepared: they had heard that a lot of rain was coming but nobody had used the word flooding, so they were surprised. This is a very telling example of how emergencies and disasters are never simply natural phenomena: they are generated by a combination of a natural phenomenon, like this exceptional rainfall, with infrastructural conditions, such as houses being built on risky places, and then, of course, also the institutional arrangements you have in place in order, for example, to make sure that the people leave the houses before they are flooded rather than afterwards. The havoc wrought by this flooding thus resulted from a combination of three things: a natural phenomenon, infrastructure that is in the wrong place and then the lack of preparedness in terms of emergency plans.

The infrastructure matter is similar, then. To go further, in well-developed urban areas in Brazil streams are mainly channelized with a very high velocity, so the water comes too fast. At the hills, we have no infrastructure and a lot of landslides, which is the main cause of deaths. This is a dramatic situation that happens every summer in some regions, at the last summer there were hundreds of deaths in Bahia, Minas Gerais and Rio de Janeiro. After 2011, after more than 800 deaths in Rio de Janeiro and a lot of jeopardizing in many cities, we were able to advance in legislation, with a national policy about disasters, with a shared responsibility with states and municipalities, to forecast, to alert, to respond to emergency and also trying to change some other laws, especially land use regulation. We tried to build something more articulated between the land use legislation and civil defense legislation, we are far away from achieving adequacy in this way, but we are now aware what has to be done and how. It is certainly a big challenge, as in the dual city the protected or risk areas are the places left for the more vulnerable people to build. It results in a double vulnerability, an environmental vulnerability and a social vulnerability together in the same place. Therefore, when there are heavy rainfalls, the possibility to deal with them is very low and the State is still not well prepared to prevent or attend to these occurrences.

Green new deal and carbon regulation

Risk is a great environmental challenge but there are other environmental challenges that need to be addressed.

There is a working group at the University of Leuven's interdisciplinary think tank, *Metaforum*, and we are addressing such issues – not just on a national level, but also wondering about the global level. When addressing carbon emissions e.g., you can say that historically Europe and United States are responsible for the bulk of the carbon emissions up till now. Europe is now developing a policy with the so-called New Green Deal, aiming at carbon neutrality by 2050. The United States, however, is a different story because of internal political tensions. That means that Europe tends to position itself as the example to follow, asking other countries to also fully reduce carbon emissions by 2050. To which, countries like China or India are reacting by pointing towards their far smaller historical responsibility, claiming that they first need more economic development before fully addressing the need for climate neutrality. This, of course, is very understandable from their point of view.

It is relevant in this respect to refer to the so-called tragedy of the commons, as discussed by Hardin (the famous article in *Science* in 1968). The tragedy of the commons refers to the idea that if you have a common good that is good for everyone, it might be in the interest of some to overuse that common good and deplete this resource. This tends to happen all too easily and it is very difficult to develop mechanisms that prohibit this tragedy from happening.

What is currently happening to the air, to fresh water systems, to the climate, or to ecological systems, is an example of such a tragedy of the commons. There is overuse of the common good, no individual feels specifically responsible, there is barely any individual penalty, so the net result is climate change. It is very hard to pinpoint who is responsible and hence very hard to agree on how to counteract climate change. It is a good thing that at least you have the Paris agreement, and the Glasgow one, and that there is a task force of the United Nations (UN), and that there are these regular reports of the IPCC.

It is commendable that all of that exists, but at the same time you see that it is very hard to implement these agreements. In many countries the commitments towards the UN within the Paris and Glasgow climate agreements are one thing and what is happening on the ground is really another thing. Here in Belgium, it is painful to watch how the international commitments do not get translated into national and regional plans that everybody agrees on. This is what we see playing out here in Belgium. In fact, the dividing lines between political parties have now to a certain extent to do with how strict we want to stick to the Paris agreement and how well we will respect the European New Green Deal and how can we cheat and maybe do less than our part. There is also a serious worry about how possible regulations and arrangements, put into place to prevent further climate change, might negatively impact the lowest income groups. That is a concern in Belgium as well as elsewhere in Europe. These are political issues right now.

In a global look, especially from Brazil, it is necessary to pay attention to the effects of this carbon protection regulations in Europe or other, peripherical countries, considering the characteristics of their economies and goods-producing activities, especially the ones related to exportation. Some activities will be able to participate, or to continue to participate in global exchanges, but part of them will not. How these countries will do the transition without the global financing, once the funds created in global agreements such as Paris do not reach 1% of the contributions idealized at the time of their implementation, this fact makes it very difficult for innovation in the poorest countries. In this context, the walls of the carbon emissions restriction will enable the transition inside the walls, with large number of resources invested inside the walls and that will diminish the capacity of investing in transition in another countries. This would represent more a new market share than a shared responsibility to the world. If Europe is to achieve zero carbon emissions, much investment will be needed. So, how can Brazil and other countries in Africa, Asia and Latin America do their transition, with little capacity to attract external investment and to invest by their own? More than that, in Brazil, this context encounters a political situation where the whole of the state is being very diminished throughout the last couple of years, and even the environmental laws, always considered advanced worldwide, are being dismantled.

The experience with the Covid-19 crisis might be very telling in this respect. On the one hand, it was fantastic that thanks to technological advancement we had vaccines very rapidly – faster than anyone predicted beforehand – because there was a massive investment in this research. On the other hand, you had a well-intentioned COVAX scheme, meant to make sure that also middle- and low-income countries would get their share of vaccines. In reality, however, the rich countries had an "us first" reflex – first America, first Europe, first Israel, etc. and this reflex prevented the COVAX scheme from working very well. As a result, the virus could develop new variants in countries with low vaccinations ratios, and these variants then threatened the rich countries too. Whereas solidarity among nation states, among countries, is thus absolutely necessary it is nevertheless not an easy goal to reach. It is similar, it seems, for climate change. It is a global threat; it is not something that you can address only on a local level. We need to indeed share the responsibility and help each other out in fighting these phenomena, because if in one half of the world carbon emissions are allowed to go rampant whereas in another part of the world they are not, climate change is still worsening. It is very difficult, however, to understand all of this and to comprehend how these global mechanisms work. Hence people have a hard time to get to terms with this, and to adjust their behavior and their political choices.

The mechanisms that drive climate change or that enable the pandemic to spread across the world, are complicated. You need to be well educated and to believe in science in order to understand what is happening. Similarly, the mechanisms that institutions develop to counter these phenomena (climate change, or the pandemic) are also very complicated. For example, even to a well-educated and a well-informed person, it is difficult to understand the ETS-system (the European Trading System for carbon emission). We know that it works and that it contributes towards reducing carbon emissions, but not being an economist, we cannot really tell exactly how it works. This means that we have a global European policy in place that more or less helps us to reduce carbon emissions but at some level, it works very counterintuitively. For example, supposedly to reduce your ecological footprint, it is preferable to take the train rather than a plane. Nevertheless, within Europe, due to this ETS-system, it really makes no difference whether one takes a train or a plane (because the carbon emission reduction will happen elsewhere, where it is easier and cheaper). This is very hard to explain to people, hence it is also very hard to motivate them to change their behavior, to adapt their lifestyles, or to make other political choices.

It is indeed complicated to explain all the relationships and to motivate people but maybe we are probably going to be motivated by tragedy, with the recrudescence of deaths and economic losses. But the thing is that people are already suffering a lot, but the huge changes needed in our way of building cities don't go much further than discourses. Doing the transition, especially the just transition, seems a lot more distant than we would like. Even the little advances made in some sectors resulted in increasing inequalities.

Multidimensional inequalities

These inequalities, although present in both countries, Brazil and Belgium, display different conditioning factors and characteristics, which necessitate an intersectional approach. The elements that characterize the most vulnerable social groups in each country are slightly different, or partly different. Since the beginning we were highlighting inequalities, by now, we can go a little bit in this intersectional analysis, especially considering the issues of gender, nationality – with emphasis in Belgium context – and ethnicity. This is indeed a big worry.

From an ecological point of view, it is argued that policies should make fuel more expensive, in order to urge people to use less and to help reducing carbon emissions. Now, of course, raising the price of fuel is most problematic for people who have cheap and old cars that use a lot of fuel – and these tend to be the lower-income people. Hence, they are the ones who suffer the most if policies make fuel more expensive. We now have this issue in Belgium, since in some city centers it is forbidden to enter with old diesel cars because they have a huge carbon emission and are much more polluting than more recent cars. The ones suffering the consequences are people in the lowest income group, because they are the ones with cheap second-hand cars of 15 years old. They are the ones who cannot use their cars any longer under such rules.

It is similar when talking about buildings. There is now a policy in place that we should move towards energy neutral buildings. It is, however, very expensive to build these things, or to renovate one's house in such a way that it is in line with these new standards. It means that rents go up. For middle class people who own the house they are living in, renovating their house towards climate neutrality might make a lot of sense, because in the long run they have a return on investment (due to lower energy consumption). For people who see their rent go up, however, it might be a huge problem because the higher rent might not be immediately compensated by lower energy costs. For policy makers, it is often really difficult to find a good balance between measures that make sense from an ecological point of view, and on the other hand, the consequences of these measures on low-income groups. The yellow vest protests in France had to do with this lack of balance. These were groups of French people who really felt left behind because of what the people in Paris were deciding. They felt that they were the ones suffering the consequences of all these decisions and they certainly had a point.

In Belgium we are also confronted with difficulties regarding policies that would benefit the lowest income groups. Belgium is a very well-organized welfare state: we have excellent welfare policies – pensions, medical care, child support, free education (or almost free education) – all these things are well organized but the people who benefit most are those from the middle class. We have a huge middle class but still there is around 15% of the people who are living below the poverty level. One sees that among these 15% there are proportionally more immigrant families and more one-parent families – hence intersectionality is at stake here. What you see in a country like Belgium however is that it is very hard to make a political coalition that would aim at developing mechanisms that would benefit this lowest income group. For example, a couple of years ago we had a reform of child support system and the system that was adopted, against the advice of the experts, was that each and every child gets the same amount of money, regardless of the income of the parents or the number of children a family has. That made the system worse rather than better for a lot of low-income families – and poverty experts see this as a missed opportunity to really alleviate poverty. The problem is that we do not develop policies that avoid the reproduction of poverty. Children that are growing up in poverty often do less well in school and end up not being so highly educated, although education supposedly is for free. There are a lot of cultural factors and social factors that play a major role in education, but they are barely addressed. Hence many of these children become adults without finishing school, and that means they are not well employable. This is how poverty gets reproduced.

My example was about child support but one can make a similar analysis for all the interventions and the subsidies now created for fostering energy transition.

There are, for example, subsidies for investment in solar panels. People who put solar panels on their roofs and benefit from these subsidies are mostly middle class, higher educated people. People on the lower end of the income ladder do not have the means to invest, so they do not receive any subsidies and neither will they in the long run benefit from lower electricity bills. We have a name for this mechanism: we call it the Matthew effect (this is after the biblical story in Matthew where workers who start later in the day nevertheless get the same amount of money for working only part of the day as the ones who started very early). The Matthew effect refers to the idea that those who have, will be given more and the have-nots will be given less. Such mechanisms unfold again and again in our system, also because the system is so complicated that a lot of people do not understand what they are entitled to. The administration requires a lot of effort in order for you to receive the benefits that you are entitled to, so there are a lot of thresholds. The better educated you are, the more de facto access you have to all types of benefits and subsidies, even if these were originally devised for lower income groups.

The fact that lower income groups disproportionally consist of people with a migration background, complicates matters. It is difficult to have more benevolent policies, for example, in social housing. We do have social housing in Belgium which is very affordable and very good, but it is only 6% of the housing stock (and remember 15% of people live below poverty level). Within social housing there is now an over-representation of immigrant families (because they are also overrepresented in low-income groups). The effect, however, is that it is almost impossible currently to really effectuate a policy to construct more social housing than we already have. That is because this huge middle class thinks it is for these immigrant people and they feel that immigrant people are pampered and hence they do not vote for parties who intend to build more social housing. From an expert's point of view, it makes sense to think that it is a very good thing if immigrant families and children receive serious benefits. In the long run that will have very positive effects, because they will be better integrated and they will become well educated, and get better jobs, etc. This is however a long-term effect, and many people see only the short-term effects that such policies cost money that they are not prepared to pay. Hence, we have a strong right wing in Belgium, and these are the parties that refuse to invest in social housing. Still the reality is that there are twice as many families entitled to social housing than there are units available. 170,000 families are currently on the waiting list.

The similarities are many, the Brazilian housing deficit is fully known, now, furthermore, as said before, property is very concentrated and there are no incentives for it to be more distributed. One of the issues lies in the fact that one no longer pays taxes, in Brazil, to have a second home. There are people who own thousands of properties. For an individual in Belgium, it is almost impossible to have a lot of houses. Currently there are real estate companies that are building up their portfolios, but it is much more common that people have one or two homes (maybe two because it is seen as an attractive way of investing money because the stock market is not doing so well and in Belgium buildings have always been seen as a good investments). More than 70% of household own the house they are living in; the other 30% are renters.

The proportion of people living in their own homes has changed a lot in Brazil, the number of renters is increasing as the financial market is catching up with the real estate market. This combination of financial market and real estate market is contributing to change the standard of owning a house or renting a house. In São Paulo, the logic and process of space production led to a trinomial: irregular subdivisions, with little infrastructure and self-built houses, in the peripheries, but this has become more complex. The city of São Paulo is coming down to the ground, with a sudden change in the built heritage, a lot of demolitions and a lot of new buildings being built, with great participation of the financial market. These buildings are being produced mainly in central areas and high-income neighborhoods, with very high values, reaching more than R$20,000 per square meter. Who will buy these properties? At the same time, and even because of this continuous valorization of the central areas, the process of urban expansion and gentrification continues. During the pandemic, many people left the center or their rented houses to live in new informal and precarious settlements because they could no longer afford to pay their rents. In other words, there are transformations underway for rich and poor and none of them seem to lead to a less unequal and more adapted city. It is shocking that we are in the transition to something that maybe produces a more unequal city than before and maybe we will be broken in a few years, but here is for me where the ethics of care comes in, we mentioned the term at the very beginning of our conversation.

Our concerns are on the one hand about the planet and climate change and we should include biodiversity and fresh water and all other elements that support human life, and on the other hand it is about these issues of equity and fair distribution. I absolutely subscribe to this ethics of care but it is very hard to translate that into a viable policies and viable guidelines as to how to apply it legally and in terms of political arrangements and coalitions. In both our countries, there is a capitalist logic that is underlying the whole political and legal system. Capitalism works well in certain ways, for example, for advancing technological development. The free market in many circumstances works well, for example, in making sure that production and consumption are balanced out and so on. At the same time, it is very hard to reconcile an ethics of care within capitalist logic. Hence, I don't have the answer as to how to elaborate this ethics of care in a way that you would have a system for organizing society and organizing the economy and organizing everything that works well on the one hand – that it is transparent, fair and efficient, that it uses the resources in the best way – and then still adhere to this ethics of care on the other.

Regarding the risks and the jeopardizing of nature that we saw in urban development and regional development as a global issue, maybe we can focus on urban development because it will be a little easier for us to figure out how to alleviate distributive asymmetries based on popular solution and state action.

The state is very important, when it articulates policies to relieve inequalities, poverty and organizes a welfare policy, in terms of regulation and as an actor. Besides that, we have to avoid a discourse even made by the left wing, that the popular solution can face these asymmetries. Popular solutions have some limits especially because popular solution doesn't have a financial capacity to build infrastructure, to build housing, act in mobility, etc. They must organize themselves to be heard in their demands; they can help to draw the solutions but they will not be able to implement them. Without the state and its institutional and financial capacity the transitions and reducing asymmetries will not be possible. But we must rethink the state and its relation to civil society. The solutions should be thought for the territory and from the territory. The territory, as the platform to political action and also the territory, as an actor important to define this political action with the State.

There is a real difference between Brazil and also the state of Sao Paulo and Belgium because the Brazilian condition is dual – it is not the same way in Belgium. In Brazil there is much more of a gap between the haves and the have-nots (to use these simple terms), whereas I would describe Belgium rather as a middle class situation where 70–80% of the people are really middle class. There are not that many extremely rich people, nor are there that many extremely poor people. Most people are middle class – lower to higher middle class – and then you have this group of 15% that are below poverty level. This means a popular movement in Belgium would really be a middle class movement. The state is a framework that is highly organized, so highly that it becomes very complex. This complexity comes forth from the need to take into account a lot of balances between different forces. We have in Belgium people with different languages (Dutch, French, German), who do not really belong to a different ethnicity but who do have let's say a different sensibility and belong to a different community. Then, we have Brussels in the midst which is officially bilingual, but with more francophone than Dutch-speaking folk. Brussels however is home to many more people coming from elsewhere, who do not have French or Dutch as their first language. Brussels therefore is a cosmopolitan city in the midst of these more homogeneous regions in the North and the South.

That reality is well covered by the federal state organization, but this organization has made itself very complex by always adjusting. The adjustments are by now so complicated that if you are not a political scientist you don't understand very well how it works and that means that, for example, in emergency situations you have this tension between the federal national level and the regional level. Nevertheless, the whole thing worked rather well in the Covid-situation, e.g., in terms of providing vaccination centers and handling health care with high pressure on the hospitals. Belgium is also part of the European Union, which is also very important. The European Union is really functioning well, at least with respect to this challenge of climate change (we spoke already about the New Green Deal). At the same time the EU is not popular: a lot of people have the feeling that EU is a kind of authority far away at a huge distance from people's life and these are bureaucrats that are making all these kinds of weird decisions that as a simple fellow you don't understand but have to live with – that is a bit the dominant image. So, on the one hand, they are doing fantastic work and on the other hand, they are not popular: that is a tension that almost seems inevitable in this complicated world.

Again, you see that it is not easy to strike the right balance, all the more so when you also try to address these asymmetries between high- and low-income people, or between citizens and non-citizens (I would say that the immigration policy of the European Union is a disaster). All this also plays out in terms of housing and urban development. Also in this respect, it is very hard to device policies that are on the one hand ecologically sound (for water, for climate change, for mobility, etc.) and on the other hand socially responsible. It is very difficult to implement this ethics of care approach, simply because the whole underlying system is based on another logic. One of the reasons European countries tend to be well organized has to do with the reliability and transparency of our legal frameworks. These, however, are 100% based on property rights and they are very rigid in this respect. That means e.g., that if people got the right to build on a plot of land maybe 50 years ago, they continue to have that right and the state can only take it away, if they offer a financial compensation. These rigidities in the system make the transition towards a more ecologically robust system very hard indeed.

There are inertias built into the system that will always be necessary to work with in our contexts and, on the other hand, we have the transition agenda, in different stages of implementation. In Brazil, the challenge is to do this with an increasingly reduced institutional capacity and the diminishing role of the State at all levels. The situation is further complicated considering the many inequalities. If the State is not going to be the actor to make a more distributive policy, who will in fact be?

References

European Environment Agency and Swiss Federal Office for the Environment. Urban Sprawl in Europe: Joint EEA-FOEN Report. Luxembourg: Publications Office, 2016. http://bookshop.europa.eu/uri?target=EUB:NOTICE:THAL16010:EN:HTML.

Gaard, Greta. Ecofeminism and Climate Change. *Women's Studies International Forum* 49 (March): 20–33, 2015. https://doi.org/10.1016/j.wsif.2015.02.004.

Gilligan, Carol. *In a Different Voice: Psychological Theory and Women's Development.* Cambridge, MA: Harvard University Press, 1982.

Schlosberg, D. *Defining Environmental Justice: Theories, Movements, and Nature.* Oxford University Press, 2009. https://books.google.com.br/books?id=SBkUDAAAQBAJ.

Sze, Julie. *Sustainability: Approaches to Environmental Justice and Social Power.* NYU Scholarship Online. New York: University Press, 2018.

Tronto, Joan C. *Moral Boundaries: A Political Argument for an Ethic of Care.* New York: Routledge, 1993.

5

CHALLENGES OF THE GLOBAL SOUTH FROM A DECOLONIAL PERSPECTIVE

Carolina Cristina Alves and Fernanda Graziella Cardoso

With the consolidation of the Industrial Revolution, the nations of the world were divided into two large groups, the developed nations and the underdeveloped nations. According to Furtado (1967), it is in this context that the origin of underdevelopment is located, especially by countries that had previously been colonies of exploitation of a good part of the countries that then started to appear as developed countries. The developed countries were thus defined as symbols of civilizations to be followed, considering therefore the standard of living – and its respective consumption profile – of advanced industrial societies as synonymous with development (Furtado, 1978).

According to Furtado (1967), development and underdevelopment are contemporaneous phenomena, underdevelopment not being a phase that precedes development but rather a result of the very way the world power system was historically organized. So, if the predominant mode of production (the capitalist one) is maintained, how to break with the underdevelopment condition?

This is an issue that has been the object of concern of both Northern authors – for example, the classical developmentalists of the Anglo-Saxon tradition – and Southern authors – for example, Latin American structuralists or Pan-Africanists – with a greater or lesser degree of permanence of Eurocentric traits, both with regard to the strategy indicated to achieve development and the development goal to be pursued – which involves what is defined as development (Reis; Barbosa; Cardoso, 2019). The variety of perspectives also points to greater or lesser faith with respect to the possibilities opened by the capitalist mode of production to nations that have fallen behind in the race for development, trapped in the underdevelopment trap (Furtado, 1992), of which the dependency perspective, both Latin American and Pan-Africanist, is also worth highlighting (Reis; Barbosa; Cardoso, 2019).

DOI: 10.4324/9781003384366-6

The organization of the production matrix, the development of the domestic market, the pattern of internal insertion, the confrontation of inequalities, especially between nations and classes, have figured as a concern of the authors who have addressed the issue of underdevelopment. More recently, the environmental issue has also consolidated its space as central to the debate on development in the 21st century, making the scenario even more challenging for nations that have not yet faced deprivation or basic socioeconomic problems.

Since the 2008 crisis, a new technological paradigm of production, consumption, and international trade has emerged worldwide, causing profound global transformations. In this new context, responses to the challenges posed to development, democracy, and sustainability have become even more complex, if not conflicting, especially in the periphery or the Global South.

In this chapter, the authors focus especially on the issue of sustainable development and the challenges that are imposed on the periphery, in the search for breaking the chains of thought imposed by the Eurocentric paradigm. The text starts from a perspective of decolonization and diversification of thought, seeking inspiration in the voices of thinkers from the Global South.

The chapter is divided into five sections, in addition to the introduction and conclusion, which discuss the following themes: the decolonization and diversification of the economy; the productive, technological, and financial transformations in process; the manifestation of interstate disputes and environmental challenges; the distributional consequences and the intersectional perspective; and the possibilities for alleviating distributional asymmetries, based on popular solutions and state action.

Decolonization and economic diversification: new paths for development reflection in the context of the Global South

The authors assume that, from now on, to discuss the Economics it is necessary to look closely at and give voice to what is intellectually produced, studied, and discussed in the Global South. This is the goal behind the idea of decolonizing the Economics, with the observation that it is important to separate the idea of decolonizing the Economics from the idea of diversifying the Economics. Although the two aspects are linked, it should be noted that they are different processes.

The idea of decolonizing Economics causes much resistance and confusion. Beyond Economics, the idea of decolonization has been happening for some time in other areas and is related to a critique of the curricular structure and the university itself (Bhambra; Gebrial; Nişancioğlu, 2018). This discussion implies looking at the period of modernity, of the Enlightenment itself, to understand that the world economy that emerges in that period, the issue of exchange between societies, and the conception of the nation-state, happen along with the Western world taking the lead (Anievas; Nişancioğlu, 2015). This process will cause many changes and challenges about how knowledge is produced, and will also lead to many methodological developments.

Many disciplines, especially history, philosophy, and international relations, began to analyze this period and realize that much of the thinking about how the world worked was informed by views and assumptions that had a perspective that justified colonial rule in Asia, Africa, Latin America, and the Middle East. In other words, the 1700s and the Age of Enlightenment occurred along with assumptions about racial and civilizational hierarchy that was then forming the thinking and knowledge produced.

It is in this sense that discussions about decolonization of the curriculum or decolonization of the university have been going on for a long time. The idea is not only to bring in authors who are from the Global South; but to understand why there is this dominance of Western authors and white men in the academic curriculum and why there is Western hegemony in academic and knowledge production. This discussion is also part of what happens in the 1970s with the emergence of postcolonial theory that flourished in various disciplines, and became an institutionalized force in academia in the late 1970s. Initiated in literary and cultural studies, over a period of about three decades, postcolonial theory has swept the spectrum of the social sciences and humanities, including disciplines such as Geography, Anthropology, Political Science, and Sociology. The central unifying theme in postcolonial theory "is the analysis of representational constructions of culture and subjectivity in and through colonial discourse" (Kayatekin, 2009, p. 1114, our translation).

An important point here is to understand why Economics was not part of this; where was Economics? How did it resist this process of contestation of hegemonic Western thought? We can answer this question by considering two aspects: the ambition of Economics to become a science, and the relationship of the discipline to the development of capitalism itself (Kayatekin, 2009).

Regarding the first aspect, from the classical political economy period to the marginalist revolution and the formalization of economics in the 1950s, the social and historical contexts were increasingly removed from the discipline of economics (Alves; Kvangraven, 2020; Milonakis; Fine, 2009). Economics embarked on an ambition to become a science, from which the development of economic principles abstracted from society and considered on the one hand as apolitical and ahistorical, and on the other as an objective, neutral, and universal truth was observed. Here "the other and his theories" become inferior, not rigorous – and even, uncivilized or backward, which may have contributed to the discipline resisting decolonization discussions. This methodological and theoretical development in economics stopped looking at issues that political economists were trying to deal with; which included a less harmonious view of society, with a more historical and political edge, taking as a starting point a society permeated by conflicts, represented by class struggle. Of course, this process also made economics increasingly *inner looking* and less interdisciplinary, which may also have contributed to the lack of communication with the disciplines that were embarking on the decolonization investigation.

The second aspect is related to the naturalization of the capitalist mode of production. The origins and roots of the field of economics are embedded in a specific mode of production called capitalism. The history of capitalism itself and the processes surrounding its developments are subject to endless disputes and debates. Persistent themes in these debates involve the role of technological change, social class, the state, capitalism's relationship to European imperialism, colonialism, and the transatlantic slave trade. However, the discipline distanced itself from these debates and not only took a biased stance toward capitalism, but also hid its relationship to oppression, violence, and the slave trade. See, for example, the field's dedication to studying black slavery in the United States and trying to understand if the Southern plantations in the United States were more productive or not, using the method of cliometrics, without discussing or analyzing the relations of oppression that were there and their implications mainly for African Americans.

In this context, decolonization of Economics means a process of investigating the production of knowledge in Economics and its relationship to slavery and colonialism (Alves et al, forthcoming). There is no short and simple definition for what decolonization of Economics is because it is a process, an attempt to understand how theories and methods in Economics have been informed by a worldview with certain assumptions about racial and civilizational hierarchy. That is, they were informed by a Eurocentric worldview. How can we be sure that issues of racism, colonialism, and imperialism are not lubricating the engines of knowledge production in the field of Economics? The investigation of knowledge production in Economics and its relation to slavery and colonialism is way behind. We, the economists, should have been the first to do so. The same goes for the need to widen the lens of the discipline and to challenge the understanding of capitalism.

Here, it is possible to relate to the diversification of the Economy, while demonstrating that diversification and decolonization are different processes. The development of the field, as described above, results in an economy that is formed by and values white Western men. The Eurocentrism observed at the center of the profession derives from two main sources. The first is that economic theories that have developed in Europe have taken European conditions as their starting point, but claim to be universal theories. To some extent, this is the case for conventional theories and many heterodox theories (for example, theories associated with Keynes, Hayek, and Marx). The second, is that only studies that pertain to Western societies are valued. Moreover, scholars from the non-Western world can actually do well professionally if they apply the dominant contemporary theories to study Western issues. Thus, while the inclusion of these non-Western scholars may make the field more diverse, it does not necessarily challenge the Eurocentrism embedded in it. In fact, non-Western scholars trained in the dominant school of thought are likely to perpetuate the Western-centric nature of the discipline and, consequently, the continued exclusion of women, black and other ethnic minorities, and non-Western scholars (Alves et al., forthcoming). So, one has to be very careful about this issue of diversification and decolonization. Although they are so integrated, it is important to pay attention to this difference, and separating them is more difficult.

If we want a more just and inclusive economy and society, we need the deepening of this investigation in the discipline of economics. It is not about moralizing the curriculum or seeking another objective truth. A discipline that excludes other approaches, other authors, cannot give us satisfactory answers about how we will build a better society.

The main productive, technological, and financial transformations in process

In the previous section, the ideas of decolonization and diversification of the economy were presented and differentiated, although they are mutually reinforcing. Reflecting from these perspectives, this section returns to the following question: what are the main productive, technological, and financial transformations in process? Having the perspective of decolonization and diversification in focus, the answer to this question will not be conventional, since the perspective of the problems of the Global South will be privileged in pointing out what is or is not a priority or fundamental to be highlighted.

This question is interesting because it really pushes you out of your comfort zone because it is one thing to define decolonization, but it is another thing to practice decolonization. When we talk about productive and technological transformations, these transformations have to do with the progress of capitalism itself. In general, economists do not view this information critically. Looking, for example, at six important technological transformations in the last three decades – (i) electricity and alternative forms of energy such as solar, wind, hydro, marine, geothermal, and biomass; (ii) the laser (discovered in the 1960s) and its application from medicine to consumer electronics and manufacturing; (iii) semiconductor chips (electrical circuitry with many components such as transistors and wiring) that opened the door for the evolution of the laptop, followed by the smartphone and tablet; (iv) quantum computing leading to the computer that uses quantum mechanics to massively increase processing power, marking a new realm of potential applications to be explored; (v) the Human Genome Project (finished in 2003) which caused a breakthrough in science never seen before, transforming medicine radically, opening the door to medical studies on genes associated with disease and leading to the flourishing of biotech companies looking to find new health applications; (vi) the Global Positioning System - GPS (invented in 1973, but available to the market only in 1995) which is a technology that uses satellites to pinpoint a location and help us navigate – how can we be critical of this as it demonstrates the wonders of progress?

The decolonial perspective in this context is critical, considering the particularities of the countries, questioning how innovation happens and how it is distributed and, of course, given this historical moment, seeks to understand the relationship between innovation and the ecological issue. Technological transformations are linked to productive transformations and usually lead to other important technical advances, becoming the springboard for countless other innovations. For economists, this progress has to be seen from at least two important angles. One is the old problem of how these innovations affect the process of economic growth. And another, often overlooked, is who controls and gains directly from these innovations – that is, how these innovations are used in society and for what purpose.

In this sense, some problems taken up by Marx and the Marxist literature remain valid. Marx analyzed long-term development in capitalism in which technological change is essential. For him, most new technologies are introduced to reduce labor-intensive production and to increase productivity. This is basically a process of relative surplus value extraction. The idea is to increase productivity while decreasing the value of the means of subsistence. This leads to another point emphasized by the Marxist literature: the form that this innovation takes in the capitalist condition. Marx, in the *Grundrisse* pointed out that capitalism's tendency to progressively replace labor with machines would lead to some kind of liberation/ transition to something other than capitalism (post-capitalism). However, an important point here is that for this to happen, we need a context where the extraction of profit/surplus is no longer the central goal. For Marx, there is an issue that concerns not technology itself, but its application in capitalism. Innovation is not necessarily aimed at practicality (improving the living standards of workers or the needs of society) because of private ownership over the ideas themselves. In other words, the focus is on increasing productivity rather than raising living standards.

A decolonial perspective on productive and technological transformations would focus on this last point, challenging the positive linear relationship between increased productivity, wages, and standard of living. Precisely because this perspective does not consider that underdevelopment is a phase that precedes development but rather a result of the very way the world power system has been historically organized (Furtado, 1967), which results in a model in which production in the periphery meets the demands of the center, transferring value to the latter, and affecting wage relations in the periphery, which can lead, for example, to an overexploitation of labor in the periphery (Bambirra, 2013; Marini, 2017).

The decolonial perspective also questions how this process happens in countries like Brazil, for example. There are no economic principles that can be applied universally. Can we really save labor and increase productivity and that's it? As said before, technological development increases productivity and impacts wages, but it can also lead to technological unemployment, for example. In countries like Brazil, this will happen in a very different way than in countries that have already gone through the industrialization process. What would then be the implications of this? How should the technical progress be implemented in this context?

Moreover, we cannot forget that our historical moment demands that we think about the productive and technological transformations considering the ecological and environmental issue. The advance in alternative forms of energy is basically related to harnessing the power of nature for technical advancement. Despite being progress, this does not solve the question of why and for what we need this energy – which, in turn, is related to the issue of innovation not necessarily aiming at practicality or increasing the collective well-being, but profit. Technological and productive innovations must be contextualized with the problem of sustainability, which involves revising our understanding of consumption and production. Technological advances, including new forms of energy, should not be seen only as a means to produce more, more cheaply.

Overall, the decolonial perspective is a perspective that problematizes the analysis by trying to consider the particularities of developing countries. It is a perspective that also has a more critical bias, which includes questioning capitalist innovation itself. That is, questioning the form that innovation has taken in capitalism. As we said before, Marx has the idea that the tendency is to progressively replace labor with machines leading to the liberation of labor. However, a critical look shows us that innovation in this unequal capitalism will not lead to this liberation happening so easily.

With regard to financial transformations, these are also often seen only from a positive perspective. Since the 1970s, we have observed the proliferation of new financial instruments that are the result of changes in regulatory frameworks in the structure of banking and financial markets over the last thirty years (Lindo, 2013), and also the advent of new technologies that favored the development of financial activity, especially computer and telecommunications (Dos Santos, 2009; Lapavitsas, 2009; Mcnally, 2009).

The growth of new technologies, in particular the Information Technology revolution, has had important consequences for both the sphere of production and the sphere of circulation. The new production techniques arising from this development have made labor savings possible and contributed to wage suppression, increased productivity and the internationalization of operations. In the sphere of circulation, these technologies, particularly in information technology and communication, have made possible the massive trade in financial assets, the expansion of this trade across continents and the development of various financial instruments. The speed of the Internet and telecommunications made trading virtually instantaneous and brought financial markets together. Advances in computing have made it possible to handle huge sums of funds from a large number of individual borrowers and large amounts of data, as well as extremely complex pricing, risk management and other models (Lapavitsas, 2009).

However, the literature that discusses financialization considers this technological revolution in the information process that occurred in the 1970s as fundamental for the increase in financial transactions, but in a critical way. That is, understanding that the multifaceted character of finance and the tension (and possible dissociation) between the financial sphere and the productive sphere, which can lead to financial crises, such as the ones we have experienced since the late 1990s. Interestingly, this discussion is also related to the technological and productive transformations that led to the end of the Fordist regime of production in the 1970s, and the difficulty of understanding – and having a consensus on – what the post-Fordist regime is. The literature presents an initial emphasis on flexibility and then on information and communication technologies as driving forces of the accumulation regime. Financial factors in this context receive more attention (Boyer, 2000, 2005, 2009; Petit, 1999). The idea of a finance-dominated or finance-led accumulation regime emerges as an attempt to connect all these changes while highlighting those financial developments crucially shape the pattern and pace of accumulation.

This is the context from which we must critically analyze the financial transformations that, combined with a decolonial perspective, forces us to look at how this development happened in the periphery. If financialization happened in the periphery, how did this process happen? What are its mechanisms?

We know that the financial development described above coincides with developing countries opening their doors financially and commercially in the 1990s, which made it possible for these countries to handle sums of money never imagined. But this does not mean that these transformations followed the same patterns as in the central countries. For example, although growing the increase in personal debt as a significant feature of financialization should be viewed with caution, given the depth of the banking system in each country. There is not enough evidence to argue that financialization in Brazil had the same characteristics as in developed economies in terms of the expansion of finance driven by indebtedness based on the flow of household income to financial markets. A similar point is valid for the banking system, in terms of the securitization process. In Brazil, the securitization market is very small compared to that of the United States, so one must be cautious in seeking to understand what happens in the periphery using a lens that fits to analyze what happens in the center.

Overall, the decolonial perspective does not take these financial innovations in a neutral and only positive way. This is where the literature of financialization helps, but we also have to point out that this literature is born in the Global North and does not necessarily pay attention to the specificities of the Global South.

The manifestation of interstate disputes and environmental challenges

If science is not neutral, neither are technological progress and the generation of innovation neutral. Thus, incorporating the perspective of decolonization of knowledge production seems a really promising path because we can no longer naturalize processes that are not neutral. The decolonization perspective illuminates many questions, including the type of development we want to build. That is, what kind of society we want and for whom.

The naturalization of all these processes that comes in the wake of the advance of capitalism and its endless quest to renew its forms of accumulation and exploitation, does not allow us to break with a path that is a generator of inequalities. It is worth remembering some questions posed by Furtado (1978): what is knowledge for? To which path are we directing knowledge? Is it really seeking to provide a better life for all the people in the world? Or is the knowledge generated reinforcing and reproducing the excluding and exploiting logic of capitalism?

The generation of innovation and knowledge, and the protagonist generation of technological progress, are central elements for development. This protagonism, according to Prebisch (1949), defines what is a central country and what is a peripheral country and, consequently, impacts sovereignty over its decisions regarding strategic choices to promote development.

Here, we also recall that development is a national question, so we cannot discuss it without considering the role of the state and the dynamics instigated by interstate disputes. Moreover, considering the most recent context, we must inquire how interstate disputes and environmental challenges manifest themselves in this context of transformations.

This is not a simple question to answer, especially since economists have stopped trying to understand and theorize about states. The state has come to be seen, in economics, only from the point of view of market failures. This has consequences not only for understanding the state in the domestic space, but also the relations between states and the inequalities not only economic but also of power between them.

A decolonial perspective demonstrates the cracks in the universalizing narrative about capitalism in economics and explores how capitalism developed in other parts of the world. For example, to understand unequal development trajectories, it is important not only to look at how England profited in crucial ways from the slave trade and colonialism, but also how competition from large-scale British industry broke industry in the colonies and how capitalism developed in particular and diverse ways in the periphery. A decolonial perspective, does not disregard the consequences and deleterious effects of imperialism and colonialism.

From a decolonial perspective, it is possible to reflect on interstate disputes in a much more complex way. A decolonial account of capitalist development focuses on power relations in its analysis of how capitalism developed, and therefore pays attention to the unequal impacts around the world, as well as to Southern views on the subject. This means having a historical perspective and also understanding the historiography of capitalism. It is in this way that the manifestation of interstate disputes must be analyzed. That is, power relations – the unequal distribution of power – must be the central element, the starting point.

The same goes for environmental challenges. The environmental discussion is dominated by the Global North and also by an orthodox view. Do those who lead these debates really know what is happening in the periphery? What we observe is that developing countries are internalizing an environmental agenda that is not theirs to solve a problem that is not theirs either. That is, the environmental challenge led by the North has an energy centrality, and the periphery has incorporated this agenda without questioning that much of the energy in the periphery is renewable or that they would have much easier access to renewable energy. The wind energy agenda does not belong to the periphery. It is an agenda for those who have been burning coal and oil to generate energy for a long time. It is, therefore, a European and North American agenda.

Besides this, the environmental agenda coming from the Global North has a more orthodox vision. That is, this agenda is being incorporated in countries like Brazil, for example, looking at the economy from the supply side. That is, the periphery has to consume wind and solar energy. The Global North sells this economy of the environment, without considering the history and what is happening in the periphery.

The economics of the environment, for the countries of the periphery, is passively reproducing the ideas and forms of sustainable energy from the Global North. There is thus an imposition not only of the idea of sustainable development, but also of the very type of energy that they want to be sustainable energy. Therefore, it is an agenda that sees the economy from the supply side and places the Global South as a mere consumer. The decolonial perspective questions the environmental agenda that is being sold to the countries of the Global South. This decolonial perspective considers the particularities of countries like Brazil and questions what is the urgent national agenda. In the case of Brazil, it involves, for example, the Amazonian issue, the issue of mining contamination, and deforestation. Brazil's agenda also involves paying more attention between the environmental issue and economic development, which implies rethinking economic development starting, for example, from inequalities, at several levels. Finally, it is necessary to have a vision that no longer imposes an environmental economy conceived in (and for) the Global North.

This brings us back to Furtado (1974) who, when discussing capitalism and the options available to underdeveloped countries, highlights that we cannot dissociate the predatory character of the civilization process engendered by the Industrial Revolution from the creation of economic value. Although technological advances help solve some of the environmental issues, the paradox is that, for Furtado, the very acceleration of technological progress can contribute to aggravating these problems. Therefore, for the author, we have to face and recognize that the generation of economic value implies irreversible processes in the physical world.

Furthermore, consumption patterns are also a major problem for Furtado (1974). The accumulation process has tended to increase the distance between the center and the periphery; the center has become increasingly homogenized, while in the periphery disparities continue to intensify. This has two main implications: one is how overall economic growth depends more on the introduction of new finished products; the second is how this increasing concentration of income at the center of the system constitutes an additional factor in increasing pressure on the non-renewable resources of the periphery. These points made by Furtado in the 1970s are still fundamental

Distributional consequences and the intersectional perspective

The 2030 agenda defined the 17 Sustainable Development Goals for all countries in the world. A positive aspect of this agenda is that it has placed sustainability at the center of the debate, that is, that we can no longer talk about development in the 21st century apart from sustainability. Development and sustainability are organically interconnected issues.

However, despite this positive aspect, the 2030 Agenda makes us question the very viability and universal suitability of the agenda. Do those goals really apply to any context? Is it possible to make it viable without having a great deal of global cooperation?

It will only be possible to solve all the problems of all the people in the world, if we reconfigure the way in which interstate disputes take place. By not critically discussing this agenda, we run the risk of naturalizing it. By naturalizing it, and understanding it as universalizing, it leads to countries shaping themselves to solve problems that are not necessarily theirs or to fight a fight that is not necessarily theirs to fight. Especially the countries of the Global South have their own urgencies, which do not always coincide with what is recommended by the Agenda 2030.

Uncritical naturalization undermines awareness of what the pressing problems are, diverting attention away from what really matters. The use of inappropriate lenses prevents one from seeing or misrepresents the observed reality. As Quijano (2005) states, it is necessary for the countries of the Global South to stop seeing themselves through the Eurocentric mirror that necessarily distorts their images.

One of the central issues in this context is inequalities and their intersectionalities. Much of the literature, including Marxist and Latin American structuralist literature, has stopped the discussion of inequalities at the level of nations or classes. However, even as a result of the processes of economic and social formation of the countries of the South, the observed inequality involves elements that the cut-off of classes, for example, does not allow us to reach, such as race and gender.

What about the decolonial perspective in the context of intersectionality? Intersectionality has to be part of the analysis, considering, for example, the differences between women from the North and the Global South. A Brazilian black woman is different from an American black woman, in relation to what she receives, to the state structure that supports her, among other elements. Here, we must also question ourselves about the intrinsic relationship between capitalism and racial oppression. Is this connection, a coincidence (contingent) or a permanent (structural) feature? Given the development of capitalism and its relationship to the two, imperialism and colonialism, one could argue that the origins of capitalism set in motion a path to divide populations by race. Still, even if this is the case, would racism be embedded in the deep structure of contemporary capitalism, as asked by Fraser (2019)?

In any case, these questions do not have much room in Economics. In this discipline, there is no way to discuss the distributive issue without overcoming the definition of the representative agent. Feminist economists, such as Nelson (1995, 1996) and Folbre (2009), have long criticized this particular concept of the individual, along with the connected notion of the purported objectivity it offers. The axiomatization of individuals avoids discussion of gendered experiences and limits economists in their analysis, as fixed points and equilibria are privileged ahead of context, ethics, and values (Nelson, 1995). Differences such as gender, race, class, and culture are swept "under the epistemological rug" (Kaul, 2008).

It is necessary to consider how economic policies affect blacks and women differently. Intersectionality is very important in this sense, and this does not mean that there is no more room for issues involving the conflict between labor and capital. The issue of income itself is still central, but there is a confluence of class, race, gender, sexual orientation, and other elements. The representative agent is unable to capture these differences and the complexity that emerges from them.

Yes, it is also necessary to emphasize the racial issue. Historically, economics has dealt with the issue of economic and racial inequality in such a way that race was an exogenous variable in the models. Assuming that the marginal productivity of labor is valid, and that what individuals get from it depends on it, and therefore everyone gets what they deserve, it becomes very difficult to explain black–white wage inequality. Moreover, in the long run, from these models, this wage gap would disappear. However, it is known that not only does it not disappear, but it increases. Thus, the intersectionality perspective challenges this economic theory. It considers race as a social construct that should be an essential part of our analyses. The decolonial perspective helps to challenge this theory by reviewing what and with whom this representative agent pointed to as universal in our models looks like.

Alleviating distributional asymmetries: state action and popular solutions

There are many challenges that point to the Global South's search for its own development path. These challenges are theoretical, methodological, cultural, political, and geopolitical. Especially regarding the political challenges, it is important to reflect on how popular actions and state action can alleviate the diversity of asymmetries pointed out in the sections of this text.

As stated earlier, the way economists discuss the state is limited. However, the recent pandemic context has reignited the debate. During the pandemic, an increase in state action in general was observed. The pandemic is forcing economists and social scientists to understand that the active state is necessary in the capitalist system for a variety of reasons, which go beyond the limited perspective of market failure.

The fundamental role of the State and State action can no longer be denied when it comes to alleviating the asymmetries promoted by the laws of the market, and to reducing poverty and inequality. The Welfare State consolidated in developed countries was the main responsible for reducing poverty. That is, we need this state transferring and distributing income and providing continuous assistance to the vulnerable. This goes back to one of the principles that organize modern society for Karl Polanyi, which is the principle that the State has the duty to offer social protection and intervene in production with external laws and restrictions (Polanyi, 2001).

However, beyond this, in line with what is being discussed in this chapter, can the state be a revolutionary agent, contributing to more radical change? Or is the state constituted only to maintain and control the class struggle? This question is fundamental to be answered because the limits of state action are not only related to assuming or not a more active state, especially with regard to distributive issues. Together, the question of whether and how it is possible to control capitalism itself emerges, because the contradictions of capitalism can lead us to challenges that go beyond the distributive issue.

In this sense, the discussion about what is the state and its role in the development process must go through a critical analysis of what the state represents and does in capitalism. This becomes even more fundamental when we assume a perspective of the theory of unequal and combined development of capitalism, which leads us to the particularities of capitalism in the periphery and, therefore, to the importance of the relations between the national and the international, between the national and international bourgeoisie, different processes of proletarianization of society, different social times, etc. (Löwy, 2013).

In relation to popular actions, we must consider that, most of the times when we discuss development, we ignore popular actions. However, these actions are fundamental, even to give legitimacy to decisions involving development and the type of social protection offered by the State. According to Fernandes (1975), in capitalism, popular pressures for income redistribution are legitimate and important, being a crucial part of the demands that led to the creation of the Welfare State in Europe. These popular actions can communicate with, or even pressure, state action, because popular actions present a constant challenge, constantly putting pressure on the *status quo* and the institutions that sustain them. Therefore, they can redirect the priorities to be listed, in terms of development.

As argued by Furtado (1964), the political objective that must be sought by peripheral countries, in order to ensure development in a pluralist democratic society, is to allow workers to have an effective participation in the process of power formation, so that the behavior of the working mass must be incorporated into the political process. And just as Furtado asked in 1964, on the eve of the civil-military coup that devastated Brazil, we can recapture his observation, extending it to the other countries of the Global South: "There is no doubt that a time of social revolution has opened for us. It remains to be seen whether this revolutionary process will develop under the form of critical practical activity, or as the tragedy of a people that has not found its destiny" (Furtado, 1964, p. 87–88).

In other words, the effective participation of workers in the process of debate and of choices of priorities concerning development in particular, by also contributing to the diversification of perspectives, seems to be an effective way to free the countries from the chains of thought and action implied by the Eurocentric perspective, translated into choices of economic policy and development agenda that hinder the confrontation of the real problems faced by the peripheral population.

In this sense, the pressure for solutions that are popular and appropriate to the context in which they are intended to be applied is also an effective pressure force to challenge outdated theoretical perspectives, led by actors who represent a worldview with a notably Eurocentric and/or dominant bias. For this movement, the decolonial perspective has a great potential contribution, because, from the start, it seeks to break with supposed universalizing theoretical and methodological standards, but which, for their construction, have neutralized and naturalized contradictory issues crucial to understanding and facing the problems historically rooted in the periphery.

Final considerations

The chapter sought to demonstrate the importance of the decolonization and diversification movements in the economy to reflect on the challenges for the development and sustainability of the periphery in the 21st century. To this end, it addressed issues such as: the productive, technological, and financial transformations in process; the manifestation of interstate disputes and environmental challenges; the distributional consequences and the intersectional perspective; and the possibilities of alleviating distributional asymmetries, based on popular solutions and state action.

Without diversifying the actors and actresses that play the leading role in the development debate – from a theoretical or political point of view – the possibilities of breaking the underdevelopment condition of the countries of the Global South seem increasingly distant. But diversification is not enough, because diversification must be accompanied by the capacity for criticality, a condition satisfied by the decolonial perspective.

Decolonizing the knowledge construction process can help drive the diversification required for the development discussion. Thus, while decolonization and diversification are not entirely coincidental processes, they can be mutually reinforcing.

The permanent questioning of what the Economy is for should not abandon us, because it is the Economy that signals the priorities and objectives to be achieved through the construction of theories, on which economic policies and development strategies are inspired.

For the construction of a true, inclusive, and popular development, it is necessary to build paths different from those followed up to now. According to Furtado (2002), without boldness and creativity, this mission is doomed to fail. The rupture with old consensuses and traps of thought, the construction of new mirrors and the adjustment of the lenses through which we view the reality of the Global South are necessary conditions for the dispute for a new future.

References

Alves, C., & Kvangraven, I. K. Changing the narrative: Economics after Covid-19. *Review of Agrarian Studies, 10*(1), 147–163, 2020.

Alves, C., Kesar, S., & Kavangraven, I. H. Kvangraven. "Decolonising economics — An introduction" (Polity Press, forthcoming 2022). Available at: https://www.international.ucla.edu/institute/article/251563

Anievas, A., & Nişancioğlu, K. *How the West came to rule: The geopolitical origins of capitalism*. Pluto Press, 2015. Available at: https://www.international.ucla.edu/institute/article/251563

Bambirra, V. O *Capitalismo dependente latino-Americano*. Florianópolis: Insular, 2013.

Bhambra, G. K., Gebrial, D., & Nişancioğlu, K. *Decolonising the university*. Pluto Press, 2018. Available at: https://www.international.ucla.edu/institute/article/251563

Boyer, R. Is a finance-led growth regime a viable alternative to Fordism? A preliminary analysis. *Economy & Society, 29*(1), 111–145, 2000.

Boyer, R. From shareholder value to CEO power: The paradox of the 1990s. *Competition and Change, 9*(1), 7–47, 2005.

———. *How new will the next regulatory regime be?* DIIS Working Paper, 29, 2009.

Dos Santos, P. L. At the heart of the matter: household debt in contemporary banking and the international crisis. *Ekonomiaz, Basque Economics Journal, 3*, 54–79, 2009.

Fernandes, F. *A revolução burguesa no Brasil: ensaio de interpretação sociológica*. Rio de Janeiro: Zahar, 1975.

Folbre, N. *Greed, lust & gender: A history of economic ideas*. New York, Oxford: OUP Oxford, 2009.

———. Is capitalism necessarily racist? *Politics/Letters Quarterly*, 2019. Disponível em: http://quarterly.politicsslashletters.org/is-capitalism-necessarily-racist/

Furtado, C. M. *A dialética do desenvolvimento*. Rio de Janeiro: Editora Fundo de Cultura, 1964.

———. *O Mito do Desenvolvimento Econômico*. Rio de Janeiro: Editora Paz e Terra, 1974.

———. *Teoria e Política do Desenvolvimento Econômico*. São Paulo: Companhia Editora Nacional, ([1967] 1977).

———. *Criatividade e Dependência na Civilização Industrial*. São Paulo: Círculo do Livro, 1978.

———. *Brasil - a construção interrompida*. São Paulo: Paz e Terra, 1992.

———. *"Que futuro nos aguarda?"* em Furtado, Celso, *Em busca de um novo modelo – reflexões sobre a crise contemporânea*. Rio de Janeiro: Editora Paz e Terra, 2002.

Kayatekin, S. A. Between political economy and postcolonial theory: First encounters. *Cambridge Journal of Economics, 33*(6), 1113–1118, 2009.

Kaul, N. *Imagining economics otherwise: Encounters with identity/difference*. London: Routledge, 2008.

Lapavitsas, C. Financialisation, or the search for profits in the sphere of circulation. *Ekonomiaz, Basque Economics Journal, 3*, 98–119, 2009.

Löwy, M. Introdução Dialética revolucionária contra a ideologia burguesa do progresso. In Marx, K. & Engels, F. (Eds.), *Lutas de classes na Rússia*. São Paulo: Boitempo, pp. 9–16, 2013.

Marini, R. M. Dialética da Dependência. *Germinal: Marxismo E educação Em Debate, 9*(3), 325–356, 2017.

Mcnally, D. From financial crisis to world-slump: Accumulation, financialisation, and the global slowdown. *Historical Materialism, 17*, 35–83, 2009.

Milonakis, D., & Fine, B. *From political economy to economics: Method, the social and the historical in the evolution of economic theory*. London: Routledge, 2009.

Nelson, J. A. Gender, metaphor, and the definition of economics. In Humphries, J. (Ed.), *Gender and economics*, Aldershot, England Brookfield, Vermont, US: Edward Elgar, pp. 103–125, 1995.

———. *Feminism, objectivity and economics*. London: Routledge, 1996.

Petit, P. Structural forms and growth regimes of the post-Fordist Era. *Review of Social Economy, 57*(2), 220–243, 1999.

Polanyi, K. *The great transformation: The political and economic origins of our time*. Boston: Beacon Press, 2001.

Prebisch, R. O desenvolvimento econômico latino-americano e alguns de seus principais problemas em Bielschowsky, Ricardo (org.), *Cinquenta anos de pensamento da CEPAL*, Rio de Janeiro: Record, vol. 1, pp. 69–136, ([1949] 2000).

Quijano, A. "Colonialidade do poder, eurocentrismo e América Latina" em *A colonialidade do saber: eurocentrismo e ciências sociais. Perspectivas latino-americanas,* 2005. Disponível em: http://biblioteca.clacso.edu.ar/clacso/sur-sur/20100624103322/12_Quijano.pdf.

Reis, C. F. B.; Barbosa, M., & Cardoso, F. G. The South's thoughts on development: Links between Latin America and Africa. *Revista de Economia Mundial, 52*, 191–216, 2019.

6

DEPENDENCY IN A WORLD SYSTEM OF GLOBAL VALUE CHAINS LED BY TRANSNATIONAL CORPORATIONS

Cristina Fróes de Borja Reis and Ingrid Harvold Kvangraven

In this dialogue, we discuss global value chains (GVCs) and some actual changes that took place during the Covid-19 pandemic that are likely to endure after the pandemic. There were many disruptions during this event in global chains, hierarchically-led by transnational corporations (TNCs), including in pharmaceutical and also health care chains that deeply jeopardized the economic, political, and social dynamics in many countries both from the Global South and North (UNCTAD, 2020; 2021).

Since the 1960s, international production started to be structured along the lines of GVCs, meaning activities and tasks related to production have been spread across the world, with international corporations 'slicing up their supply chains in search of low-cost and capable suppliers offshore' (Gereffi 2014, p. 10). GVC can be considered the other face of the international division of labor, meaning the way that the production is organized internationally, led by TNC that are mostly from developed countries. We both approach this international division of labor critically, and we therefore consider it to be important to have a theoretical discussion regarding how to understand it before addressing the mains empirical and political questions of the book's dialogue.

Theoretical background

GVCs can be approached from many different theoretical angles, which is why we're excited to be able to have this kind of critical dialogue about what they mean and how we should think about them. The concept is used by the multilateral institutions, such as International Monetary Fund (see Ignatenko et al., 2019; Salinas & Muñoz, 2021), the World Bank (2020) and WTO (2021), although they often take a narrow approach in terms of focusing on how firms can upgrade within a chain, rather than exploring the political economy

DOI: 10.4324/9781003384366-7

of the chains themselves. It is often assumed that there are a set of policies and strategies firms can employ to upgrade and that any firm can follow these specific steps to become higher value-added producers. Constraints to such upgrading are often thought of in terms of "market failures".

This is very different from how critical scholars originally envisioned it. GVC came from the commodity chains approach (Gereffi & Korzeniewicz, 1994; Sturgeon, 2008), with its roots in world systems theory, which is a critical Marxist approach based on imperialism and center-periphery relations (Lenin, 1917; Braudel, 1958; Wallerstein, 2004). However, it has subsequently been co-opted by mainstream economists and other social scientists. This critical literature, as well as the dependency theories, looked at the technological content of production and its constraints, that are much more severe for firms in the Global South. Ownership of production, how that impacts the domestic economy, who can produce and who owns the technology or can access technology, as well its potential for spillover effects among different kinds of firms are really important matters for development in a broad sense (Kvangraven, 2020).

As Reis, Barbosa and Cardoso (2019) explain, dependency in the periphery was historically derived from the association of domestic to foreign elites, determining technologically and financially subordinated productive and trade relationships – and the replication of consumption, education, ideological and cultural standards, too. Dos Santos (1970, 2015) considers that dependent relationships have been shaped mainly by the interests of capital markets from the center due to their monopolistic control of large-scale capital and complex technology. TNCs have penetrated the periphery seeking cheap supply of inputs, cheap labor, and export platforms. For Latin American structuralists, TNCs' local production, as well as primary exports production, were traditionally characterized by a structural heterogeneity of wages and productivity between tradable and non-tradable sectors, binding the domestic growth dynamics (Pinto, 1976; Reis & Cardoso, 2021).

When a country enters into a GVC at the very bottom, the potential for spillovers will be very different depending on the type of industry, which is generally ignored in the mainstream GVC literature. Drawing on those the kind of traditional old critical scholars can therefore be valuable when studying GVCs, in order to broaden and deepen our critical understanding of how they operate and the implications (Amin, 2010; Foster, 2015; Kvangraven, 2021). Actually, there are quite a few scholars that are employing such critical theoretical lenses to understand contemporary GVC issues. For example, Starosta (2010) employs a Marxian view of global capital accumulation to explore the social processes of 'value creation & capture'. Crossa and Ebner (2020) draw on dependency theories to demonstrate that the growth of the export-led automotive industry in Mexico has contributed to a fragmented, precarious and dependent national industrial configuration, and not to a process of endogenous economic development. Suwandi (2019) explore GVCs in Indonesia, where she shows how imperialism is key for understanding upgrading possibilities, thus implicitly drawing a lot of the same insights of the dependency theory tradition, while analyzing the role of the state in mediating development challenges, the power asymmetries between firms, and, of course, the global circumstances that shape what kind of upgrading possibilities there are.

Furthermore, Radley (2020, p. 814) draws on the concept of *peripherality* to expand the GVC framework to understand production in the Democratic Republic of Congo. By *peripherality*, he means that producers show "heavy dependence of peripheral resource extraction on technological and industrial dissemination from centers of the global economy" along with a focus on the capitalist labor process ("considering how work is organized and the shifting balance of power between workers and managers provides an important potential counterpoint to any progress that might be observed at the firm level"). Reis and Guedes Pinto (2021), on the other hand, show that pharmaceutical value chains are clearly divided along lines of center and periphery, though they are also organized in a regional dimension due to technological and financial advantages. Lastly, the rise of China as a global power from the south adds more complexity to our understanding of GVCs at a global scale. China is a leader in certain GVCs, it has achieved high-technology development in certain sectors, but the country's population still has low income per capita. Moreover, even though China has drastically expanded its manufacturing exports based on integration into GVCs, there is no doubt that this expansion has involved a strong dependence on FDI, rapid denationalization of the export-oriented manufacturing sector and relatively low levels of domestic innovation incorporated into exports (Ferrarini & Scaramozzino, 2015; Fischer, 2015). This is why Fischer (2015) argues that even the development of China can be fruitfully understood through a lens of *peripherality*. Nonetheless, the case of China is a stark reminder that the periphery is certainly not homogenous and that it may be useful to employ the concept of semi-periphery as well (Cheng & Zhai, 2021).

Anyway, it is important to take one step back and distinguish at least two theoretical foundations that stand in opposition to mainstream approaches to understand economic and political phenomena. First, while the latter assumes *perfect* competition with market clearing mechanisms that allow for equilibrium of prices and quantities, or in its more recent variations, *imperfect* competition because of market rigidities; the structural approach does not assume perfect competition in any market, but above all not in the labor market. There is structural unemployment in the labor market, resulting from political, social and economic reasons (bargain power, technological change, wage institutions, class and social struggles in general – including gender and race issues). And there are monopolies and oligopolies in the capital market and in most, or maybe all, goods and services markets. Taking or not assumption leads to very different impacts on the development path. The second theoretical foundation is the existence of uncertainty – as brilliantly developed by Keynes (1936). Uncertainties are not fully measurable in terms of risks. However, with uncertainty can lead to changes in expectations, which in turn can impact quantities and prices of different markets in variegated ways. They actually depend on the demand side of the economy, more specifically, on the growth of investment (Serrano e Medeiros, 2001). As such, demand-led perspectives consider that the demand induces and creates the supply based on the principle of the effective demand, originally formulated by Keynes (1936) and Kalecki (1943a).

Following from these two theoretical challenges, it becomes necessary to abandon methodological individualism and perfect competition as methodological and theoretical starting points, if we want to understand economies as politically, socially, and institutionally, shaped and as evolving in a dynamic manner. That's why we prefer theories that take a structural approach. The definition of "structural" method, according to Rodriguez (2009) applies to analyses that focus the economic structure, considering its formation and transformations – and therefore it is necessarily, concomitantly, historical. This method also makes it possible to avoid reductionism, as it allows considering the economic structure in relation to institutional, social and political aspects.

Moreover, there is neither an assumption of agents' maximizing behavior in a structuralist approach, nor does it consider agents' behavior as separated from their social fiber. This is important because when much of the social sciences take either methodological individualism or methodological nationalism as their starting points – "the notions that individuals and nation states, respectfully, are the most relevant units of analysis" – the *global* structures of exploitation are missed (Kvangraven et al., 2021, p. 2). Indeed, although GVC literature originated in a body of literature theorizing about the *world system of exploitation*, this is often overlooked, unknown, or forgotten, in discussions about GVCs today. This has massive theoretical, methodological and political implications.

The implications are easily visible if we delve into neoclassical trade theory. The well-known conclusion from Ricardian trade theory – which still underlies contemporary trade theory – is that all countries will benefit from opening up to free trade (or at least that no one will lose), regardless of each country's *absolute* advantage. The reason it is possible for everyone to benefit is because in a free market, the exchange rate will move to ensure that all countries will eventually become equally competitive (alternatively the equilibration will happen through the price mechanism, which is the case in Ricardo's original example). Through this equilibrating mechanism, trade will balance in the long run. The example also works with fixed exchange rates, as *quantity theory of money* is assumed so that prices will rise in the surplus countries and fall in the deficit countries, until countries are equally competitive and trade is balanced.

However, the assumption behind Ricardo's theory is that a country's terms of trade adjust to ensure balanced trade is problematic on several accounts. One issue is that empirically we see that terms of trade tend to move against primary commodity exporters (as first observed by Prebisch in 1949sh). Another issue is that there could be completely different forces driving exchange rate movements and that there is little evidence of the exchange rate actually adjusting to ensure balanced trade (Shaikh, 1980). On the contrary, persistent trade imbalances have been observed throughout the history of global capitalism.

Still nowadays the idea of comparative advantage is very influential. For instance, the World Development Report from the World Bank (2020, 2021) explicitly talks about the benefits of comparative advantage through the lens of GVCs. Selwyn and Leyden (2021) criticize that report specifically taking a Marxist approach, arguing that the chains are a very oligopoly-driven system, so that we need to look at the power symmetries to understand the inequalities that are being produced by the market structure.

Latin American structuralist theory takes an entirely different starting point to understanding international trade and sources of development. Rather than assuming balanced trade in the long run, structuralists see trade imbalances reflecting structural problems like technological constraints, linkage effects, uneven class relations, low productivity and low wages levels, the very big amount of people that are available to work – or the labor-force excess of supply. Institutional matters are also emphasized – such as the macroeconomic regime, industrial and trade policies, State policies in general, property rights etc. (Reis, 2016).

In short, then, returning to the GVC analysis' origins in world system analysis and a worldview compatible with dependency theory, can be fruitful to understand how GVCs are embedded in relations between classes, genders and, races across countries. One of their key insights is the view of uneven development – that the tendency is polarization globally, rather than catchup. Although insights from dependency theories predate GVCs, many of the insights remain highly relevant for understanding how peripheral countries are being integrated into the global production structure.

Then, we must pay attention to the long duration history, to how institutions developed during colonialism – which were very extractive and were basically established to serve the center or the colonizer. It is difficult to get rid of them, and to just leave the markets to operate freely will only increase inequality. Finally, we emphasize also, as a specific constraint to development in the periphery, the balance of payment restrictions (McCombie, 2012). They are related to the degree of macroeconomic vulnerability to shocks from outside and the swings of the global economy's business cycle and demand from the core. The fact that peripheral countries are prevented from pursuing active macroeconomic tools and industrial policies to counter the historical legacies of colonialism can help to explain the persistence of structural heterogeneity between activities with low and high value added/wages (Missio & Jayme Jr., 2012).

What are the main productive technological and financial transformations in this process?

These key insights brought from the structuralist theories as well as dependency theories, are relevant nowadays to understand global value chains. Even if the authors were not necessarily thinking about low value activities of the chains on that time, we could try to mirror this critique to GVC analysis.

In the mainstream literature, there is this view that companies and states need to upgrade in value chains, in the sense that they need to perform tasks and activities that add more value, according to the smiling curve (OCDE, 2013). The value curve in terms of the productive process is regarded as a kind of time continuing, as if there was a natural evolution from a low value-added activity to a high value-added activity. But, as the dependency theories were saying that the developing and the developed world are both the face of the world productive system, not necessarily a continuation, the amount of value added by each activity or task of the chain are also different manifestations of this world process: there is no natural time evolution towards everyone engaging in high value-added activities. In other words, we could think about value chains at the same terms as in the dependency theory: the low value-added activities and the high value edit activities belong to the same process, and there is not anyone without another to produce a certain good or service. And they are derived not only from productive or technological differentials, but also from structural problems and inequalities between north and south or between sectors of the domestic economy.

Thinking about it in that way seems close to how developmentalist and dependency theories were talking about development and underdevelopment (Furtado, 1961). It stands so much contrast to global value chain analysis, which abstracts upgrading as a solution without discussing the fact that the productive system is closely connected to a firm holding a lot of monopoly power. So low and high value-added activities are not at the equal plane, actually they are closely connected and one is being directly exploited by the other. Moreover, as Rikap (2018) argues, monopolizing innovation can also be conceived as "the source of a lasting power relation, leading to structural differences among enterprises allowing for the emergence of GVCs" (Rikap, 2018: 69–69).

This resonates with the insights of the ECLAC structuralists, who were particularly concerned with the technological content of production (e.g. Prebisch, 1949), the ownership of production and how that impacted the domestic economy (e.g. Singer, 1950), potential for spillover effects and increasing returns of domestic production (Baumgartner et al., 1976), and how these structures relate to power, the global economy, and economic development more broadly.

During the pandemic, the power asymmetries of GVC are more than evident. And we do not need to look to heterodox or left-wing literature to read that. Many documents from multilateral institutions and from consultancy companies, too, are very clear on how small and medium sized companies (SMEs) (Gartner, 2020; WEO & Kearney, 2020), especially from developing and the least developed countries (World Bank 2020b, UNCTAD 2021b), were hit harder by the crisis. Dramatically, the Covid-19 came in times when technological and financial transformations were already unevenly reaching the weak side of the markets.

Since the international financial crisis in 2008/2009, industry 4.0 is consolidating a new technological paradigm based on artificial intelligence, digitalization and additive printing (UNCTAD, 2020), which have been accompanied by "de-globalization" of value chains. In the 2010s, both GDP, trade and investments growth decelerated in relation to the previous decade. Trade in value-added data shows the same trend (UNCTAD, 2020). That's why that same *WDR* (World Bank, 2020) sees GVC "at a crossroads" (p. xi). Before Covid-19, the World Bank had suggested that the reduction in trade costs would help developing countries to take benefit of the new technologies and upgrade in value chains, even recognizing that (a) platform firms and e-commerce unevenly benefit firms and households; (b) new production technologies had heterogeneous effects across countries and sectors; (c) robots are driving down the labor share of income and increasing the demand for skilled workers, thereby exacerbating inequality in the labor market (WB, 2020, p. 136). Once the trade costs rose significantly during the pandemic, following WB's arguments we can conclude that the new technologies and the pandemic worsened the inequalities in GVC and also increased incentives to leave GVCs, or at least, to leave some previous types of insertion into GVCs.

Though the full impact and evidence remains to be seen, there are reasons to believe that the pandemic and its disruptions in value chains can provoke trends of reshoring, nearshoring, diversification, or reindustrialization, which has begun in developed countries. We see states like the US, Germany, and China promoting industrial policies to revamp the manufacturing industry. UNCTAD (2020) argues that, on the one hand, the disruptions caused by governments' isolation measures against Covid-19 spread, on top of the rising protectionism and new demands for sustainability, have led TNC to think about alternatives to create more resilient supply chains in the long term. On the other hand, governments and societies are concerned about increasing national or regional autonomy in production capacity, especially for essential goods and services (e.g., health care-related products). As Reis (2021) explains, even for this narrative, the crisis caused by Covid-19 imposed governmental and corporate reactions to make supply chains more resilient, reducing the geographical concentration by promoting reindustrialization.

But are the developed countries really going to reshore the tangible manufacturing activities of the chains? It would definitely contradict the mainstream political narrative of free trade. In contrast, it would demonstrate how a trade "advantage" can be artificially created by the State. Indeed, this suggests that structuralist views have better explanatory power of productive and trade specialization in value chains: the reasons why a certain activity is produced in a place and its development impacts are so complex and depend on so many aspects, including financial and political ones. It is not simply a question of who has static comparative advantage at one moment in time.

How do interstate disputes and environmental challenges manifest?

The accumulation process behind the international productive system is closely related to the interstate disputes. In other words, there is competition for wealth and power relations among firms and states in the world system (Fiori, 2009). This reminds us of the controversy in international political economy (IPE) from the Anglo-Saxon countries during the seventies and eighties between the liberals (Keohane & Nye, 1987; Stopford & Strange, 1991), realists (Gilpin, 1987; Kindleberger, 1996) and Marxists (Cox, 1987; Arrighi, 1996; Wallerstein, 2004). Due to the third industrial revolution and financialization, capital was rapidly internationalizing and world production was reorganized as the power of TNCs was rapidly rising (Chesnais, 1995). It was the transition from the technological cycle based in analogical to digital technologies, in which the automotive industry loses importance in relation to informational technology industries as leaders of the economic dynamic worldwide. Then, that controversy was basically about whether and why TNCs were becoming more important than States and on the decay of American hegemony. However, that discussion paid little attention to the development challenges for the so-called second (countries and regions aligned to the Soviet Union or China) and third worlds (the countries and regions aligned to the developed countries in the West led by the US). This was the moment when developmental and dependency theories were criticizing the Eurocentric analyses and normative formulas emanating from the center. Instead, they were in search for their own diagnoses and solutions (De Sousa Santos & Paula, 2014).

Similarly, nowadays, we might be in between two cycles, facing technological change and perhaps with hegemonic change. The fourth technological revolution and the hegemonic dispute between the US and China are triggering the discussion on the competition of firms and states both in the North and the South. Shortly, the debate revamps that debate in the IPE from the 70s. The liberal narrative put emphasis in the competition between firms, believing that free markets, with less State intervention, would lead to better allocative results. The realists and nationalists put emphasis on power disputes, so that geopolitics is the most important driver of the world system. Marxists put emphasis in the class struggles, mostly related to firms, but also related to states. For the latter, the productive and distributive conflicts predominate in explaining the world system.

Retaking our previous discussion on the roles in GVC, because of the competition between capitals, specializing in competitive advantage is not necessarily going to take the periphery far. In the harsh competition of the weaker against the stronger, those in the peripheral positions are likely to lose (Shaikh, 2016). States do influence multinational corporations strongly but multinational corporations also influence states through lobbying in all countries both the periphery and the core, as Strange (1992) observed. That's really important to understand global value chains, how they work, what is produced where and why. It's not random; there are many geopolitical concerns involved in shaping GVCs.

And to describe the disputes nowadays, we must not only consider the new technologies such as 5G, but also sustainability. Everyone has to also bring in the environment to the GVCs or any economic analysis. It's impossible to just look at the economy abstracted from the environment in this day and age. Then, we could bring in the dependency theories again, as well as post-colonial or decolonial theories, to consider how historically, during colonialism and even before, extractive production structures that were environmentally very destructive were set up (Nkrumah, 1967; Fanon, 1968). Natural resource-based development in developing countries is usually led by TNC that are exploiting resources based on different rules in comparison to their home countries. The TNC came in, operated, and reshaped their historically constituted extractive structures. Indeed, it was easy for TNCs to exploit workers or firms in the periphery, with these very negative environmental and social consequences because that's how the societies were structured historically. When the mainstream analysts make recommendations about the environment for TNCs, it's often about patching or alleviating some negative effects at the margins, rather than challenging the structures that produce the problems in the first place (e.g. Archer & Elliott, 2021).

This is an interesting starting point to critically engage with the environment to analyze political, economic, and social phenomena playing out in GVCs. On the one hand, we see the firms, especially TNCs, structurally impacting and being impacted by the environment. On the other hand, the State and society shape and are shaped by these interactions as well. Today, new sustainability requirements are being pushed by many states; and many firms are obliged to publish annual sustainability reports. In parallel, governments are increasing investments in renewable sources, so that the energy matrix of many countries is changing towards green technologies. In this sense, the US and China are sending a clear message to the world: they are investing heavily in becoming carbon-neutral in 30–40 years. Then, clean energy might become one of the main industries driving the growth dynamics of these countries and, consequently, the world. As the annual report of the International Energy Agency (WER/ IEA, 2021) shows, clean energy investments must double in the 2020s to prevent global temperatures from rising 2°C, or triple to stabilize at 1.5°C (reaching $4 trillion). This will require government actions and a reshaping of financial architectures to accelerate clean capital investments and to promote technological innovations in green industries. According to the five-year plan, China aims to boost the development of new energy sources, for non-fossil fuels to grow from 15% to 20% in the energy use matrix by 2025. In the US, the Biden and Harris administration announced the Jobs and Infrastructure plan, which aims to foster the American industry with $1.3 trillion in infrastructure (over ten years) and $2.2 trillion in clean energy (in this administration alone).

Therefore, in both countries we have an expansion of the State in the economic and political, domestic and international spheres, not only because of the need for counter-cyclical measures to circumvent the Covid-19 crisis, but as a long-term inducer of investments in the strategic technologies and industries of the first half of the 21st century: the sustainable 4.0 paradigm (Reis, 2021b).

Then, we have at least four major problems. First, the consequences of the sustainability transition for developing economies that depend on natural resources.

Sustainable requirements are just binding them in ways that are highly unfair (see the chapter of Rossini and Magacho in this book). Second, the new technological green paradigm dominated by the monopolies makes it even more difficult for smaller companies to participate in this global venture. Thus, green 4.0 processes can also be a technological constraint both for developing countries and for small companies across the world (also from the developed world). According to the logic of capital and state disputes discussed before, this new technological imperative is also a strategy to concentrate and centralize capital accumulation in the most powerful TNC and states of the world system (Reis, 2021b). Then, it's not enough to just require small firms in the periphery to do certain things without actually providing the technology or related support for them. Analogously, the third problem is that just a couple of rich States are actually able to raise investments and enterprise in next-generation markets (Mazzucato, 2018). They have capital to finance new technologies and infrastructure, but most have not (see the chapter of Schutte and Prashad in this book). The availability of these financial conditions is also very uneven across countries. Furthermore, it is usually easier for the country that has the international currency (Eichengreen, 2008).

Taking the case of renewable energy, there is some hypocrisy related to the view that it can be a niche for companies from developing countries. There is a kind of opportunity here due to natural endowments, but many structural institutional conditions must be created for this opportunity to be realized. It is very difficult to capitalize on that opportunity unless there is heavy investment. China has been able to produce a lot of green energy or green energy sources and technology, but that is because of heavy investment – partly for their own sake because there is so much pollution and partly in order to become competitive internationally. Ecuador or a small firm from there might not be able to do that so easily because a lot of investment would be needed to developing technology. For advanced technology you need bigger firms, lots of scientists. Probably it is harder for developing countries to capitalize on that opportunity than in advanced countries. There are counterexamples of leapfrogging, though. Kenya famously 'skipped' phone landlines to go straight to digital payment systems and mobile phones. Not adopting 'old' infrastructures but just moving straight to new ones is another example that 'development' is not time continuous. However, adopting new technologies at a rapid speed does not necessarily disrupt the existing societal power hierarchies, on the contrary, it can reinforce them (dos Santos and Kvangraven, 2017). In light of this, mobile banking may indeed not be the 'revolution' it was first foreseen to be (Etzo & Collender, 2010).

And, fourth, we have to also consider sustainability in GVC both in the place of consumption and production. There is another hypocrisy enabled by the chains: some sustainable chains' activities rely in other activities that are not sustainable at all. Or the final product can be sustainable, but its production is not. There are many green tech products usually consumed in the rich countries rather than the poor countries. In Norway, one way the government is pushing a green economy is to aggressively promote electric cars. While this is a great way to avoid local pollution, in global terms we need to ask where these cars are being produced and how? At a closer look, we see that there are minerals like cobalt that go into electric cars that are extracted from the Congo and other developing countries. The parts of the cars that are produced at the bottom of the chain are often produced through poor working conditions and based on environmental destruction. Then the car that arrives in Norway is presented as a super clean machine, but its carbon footprint – if one considers all activities of the chain – is not taken into account.

What are distributional consequences from an intersectional standpoint?

Structuralist theories and dependency theories have always pointed to distributional asymmetries between center and periphery, as well as within the periphery. These theories were very clear in showing how there are differences between countries, but also the differences in domestic economies between classes. Structuralist or dependency Marxist theories highlight not just the inequality between center and periphery, but also the inequalities within the periphery. Prebisch (1949), Singer (1950), Celso Furtado (1961), Pinto (1976), several authors were analyzing the structural heterogeneity in the periphery: a divide where there are the export processing zones or cleavage of some production with high wages and productivity, and the rest of the economy with low wages and productivity. As explained before, they were especially concerned with how the dynamic export sector can leverage and improve the economic dynamics of the domestic economy.

However, many pioneers of these theories did not discuss gender and racial inequalities (Cardoso & Reis, 2019; Antunes Oliveira, 2021). In general, class struggle was often privileged over other struggles. But there are exceptions in Latin America, and many examples in other regions, related to the decolonial literature (see the chapter of Cardoso & Alves in this book), especially in the black radical tradition that discuss the productive and also the race relations between countries from a Marxist approach (Fanon, 1968). Decolonial traditions also point to other ways of comprehending development: what does 'development' mean? How we are going to develop, based on which productive forces? How do we improve the distribution among the different groups of society?

In this sense, we think that intersectional inequalities can be more than just incorporated into dependency theories; they must be an epistemological standpoint from which to understand the economic and political processes in course. As Crenshaw (1990) points out, working with the idea of intersections allow us to better recognize and ground the differences between people and negotiate the means by which those differences will find expression in the construction of group politics. Bringing in race, gender, and other intersections does not mean neglecting the materialist sort of structures, however. It is about looking at how global production structures tend to not just exploit workers in the periphery, but to exploit those that are already in a subordinate position (race to the bottom, as put by Smith 2016 or Latimer 2021). The way that the global production is structured reinforces the existing race and gender inequalities in the periphery. Depending on the country, black or indigenous people and women are super-exploited – in the words of Marini (1992), meaning the greatest exploitation of the physical strength of the worker in developing countries, whose labor normally is paid below its value. Analyzing super-exploitation along gendered and racial lines nowadays fits into a revised dependency approach, even if many of its pioneers did not necessarily engage with it directly themselves.

There is plenty of data showing how different wages are, across groups in society and across countries (ILO, 2019, 2021). But looking to wages is not necessarily enough to capture existing inequalities, as racism and misogyny are structural, and they manifest not only in features that are measurable through conventional means, but also through discrimination, exclusion, oppression, and other forms of structural violence that hurt and oppress certain groups. Mbembe (2018, p. 6) affirms that in times of globalization, the term "Black" was the product of a social and "technological machine (...) invented to signify exclusion, brutalization, and degradation, to point to a limit constantly conjured and abhorred" because "the Black Man, despised and profoundly dishonored, is the only human in the modern order whose skin has been transformed into the form and spirit of merchandise – the living crypt of capital". As Almeida (2019, p.15, our translation) explains, racism is always structural, so that it integrates the political and economic organization of the societies, providing "the meaning, the logic, and the technology for the reproduction of the forms of inequality and violence that shape contemporary social life".

Many feminist scholars show that the inequalities are not just about the wage; it is about the kinds of jobs for women and people of color – they're often more dangerous, less protected, more precarious. For example, it is possible to trace how GVCs are structured in ways that reinforce existing inequalities, also within countries. For example, in South Africa, black workers face particularly harsh forms of exploitation because of the historically very unequal racial structure in the country, and this can be observed also in GVCs (Newman & De Lannoy, 2015; Meagher, 2019). Moreover, there is also a gendered division of labor in the world system. Hirata and Kergoat (2018) propose a framework to conceptualize this gendered division, where they identify priority assignments of men in the productive sphere, and of women in the reproductive sphere, so that, men appropriate functions with greater social added value (political, religious, military etc.). In GVC is not any different (Quentin & Campling, 2018).

If now, during the pandemic, the system is becoming more concentrated because of the technological changes and financial improvements that are being made by the TNCs to keep or to raise their rate of surplus value extraction – their profit rates, we can thus expect class and intersectional struggles to be intensified. The power and wealth distribution has already been worsening. When this happens, historically, we observe the political positions becoming more polarized.

The power of conservative views increases while left-wing narratives about socialism and other alternative modes of organizing production arise (Kalecki, 1943b; Polanyi, 1944; see also the chapter of Berringer & Saad-Filho in this book).

How to alleviate distributive asymmetries, based on popular solutions and state action?

We hope that the radical alternatives being put forward resonate with a broad populace, to avoid top-down approaches developed by that will further intensify exploitation. In our understanding, new ways of organizing the world system must be born as bottom-up structural approaches. Indeed, that is precisely one of the greatest challenges for scholars: to participate, to contribute, to put into action truly popular projects that challenge existing and intensifying inequalities.

Especially now in a time of crisis, when somehow these popular progressive movements do not tend to do well. When there's lots of competition for resources, the conservatives tend to win because the elites have more resources to push their agenda. Marginalized workers are more scared about their paycheck than in normal times because it is a time of crisis. So, it may be riskier to go for an unknown alternative – or workers may be too preoccupied with their daily struggle. Moreover, as Saad-Filho and Boffo (2021) argue, already before the pandemics, we saw the rise of an "authoritarian neoliberalism" related to the contradictions in the restructuring of production, social reproduction, and structures of representation under neoliberalism.

Therefore, many contradictions of the world system are furthered in the wake of Covid-19. For example, the states had to play a big role to tackle the virus, deciding about the isolation measures, the anti-cyclical economic policies etc. But, in many countries, the economic policies instead of emphasizing the role of the state are actually trying to again make the state less interventionist, letting more space to the "market clearing" and to the private interests. Austerity is already happening in the developing world, supported by IMF recommendations. This is very serious in terms of consequences, but also in terms of the uneven treatment given by the multilateral institutions. It is shocking how the IMF and the World Bank were pushing austerity to the periphery countries already by the end of last year (Daar & Tamale, 2020), while center countries were recognizing the need for counter-cyclical and expansionary fiscal and monetary policies. Indeed, this inequality suggests that the discussions about the 'end' of neoliberalism may be a stable of the Global North, rather than a global phenomenon (Khurana & Narayan, 2021).

Currently, there are the third and fourth waves in many countries in a context of vaccine inequality, thus spending on health and other basic goods are urgent. What's more, austerity has proved to hit women and other marginalized groups in periphery countries harder, (see, for example, evidence from Brazil by Oliveira & Alloatti, 2021). There is also evidence that suggests that privatizing health care can worsen efficiency (Assa & Calderon, 2020) as well as access.

In order to fight inequalities, let's remember the classical solution of the Marxist theories: workers should unite forces (Marx & Engels, 1848) around the political battles within both the center and the periphery. Our task as scholars is to build coalitions globally between those non-Eurocentric approaches. As an example, the book *A People's Green New Deal* (Ajl, 2021) uses dependency theory to counter Eurocentric approaches to the climate crisis (which center on issues such as green infrastructure and shifts towards electric cars in the Global North). Eurocentric Green New Deals do not take into account all the destruction that has happened throughout colonialism and the destruction that is currently still taking place in certain parts of GVCs, negatively impacting the periphery in particular. Ajl therefore outlines what an anti-colonial Green New Deal could look like, which is surely the best way to fight climate change. As a global problem, it will never be solved just within the Global North or just within the center. It needs to be a global project where we address the particular challenges faced by each society and see them in relation to each other.

We have to jointly create strong social pacts and projects that rise into power in local, regional, national and international arenas, to reduce dependency in GVC or, more broadly, between center and periphery. This requires broad coalitions among marginalized groups, including workers across the world that are attentive to the different yet connected challenges different kinds of groups face. Though disruptive structural changes are historically difficult, it is our role to dialogue and to reflect together on how to make them possible. It feels like it is even more urgent now when the pandemic and the climate change are worsening global inequalities.

References

Ajl, Max (Ed.). *A people's green new deal*. Pluto Press, 2021.

Almeida, Silvio. *Racismo estrutural*. Pólen Produção Editorial LTDA, 2019.

Amin, Samir. *Eurocentrism*. Monthly Review Press, 2010.

Antunes de Oliveira, Felipe. Who are the super-exploited? Gender, race, and the intersectional potentialities of dependency theory. In: Madariaga, A.; Palestini, S. (eds) *Dependent capitalisms in contemporary Latin America and Europe*. International Political Economy Series. Palgrave Macmillan, Cham, pp. 101–128, 2021.

Archer, Matthew; Hannah Elliott. 'It's up to the market to decide': Revealing and concealing power in the sustainable tea supply chain. *Critique of Anthropology*, v. 41, n. 3, pp. 227–246, 2021.

Arrighi, Giovanni. *O longo século* XX: dinheiro, poder e as origens de nosso tempo. Editora UNESP, 1996.

Assa, Jacob; Calderon, Cecilia. Privatization and pandemic: A cross-country analysis of COVID-19 rates and health-care financing structures. *Working Paper* 08/2020, Department of Economics, The New School for Social Research, June 2020.

Baumgartner, Tom, Buckley, Walter and Burns, Tom. R. Unequal exchange and uneven development: The structuring of exchange patterns. *Studies in Comparative International Development*, v. 11, n. 2, pp. 51–72, 1976.

Braudel, Fernand. Histoire et sciences sociales: la longue durée. *Annales. Histoire, Sciences Sociales*, v. 13, no. 4. Cambridge University Press, 1958.

Braudel, Fernand. Histoire et sciences sociales: la longue durée. In: *Annales. Histoire, Sciences Sociales.* Cambridge University Press, pp. 725–753, 1958.

Cardoso, Fernanda Graziella; Reis, Cristina Fróes de Borja. Retomando o Estruturalismo para interpretar a desigual América Latina no século XXI. *Brazilian Keynesian Review,* v. 5, n. 2, pp. 324–341, 2019.

Cheng, Enfu; Zhai, Chan. China as a 'Quasi-Center' in the world economic system: Developing a new 'Center–Quasi-Center–Semi-Periphery–Periphery' theory. *World Review of Political Economy,* v. 12, n. 1, Pluto Journals, pp. 4–26, 2021.

Chesnais, François. A globalização e o curso do capitalismo de fim-de-século. *Economia e Sociedade,* v. 4, n. 2, pp. 1–30, 1995.

Cox, Robert. *Production, Power, and world order: Social forces in the making of history.* New York: Columbia University Press, 1987.

Crenshaw, Kimberle. Mapping the margins: Intersectionality, identity politics, and violence against women of color. *Stan. L. Rev.,* v. 43, p. 1241, 1990.

Crossa, Mateo, and Nina Ebner. Automotive global value chains in Mexico: a mirage of development? *Third World Quarterly,* v. 41, n. 7, pp. 1218–1239, 2020.

Daar, Nadia; Tamale, Nona. *A virus of austerity? The COVID-19 spending, accountability, and recovery measures agreed between the IMF and your government.* OXFAN, inequality & essential services, 12th October 2020, available at: https://www.oxfam.org/en/blogs/virus-austerity-covid-19-spending-accountability-and-recovery-measures-agreed-between-imf-and

De Sousa Santos, Boaventura; Paula, Meneses Maria. *Epistemologias do sul.* Cortez Editora, 2014.

Dos Santos, Theotonio. The structure of dependence. *The American Economic Review,* v. 60, n. 2, pp. 231–236, 1970.

Dos Santos, Theotonio. *Teoria da dependência: balanço e perspectivas.* Insular Livros, 2015.

Dos Santos, Paulo and Ingrid Harvold Kvangraven. Better than cash, but beware the costs: Electronic payments systems and financial inclusion in developing economies. *Development and Change,* v. 48, n. 2, pp. 205–227, 2017.

Eichengreen, Barry. *Globalizing capital.* Princeton Univ. Press, 2008.

Etzo, Sebastiana; Collender, Guy. The mobile phone 'revolution' in Africa: Rhetoric or reality? *African Affairs,* v. 109, n. 437, pp. 659–668, 2010.

Fanon, Franz. *Os Condenados da Terra.* Rio de Janeiro: Civilização Brasileira, 1968.

Ferrarini, B.; P. Scaramozzino. The Product Space Revisited: China's Trade Profile. *The World Economy,* v. 38, n. 9, 1368–1386, 2015.

Fiori, Jose Luis. O Poder Global e a Nova Geopolítica das Nações. *CyE* Año I N° 2 Primer Semestre 2009.

Fischer, A.M. The end of peripheries? On the enduring relevance of structuralism for understanding contemporary global development. *Development and Change,* v. 46, n. 4, pp. 700–732, 2015.

Foster, John Bellamy. The new imperialism of globalized monopoly-finance capital. *Monthly Review,* v. 67, n. 3, July-August 2015.

Furtado, Celso. *Desenvolvimento e subdesenvolvimento.* Editora Fundo de Cultura, 1961.

Gartner. *Weathering the Storm: Supply Chain Resilience in an Age of Disruption.* Stamford: Gartner, 2020.

Gereffi, Gary. Global value chains in a post-Washington Consensus world. *Review of International Political Economy,* v. 21, n. 1, pp. 9–37, 2014.

Gereffi, Gary; Korzeniewicz, Miguel (Ed.). *Commodity chains and global capitalism.* ABC-CLIO, 1994.

Gilpin, Robert. *The political economy of international relations.* Nova Jersey: Princeton University Press, 1987.

Hirata, Helena; Kergoat, Daniéle. The sexual division of labour re-examined. In: *The Gendering of Inequalities: Women, Men and Work*. Routledge, 2018. pp. 69–80.

Ignatenko, Anna; Raei, Faezeh; Mircheva, Borislava. Global Value Chains: What are the Benefits and Why Do Countries Participate? *IMF Working Papers*, v. 19, n. 18, 2019.

ILO. *Global Wage Report 2018/19 What lies behind gender pay gaps*. Geneva: International Labour Organization, 2019.

ILO. *Global Wage Report 2020/21: Wages and minimum wages in the time of COVID-19*. Geneva: International Labour Organization, 2021.

International Energy Agency. World Energy Outlook 2021. IEA: Paris, 2021.

Kalecki, Michaeł. *Theory of economic dynamics*. Routledge, [1943a, (2013)].

Kalecki, Michael. Political aspects of full employment. *Political Quarterly*, v. 14, n. 4, pp. 322–331, 1943b.

Keohane, Robert O.; NYE, Joseph. S. Power and Interdependence revisited. *International Organization*, v. 41, n. 4, 1987, pp. 725–753.

Keynes, John Maynard. *The general theory of employment, interest, and money*. Springer, [1936, (2018)].

Khurana, Ishan; John Narayan. (After) Neoliberalism? Rethinking the return of the State. *Discover Society: New Series*, v. 1, n. 4. https://doi.org/10.51428/dsoc.2021.04.0003, 2021.

Kindleberger, Charles. *World economic primacy 1500–1990*. Oxford: Oxford University Press, 1996.

Kvangraven, Ingrid Harvold. Impoverished economics? A critical assessment of the new gold standard. *World Development*, v. 127, p. 104813, 2020.

Kvangraven, Ingrid Harvold. Beyond the stereotype: Restating the relevance of the dependency research programme. *Development and Change*, v. 52, n. 1, pp. 76–112, 2021.

Kvangraven, Ingrid Harvold; Styve, Maria Dyveke; Kufakurinani, Ushehwedu. Samir Amin and beyond: The enduring relevance of Amin's approach to political economy. *Review of African Political Economy*, v. 48, n. 167, pp.1–7, 2021.

Latimer, Amanda. Super-exploitation, the race to the bottom, and the missing international. In: Ness I.; Cope Z. (eds) *The Palgrave encyclopedia of imperialism and anti-imperialism*. Palgrave Macmillan, Cham, 2021.

Lenin, Vladimir Ilich. *Imperialism: The highest stage of capitalism*. Resistance Books, 1917 [1999].

Marini, Ruy Mauro. *América Latina: dependência e integração*. São Paulo: Brasil Urgente, 1992.

Marx, Karl; Engels, Friedrich. *Manifesto comunista*. Boitempo Editorial, 1848 [2015].

Mazzucato, Mariana. Mission-oriented innovation policies: challenges and opportunities. *Industrial and Corporate Change*, v. 27, n. 5, pp. 803–815, 2018.

Mbembe, Achille. *Crítica da Razão Negra*. Lisboa: Antígona, 2018.

Mccombie, John S. L. Criticisms and defences of the balance of payments constrained growth model: Some old, some new. In: Soukiazis, Elias; Cerqueira, Pedro (Eds.), *Models of balance of payments constrained growth*. London: Palgrave Macmillan, 2012.

Meagher, Kate. Working in chains: African informal workers and global value chains. *Agrarian South: Journal of Political Economy*, v. 8, n. 1–2, pp. 64–92, 2019.

Missio, Fabricio; Jayme Jr., Frederico. Structural heterogeneity and endogeneity of elasticities on the balance-of-payments constrained growth model. In: Soukiazis, Elias; Cerqueira, Pedro (Eds.), *Models of balance of payments constrained growth: History, theory and empirical evidence*. Great Britain: Palgrave MacMillan, 2012.

Newman, Katherine S., De Lannoy, Arianne. *After freedom: The rise of the post-apartheid generation in democratic South Africa*. Beacon Press, 2015.
Nkrumah, Kwame. *Neocolonialismo: Último Estágio do Imperialismo*. RJ: Civilização Brasileira, 1967.
OECD. *Interconnected economies: Benefitting from global value chains*. Synthesis report. Geneva, 2013.
Oliveira, Ana Luíza Matos; Alloatti, Magali N. Gendering the crisis: Austerity and the Covid-19 pandemic in Brazil. *Economia Politica*, pp. 1–22, 2021.
Pinto, Anibal. *Heterogeneidade estrutural e modelo de desenvolvimento recente*. América Latina: ensaios de interpretação econômica n. 2, pp. 44–82, 1976.
Polanyi, Karl. *A Grande Transformação*. Rio de Janeiro: Campus, 2000[1944].
Prebisch, Raul. O Desenvolvimento Econômico Latino-Americano e Alguns de seus Principais Problemas. In Bielschowsky, Ricardo (ed.) *Cinqüenta Anos de Pensamento na CEPAL*, Rio de Janeiro: Record, v. 1, 1949[2000].
Quentin, David; Campling, Liam. Global inequality chains: Integrating mechanisms of value distribution into analyses of global production. *Global Networks*, v. 18, n. 1, pp. 33–56, 2018.
Radley, Ben. The end of the African mining enclave? Domestic marginalization and labour fragmentation in the democratic republic of Congo. *Development and change*, v. 51, n. 3, pp. 794–816, 2020.
Reis, Cristina Fróes de Borja. Efeitos de encadeamento e diversificação industrial comercial e produtiva: uma análise da Indonésia, Malásia e Tailândia entre 1980 e 2010. *Economia e Sociedade*, v. 25, pp. 51–85, 2016.
Reis, Cristina Fróes de Borja. The pandemic and the new technologies' boom: New narratives for justifying more power and wealth asymmetries. In: Rached, Gabriel (Org.) *States and Institutions: International Dialogues and Policies for Tackling the Crisis*. Autografia: Niterói, 2021a.
Reis, Cristina Fróes de Borja. Os impactos da pandemia nas cadeias de valor: acima de que, Brasil? *Revista Economistas*, n. 40, COFECON - Brasilia, Julho 2021b.
Reis, Cristina Fróes de Borja; Barbosa, Muryatan Santana; Cardoso, Fernanda Graziella. The South's thoughts on development: Links between Latin America and Africa. *Revista de economía mundial*, n. 52, 2019.
Reis, Cristina Froes de Borja; Cardoso, Fernanda Graziella. Center and periphery in global value chains: An interpretation based on the pioneers of Development. In Hermann, Arturo; Mouatt, Simon (orgs.) *Contemporary Issues in Heterodox Economics*. London: Routledge, 2021.
Reis, Cristina Fróes de Borja; Guedes Pinto, Jose Paulo. Center-periphery relationships of pharmaceutical value chains: A critical analysis based on goods and knowledge trade flows. *Review of Political Economy*, 2021. https://doi.org/10.1080/09538259.2021.1882192
Rikap, Cecilia. Innovation as economic power in Global Value Chains. *Revue d'économie industrielle*, n. 3, pp. 35–75, 2018.
Rodriguez, Octavio. *o estruturalismo latino-americano*. rio de janeiro: civilização brasileira, 2009.
Saad-Filho, Alfredo; Boffo, Marco. The corruption of democracy: Corruption scandals, class alliances, and political authoritarianism in Brazil. *Geoforum*, v. 124, pp. 300–309, 2021.
Salinas, Gonzalo; Muñoz, Sònia. Proximity and horizontal policies: The backbone of export diversification and complexity. *IMF Working Papers*, v. 2021, n. 064, 2021.

Selwyn, Benjamin; Leyden, Dara. Oligopoly-driven development: The World Bank's trading for development in the age of global value chains in perspective. *Competition & Change*, 2021. DOI: 1024529421995351.

Serrano, Franklin L. P.; Medeiros, Carlos A. Economic development and the revival of the classical surplus approach. In UNRISD *"The Need to Rethink Development Economics*, pp. 7–8, 2001.

Shaikh, Anwar. Foreign trade and the law of value. *Science & Society*, v. 44, n. 1, 27–57, 1980.

Shaikh, Anwar. *Capitalism: Competition, conflict, crises*. Oxford: Oxford University Press, 2016.

Singer, H. The distribution of gains between investing and borrowing countries. *American Economic Review*, v. 40, n. 2, pp. 473–485, 1950.

Smith, John. *Imperialism in the twenty-first century: Globalization, super-exploitation, and capitalism's final crisis*. NYU press, 2016.

Starosta, Guido. The outsourcing of manufacturing and the rise of giant global contractors: A Marxian approach to some recent transformations of global value chains. *New Political Economy*, v. 15, n. 4, 2010, pp. 543–563.

Stopford, John; Strange, Susan. *Rival states, rival firms*. Cambridge: CUP, 1991.

Strange, Susan. States, firms and diplomacy. *International Affairs*, v. 68, n. 1, pp. 1–15, 1992.

Sturgeon, Timothy J. From commodity chains to value chains: Interdisciplinary theory building in an age of globalization. *Industry Studies Working Paper*, 02, 2008.

Suwandi, Intan. *Value chains: the new economic imperialism*. Monthly Review Press, 2019.

UNCTAD. *World investment report 2020: International production beyond the pandemic*. New York: United Nations Conference on Trade and Development, 2020.

UNCTAD. *World investment report 2021: Investing in sustainable recovery*. New York: United Nations Conference on Trade and Development, 2021a.

UNCTAD. *Impact of the COVID-19 pandemic on trade and development: Recovering, but unevenly*. New York: United Nations Conference on Trade and Development, 2021b.

Wallerstein, Immanuel. *World system analysis: An introduction*. Duke University Press Books, Year: 2004.

World Bank. *World development report 2020: Trading for development in the age of global value chains*. Washington, DC: World Bank, 2020a.

World Bank. *Poverty and shared prosperity 2020: Reversals of fortune*. Washington, DC: World Bank, 2020b.

World Bank. *World development report 2021: Data for better lives*. Washington, DC: World Bank, 2021.

World Economic Forum; Kearney. *How to rebound stronger from COVID-19 Resilience in manufacturing and supply systems*. WEF/ Kearney, White Paper, April 2020.

World Trade Organization. *World trade report 2021*. Geneva: WTO, 2021.

7

THE DEINDUSTRIALIZATION OF THE BRAZILIAN ECONOMY

Theoretical aspects and empirical evidence

Gabriel Almeida Antunes Rossini and Guilherme Riccioppo Magacho

Currently, keeping up with Brazil's socioeconomic dynamics has become more difficult due to the changes brought about by the Covid-19 pandemic and the political-economic jolts the country has experienced since 2015. These elements are added to the growing international instability due to consequences of the pandemic, the rise of China, and the march of the so-called Industry 4.0 (Salama, 2019).

Precisely in the midst of this scenario full of uncertainties, the Brazilian economy is the protagonist of a profound process of early deindustrialization, a growing producer of goods from the extractive and agribusiness industries – with low added value and ample potential for environmental destruction – characteristics that tend to place the country in a subordinate position, such as that experienced before the so-called displacement of the dynamic center of the Brazilian economy by Celso Furtado (2009), which occurred in the 1930s (Paulani, 2021).

With these elements in mind, this chapter assumes, as a premise, the postulate of the centrality of the industrial sector to drive processes of sustained and sustainable growth, technological diffusion, and socioeconomic development in middle-income countries, such as Brazil. The text is organized around the recognition that selective industrialization, that is, industrialization centered on the most sophisticated segments, has the ability to advance the collective capacities of appropriation and multiplication of productive knowledge, to trigger innovative processes and to raise productivity and real wages, thus providing support for the promotion of inclusive and sustainable development. The centrality of the industrial sector becomes even more evident at a time when the economy is on a path of low growth, directly impacted by the different facets (political, economic, health, territorial) of a crisis that for almost a decade has taken on more defined contours and whose speed and consequences have intensified due to the Covid-19 pandemic.

DOI: 10.4324/9781003384366-8

Initially, the text addresses the existing links between economic dynamics and the industrial sector and in what circumstances, according to specialized literature, the so-called deindustrialization manifests itself. Next, we recover aspects of the medium-term trajectory of the Brazilian industry that incorporates, among other problematic elements, the negative characteristics of deindustrialization. Finally, we list some final considerations.

Before we move on, it is worth sharing with the reader the particular methodology used for the elaboration of this chapter, which results from the project *South-North Dialogues on Democracy, Development and Sustainability*, organized by NEEDDS-UFABC. The dialogues involved researchers associated with NEEDDS and guests from different research centers around the world. The interaction with external researchers aimed to contribute to the consolidation of the internationalization of some central ideas of the studies of NEEDDS associated professors and to mature concepts and perspectives, opening the way for new reflections and research extensions.

Theoretical aspects: the nexus between economic dynamics and the industrial sector

As a result of the greater enrichment of the most industrialized countries, we began to observe, from the 1960s on, the frank expansion of the share of services in terms of their contribution to GDP and their share in total employees, a phenomenon that has been discussed as a process of deindustrialization (Rodrik, 2016).

This formulation was investigated and developed by several authors who sought to explain this phenomenon in developed economies throughout the 1970s and 1980s. Central to these investigations were the researches of Rowthorn and Wells (1987), Rowthorn and Ramaswany (1999) and Rowthorn and Coutts (2004), who formulated relevant contributions on the dynamics of deindustrialization. This process, which can assume a positive or negative aspect, is the result of a long decline in the participation of manufacturing in national employment. The positive side would result from the scenario of long-lasting economic growth combined with full employment and not associated with the reprimarization of the export basket. The decline in industry would occur due to the increase in its productivity, a result of technological and scale gains and, as a result of this evolution, the workers that have become excessive in industry would be absorbed by the service sector, since this sector's demand for the labor factor is more elastic. However, the reduction in the volume of labor absorbed by the secondary sector, tends, by virtue of its increasing productivity, not to impact the value added of manufacturing (Rowthorn & Wells, 1987). The negative one, in turn, could affect countries at different stages of development and would result from prolonged recessionary processes, in which the dynamics of real income and industrial production would remain stagnant or diminish, making it impossible for the unemployed workers in the primary and secondary sectors to be absorbed by the tertiary sector. In this modality of deindustrialization, reprimarization of the export basket could occur.

In more recent work, Tregenna (2008 and 2011) has expanded the understanding of deindustrialization by stating that this process can also occur when there is a sustained decline in the share of manufacturing in GDP. The author argues that, while many of the problems of deindustrialization arise from the relative reduction in industrial employment, many others may not occur if industry is not losing its share of output (chaining effects, increasing returns to scale, *learning-by-doing,* etc.). Furthermore, the expansion of production in the manufacturing sector, which is not necessarily accompanied by an increase in employment is capable of relieving restrictions in the balance of payments, due to the fact that its global demand has greater elasticity than that of the primary sector (Tregenna, 2008).

In addition to the previous approaches, others have shown that the causes of this phenomenon are diverse and change as a result of the moment under analysis, the degree of development of the countries, and the way they are inserted into the global scenario.

Palma (2014) shows that the economic reforms implemented by Latin American countries obstructed the transition to a self-sustaining industrialization. To the extent that they carried out liberalizing reforms in the early 1990s, their trade insertion became conditioned by the production of primary products with low added value to the detriment of the production of manufactured goods with higher technological content. Such scenario causes a certain premature deindustrialization, because despite the fact that these countries have low *per capita* income, they are deindustrialized due to: the inability to keep up with the evolution of the productive forces; the deterritorialization of parts of their production chains to countries with cheaper labor; and the economic policy adopted since the 1980s. Such scenario of premature deindustrialization removes, according to Rodrik (2016), the main channel of accelerated growth and decreases the possibilities for underdeveloped economies to converge to the income pattern of developed nations. For the author, a large portion of underdeveloped countries face deindustrialization processes before they have achieved a high-productivity industrial fabric.

Some authors also argue that the phenomenon of deindustrialization can result from the concentration of manufacturing activity in less sophisticated activities, i.e., due to a certain regressive specialization in less productive sectors that allow for lower value added. As Tregenna (2015) emphasizes, in addition to the general diagnosis of deindustrialization, given the great heterogeneity of the industrial sector, it is necessary to identify which manufacturing sectors are losing relevance. This movement is central, since there are sectors with high technology, productivity, productive chains, high wages, and requiring a high level of education for workers. These coexist with industrial activities characterized by low productivity, low wages, rudimentary technology, and partial or limited dynamic chaining effects (Maia, 2020).

Brazilian authors linked to the so-called new developmentalism, such as Palma (2014), also recurrently associate Brazilian deindustrialization with the "Dutch disease" (Bresser-Pereira, 2008). According to Torres and Cavalieri (2015, p. 862), the Dutch disease is defined as the situation in which the wide availability of natural resources of a country enables comparative advantages, such that their export can cause repeated trade surpluses and, by extension, exchange rate appreciation and a decrease in industrial investments, because imported products become more competitive. The tendency for exchange rate overvaluation does not result, however, only from the reprimarization of exports. Palma (2005), Oreiro and Feijó (2010) and Bresser-Pereira and Marconi (2010) recognize that other factors contribute to exchange rate appreciation, some market factors, other economic policy factors such as the adoption of high interest rates and the opening of the capital account.

In addition to the previous aspects, the displacement and deterritorialization of production to countries with lower labor costs, with the consequent deepening of global value chains (GVC) and the so-called statistical illusion arising from the outsourcing of industrial services – such as cleaning, security – also play an important role. With regard to the statistical illusion, it is worth noting that while the central countries insert themselves into these chains by expanding their exports of sophisticated services, the peripheral countries recurrently participate through the repeated reprimarization of their export schedules.

Aspects of the recent dynamics of the Brazilian industry

The Brazilian manufacturing park has developed differently from the parks in Asian countries, which today are the most relevant. The Brazilian industry consolidated itself by directing its efforts toward the domestic market. Brazil has sophisticated and diversified its production, but its exports, with some exceptions, have not been organized around more sophisticated goods, as has occurred with Japan and South Korea and, more recently, with China and Vietnam.

Brazil, as well as most Latin American countries, faced difficulties in organizing an export industry of more sophisticated goods. Most countries in the region had, and still have, export agendas dependent on agricultural and mineral *commodities*. With the advent of the oil shocks of the 1970s and the increase in the North American interest rate, which occurred in 1989, these countries became extremely indebted and without access to the necessary foreign exchange to make imports, since their respective export agendas were not very diversified and *commodities*, with the exception of oil, were those that suffered most negative shocks.

This scenario, adverse for the peripheral countries in general and for Latin American countries in particular, was aggravated by the rapid transformations of the technological base, especially as a result of new possibilities opened up by electronic innovations. Brazil, for example, tried to insert itself into this new paradigm by means of a set of relevant policies that involved the protection of the domestic market and incentives to export more sophisticated goods. The policies implemented meant that the country, at the time, did indeed flirt with the possibility of becoming a major electronics production base. However, due to the significant indebtedness, resulting from the state taking over private sector debts, the promotion of external insertion by selling more sophisticated goods to the rest of the world was unsuccessful. This result was largely due to the significant devaluation of the exchange rate in order to obtain a greater volume of foreign exchange and to equate the financing of imports, and also to the drastic reduction in government investment, discouraging private investment and causing a large part of the demand, necessary to make possible the transition to the new technological paradigm, to be depleted. Thus, there was not enough growth dynamics to sustain the Brazilian industrial conversion throughout the 1980s. The crisis of this decade, which lasted at least until 1996–1997, completely undermined the capacity of the Brazilian industry to catch up in a crucial moment.

With high inflation and problems with its foreign debt, Brazil, in the late 1980s, remained apart from the international financial market. Seeking to remedy this situation, Brazilian governments pursued the creation of conditions for the country to become a more attractive market for international investments and, to this end, some reforms were carried out (Paulani, 2017b), such as: staggered reduction of non-tariff barriers and import tax (pillars of the protection of domestic industry); opening of the capital account; internationalization of the Brazilian securities market; tax subsidies to owners of shares and financial gains of non-residents; legal changes aimed at protecting the state's creditors (Fiscal Responsibility Law), and privatization of the relevant state-owned companies in the petrochemical and steel industry – segments that concentrated more than 90% of the state's presence as a direct producer in the manufacturing industry (Bielschowsky, 1998) – as well as of the state-owned companies that offered public utility services (public transportation, electricity, gas, telephone).

The wide opening of the Brazilian economy, initiated in 1989 and deepened by Fernando Collor and Fernando Henrique Cardoso, drastically reduced the degree of protection of the national production park in face of foreign competitors. The macroeconomic framework resulting from the Real Plan (1994) – rigidity of public spending, adoption of high real interest rates and an overvalued exchange rate to ensure price stability, in addition to privatizations – produced a new competitive context for the domestic industry and prevented the promotion of consistent cycles of investment in new production plants. This fact is largely explained by the existing relationship between high interest rates and the dynamics of short-term profitability, which makes the price of shares and the distribution of high dividends become the key variables around which corporate management began to organize, separating profits from investment (Guttmann, 2008) and expressing the existing unity between productive capital and financial capital (Chesnais, 2016).

Strictly speaking, we can say that we were in the wrong place at the wrong time. In the 1990s, we insisted on mistaken policies. Precisely when we remained technologically outdated, exactly at the moment when we were susceptible to the entry of foreign companies, mainly Asian, an abrupt commercial opening was carried out. As a result, even the companies that could compete internationally lost the capacity to do so.

This new reality caused companies, in general, to implement, throughout the 1990s, a certain defensive adjustment that promoted a broad "non-creative destruction" (Tavares, 1998), characterized by cost cutting, through layoffs, import of inputs, and outsourcing of activities – cleaning services, security, technical assistance, etc. – resulting in reduction of industrial employment, which Palma characterized as "statistical illusion" (Palma, 2005, 2014), in addition to denationalization of industrial sectors, company bankruptcy and restructuring of segments of industry, resulting in reduction of industrial employment, which Palma characterized as "statistical illusion" (Palma, 2005, 2014) – in addition to denationalization of industrial sectors, bankruptcy of companies and destructuring of segments of the Brazilian industrial park. There has also been a retraction in research and development (R&D) activities, a widening of the gap between product and employment, and regressive specialization in the pattern of foreign trade, with an increase in the weight (see graph 2) of simpler products in exports (footwear, leather, hides, and sugar) and of more sophisticated products in imports (electronic equipment and electrical material) (Kupfer, 2003).

There was, moreover, low average GDP growth (in the 1990s, the average annual increment was 2.85%), a new reduction in the participation of industry (just over 20% of GDP in the year 2000) and, according to Morceiro and Guilhoto (2019), a fall in the volume of jobs in the manufacturing industry (12.3% in 2001, against 15.2% and 16.1% in the years 1990 and 1980, respectively). Finally, in this new scenario, the deterioration of the Brazilian trade balance occurred until the exchange devaluation of 1999, which promoted voluminous net inflow of foreign capital, which rebalanced the Balance of Payments and expanded the degree of dependence of the national economy in relation to the global financial system (Carvalho & Kupfer, 2008; Morceiro, 2012).

When, in 1999, it was no longer possible to sustain the excessive valuation of the Real, another strategy was implemented. A systematic increase in interest rates, which reached 50%, prevailed, which once again deepened the problems faced by the Brazilian industrial sector, since, with the possibility of large gains arising from the financial sphere and with the increase in the cost of long-term loans, the expansion of the Brazilian productive capacity was once again discouraged. Since the first years of the Luiz Inácio Lula da Silva administration (2002), social scientists from different theoretical positions outside the *mainstream* were dismayed by the maintenance of the macroeconomic policy design formulated by Fernando Henrique Cardoso's team (1995–2002) after the crisis of the real in 1999. There was the maintenance of the tripod based on inflation targets – to this end, in March 2003, the interest rate reached 26.5% per year – a floating exchange rate and a fiscal policy conditioned by the achievement of a high primary surplus (beyond the levels demanded by the International Monetary Fund (IMF), which more than compensated for the nominal deficit of the public accounts. Critics of the conduct of economic policy highlighted that this arrangement hindered industrial and income transfer policies necessary to enable the resumption of growth and the reduction of inequality of income and wealth in the country (Carvalho, 2003; Morais & Saad Filho, 2011; Paulani, 2008; Sicsú, 2003).

At the international level, powerful dislocations were taking place, repositioning the global balance of power. The growing US fiscal and trade deficits fed a global scheme to recycle financial surpluses, whereby the trade surpluses of US creditor countries were absorbed by *Wall Street* and brought back into the international circuit via additional demand for European and Asian financial products, profits, and income, at the cost of accumulating gigantic debts (Paulani, 2017b). The resulting financialization constitutes the background of the recent phenomena of intensification of deindustrialization in much of the world and also in Brazil.

Before the 2008 crisis, the changes in external conditions that the Brazilian economy had been facing since 2003 – embodied in the increase in *commodity* prices resulting from higher Chinese demand (see graph below) –, high real interest rates and the process of national currency appreciation deepened the financialization of the economy and made the country a locus of rentier gains. From the end of 2008, as a result of the financial crisis produced by the *subprime* mortgage market in the United States, Brazil felt the financial collapse intensely: in contrast to the 6.1% growth in 2007 and 5.1% in 2008, the impact of the crisis caused the Brazilian economy to shrink by 0.2% in 2009. After the crisis, the small devaluation of the real was unable to offset the high real interest rates practiced then, notably in a context of very low or negative international interest rates. This scenario was only partially and momentarily reversed during the Dilma Rousseff administration, throughout 2011 (Mazzucato, 2018; Paulani, 2012).

Despite the adverse scenario, approximately between 2004 and 2012, the country set in motion a sequence of three major industrial policies. Two of them, given the prevailing political and economic conditions, were very well designed. These are the Industrial, Technological and Foreign Trade Policy (PITCE) and the Productive Development Policy (PDP). If not a greater stimulus to industry in relation to other sectors, such initiatives sought to mitigate the higher taxes levied on investments in the productive sectors. In addition, such actions tried to promote block investments, which is fundamental, because to be successful, many times, the expansion of productive capacity must create simultaneously suppliers, demanders, etc.

There are, moreover, two other elements that explain an important part of the national economic scenario at the time: the fiscal adjustment implemented by Joaquim Levy in favor of "regaining confidence" of economic agents – guided by an idea dear to the neoliberal discourse, although already quite worn out: "*there is no alternative*" – and the mistaken option made by Dilma Rousseff, of prioritizing private investments over public ones, through the expansion of tax exemptions and subsidies (Orair & Gobetti, 2015). According to Carvalho (2018), as of 2011, the fact that Brazilian industry was not growing like the service sector, due to competitiveness problems aggravated by the appreciated real, led to a change in economic policy guided by the almost full adoption of the so-called "Fiesp Agenda", which had as central elements: devaluation of the real, reduction of the interest rate, fiscal adjustment, payroll tax breaks, and reduction of energy tariffs.

However, as is well known, the private sector has not become the protagonist of the growth process. This fact is explained, in part, by the scenario formed, on the one hand, by the contraction of international trade resulting from the crisis in the European periphery in 2012, the slowdown in the Chinese economy, and the tenuous North American economic dynamics. On the other hand, by the retraction in domestic demand resulting from the decrease in public investment and the fiscal adjustment then implemented. Since 2011, a slowdown in industrial production and investments was observed. Moreover, as Carvalho (2018) states, the government insisted on making the mistake, granting more and more benefits as a way to try to awaken investments. This had a high fiscal cost and contributed to deteriorate the situation of public accounts, already damaged due to lower economic growth – even considering that expenses were growing less than before and public investment remained stagnant throughout the first Dilma Rousseff administration.

When international conditions deteriorated and the economic policy advocated by the "FIESP Agenda" proved unsuccessful, the model sustained by the increase in consumption through credit expansion began to cool down and the dispute for public funds became more intense. At the same time, the unwillingness of the elites to maintain a government that advocated some intervention and implementation of social policies grew. Although the policies adopted until 2014 had managed to keep the unemployment level at the lowest levels of the historical series, the set of elements indicated above caused "the crisis to explode, not only from the economic point of view, but also politically, given the worsening of public accounts, a stony clause of the orthodox-liberal canon that regulates the economic policy pro-financial valorization" (Paulani, 2017b, p. 37).

As a consequence of this adverse scenario, there was once again a deepening of the process of deindustrialization and reprimarization of our exports. As shown in Figure 7.1, the share of industry in the GDP fell from 35.9% to 26.8% between 1985 and 1994, and subsequently continued to decline, reducing its share from 16.8% to 11.3% between 1995 and 2018, something that is verified both when measuring the share of industry in current values and when discounting the change in relative prices. The information regarding foreign direct investment (FDI) in Brazil is an expression of this movement. While in the 1980s the participation of manufacturing industry in total FDI was around 75%, in the 1990s this figure fell to 60% and fluctuates between 30% and 40% from 2001 on, reaching, in 2017, a little over 33%. In contrast, the share of FDI in the services sector, between 2006 and 2017, reached an average of 65% (MIDIC/CAMEX, 2018).

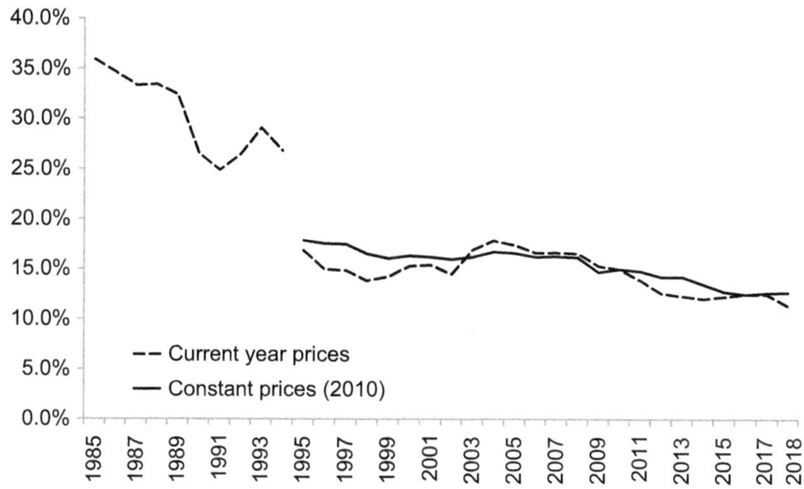

FIGURE 7.1 Manufacturing Industry (% in GDP), 1985–2018.
Source: Ipeadata; Own elaboration.
(*) Due to a methodological change, the 1994 figure cannot be compared to the 1995 figure.

In terms of the reprimarization of the export agenda, the data are even more alarming. According to the Ministry of Industry, Foreign Trade and Services, the share of manufactured products in exports fell from 59% in 2000 to 36% in 2018, and the share of basic products jumped from 22.8% to 49.8% in the same period. Thus, the negative impact of economic policies practiced over the past decades in Brazil, combined with low growth rates and the absence of consistent strategies to boost and develop technology, resulted in the systematic decline of medium- and high-tech industrial exports and the correlated increase in imports of inputs and tradable components of manufacturing industry. Furthermore, the trade liberalization and productive insertion caused practically all sectors to substitute national inputs for imported ones. However, while in agriculture, mining, and low-tech manufacturing, the increase in exports offset this negative effect on demand; in medium- and high-tech manufacturing, the increase in exports was unable to offset the perverse effects of productive disarticulation (Magacho, Mccombie, & Guilhoto, 2018).

In addition to recalling the relevance of macroeconomic policy design for the dynamics of Brazilian industry, it is worth, in order to achieve our objectives, to briefly compare the Brazilian industrial performance with the international one, which can be partly glimpsed in the graph below. To this end, it is important to keep in mind that the competitive, productive, technological, and asset mutations of great significance, which occurred in the global economy, are fundamental for us to understand the dynamics of Brazilian industry (Chesnais (1996, 2010 and 2016); Sarti and Hiratuka (2015, 2018)). Such transformations and the resulting technological, knowledge, and learning asymmetries are a condition, as emphasized by Latin American structuralism, for us to understand some of the specificities that guided the movement of Brazilian and global industry. However, this is not to omit the acuity of internal factors, but to perceive that the strategies of global oligopolies and transnational companies do not condition exogenously the accumulation of peripheral countries, but articulate with it and transform it from inside (Tavares, 1985; Figure 7.2).

To take this a step further, we put in the foreground the fact that the adverse dynamics faced by Brazilian industry over the past decades meant that in 2019, among other things, the sector that covers the plastics, food, beverage, metallurgy, and textile industries, among others, represented only 11% of economic activity. This result evidenced that the Brazilian industry was one of those that presented the largest retraction, between 1970 and 2017, according to a survey involving 30 countries and using the United Nations *National Accounts Main Aggregates Database*, updated in December 2018, by the Institute for Industrial Development Studies (IEDI). The study concluded that the share of industry in Brazilian GDP fell from 21.4% to 12.6% between 1970 and 2017, causing the country to experience the third largest contraction in the sector – ahead only of Australia and the United Kingdom – and deep premature deindustrialization process (IEDI, 2019). The broad industrial setback, for more, is also evident when we look at Brazil's share of global manufacturing value added. The country's industry went through a "forced march" growth phase until 1980, which involved extensive planning by the state. In that year, Brazil held about 4.0% of global industry, that is, an industrial production park then larger than China, Korea, and India combined. In 2017, the industry of each of these countries was

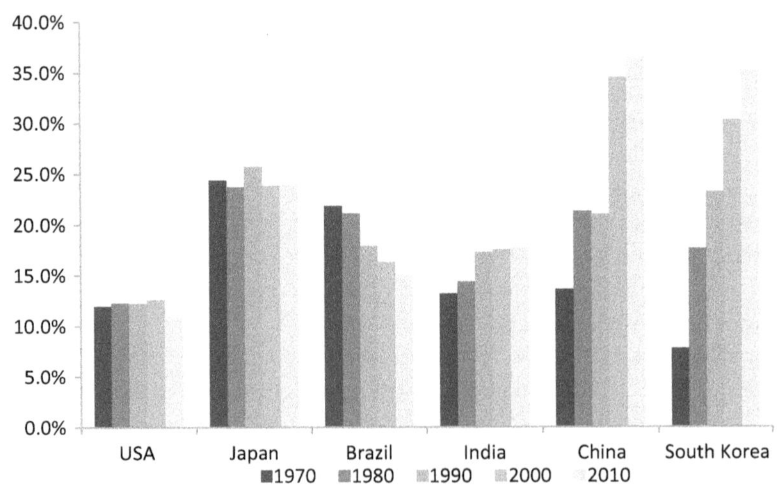

FIGURE 7.2 Manufacturing Industry (% of GDP), Selected Countries.

Source: GGDC 10-Sector Database Timmer et al. (2015) and Ipeadata; Own Elaboration.

(*) Data at 2005 prices from GGDC 10-Sector Database, except for Brazil in 2000 and 2010, whose source is IPEADATA and data are at 2010 prices.

already significantly larger than Brazil's (Idem). According to the cited study (IEDI, 2019, p. 49):

> Brazilian manufacturing grew only 24% between 1980 and 2017, while world manufacturing grew 204% and the world, excluding China, grew 135%. [...] In China, the industrial park has multiplied by 44 and in South Korea by 18, being the leaders in industrial growth since 1980. It is worth noting that both countries have conducted robust industrial policies focused on innovation, exports, and internationalization of domestic companies, with the state acting in conjunction with the private sector to significantly enhance development, in addition to following macroeconomic policies favorable to industrial growth.

Finally, we point out that the deep process of Brazilian deindustrialization causes apprehension, due to its precocity (which began in the 1980s and with *per capita* income below US$ 4,000) and the obstacles it creates for economic development. This concern results from the understanding that industry is a catalytic sector, in the long run, for economic growth, due to: (i) its potential to enable product and investment chaining effects; (ii) the increased generation and diffusion of R&D and innovations that can boost the productivity of industry and other sectors; (iii) the potential of static and dynamic economies of scale; (iv) the higher income elasticity of demand for industrial products, mitigating the external restriction of the manufacturing exporting country (Ferraz, Kupfer & Iooty, 2004; Oreiro & Feijó, 2010; Torres & Cavalieri, 2015). Moreover, it corroborates the promotion of regional development.

Final considerations

Despite the occurrence of decades of intensive and integrated industrialization that were able to originate vigorous and diversified industrial production, the continuous falls in the participation of this sector – especially, of the transformation industry in the Brazilian GDP, as well as of industrial employment in total employment, besides the reprimarization of the country's export portfolio – shows a deep process of early deindustrialization, with a *per capita* income level that, according to specialized literature, does not explain this process. As we emphasized, this goes back to the crisis of the 1980s and the continued loss, since then, of competitiveness of the country in the international market of products of higher technological intensity, a potentially deleterious process, since, as Singer (1950, p. 477) emphasized, "the most important contribution of an industry is not its immediate product [...] nor even its effects on other industries, but [...] its effect on the general level of education, skill, *way of life,* inventiveness, habits, stock of technology".

Such a scenario makes it impossible or at least substantially hinders the country's adoption of consistent development strategies, which must be "sectoral specific" (Reinert, 2016, p. 80), requiring persevering direction and strategy, grounded in solid political alliances capable of sustaining actions that transcend government mandates. Put bluntly, development should be conceived "as a process of productive transformation, led by the expansion of collective capabilities and resulting in the creation of good-quality jobs and sustainable structural change" (Andreoni & Chang, 2017). Such an approach does not imply, as pointed out in the introduction of this paper, that the recovery of developmentalism leads to privileging only the material dimension of development – technological, political, institutional, environmental, and democratic aspects, as well as the fight against inequalities, are, likewise, crucial for addressing the issue today.

The "Brazilian way" of the last decades – in spite of some important but discontinued experiments – has harmed activities of growing income and synergic effects, as well as neglecting investment in collective productive capacities, which lead to increased income and employment. However, it is worth pointing out that Brazil still has many potentialities, competences, and opportunities to develop productive development policies, make investments in technological infrastructure, etc. Besides, as is well known, we still have to face very traditional problems, arising from the 19th century (investments in infrastructure, in sanitation, in transportation, etc.), which may bring beneficial solutions to the country's socioeconomic dynamics.

As we have tried to emphasize, an assertive trajectory of economic and social development, with an emphasis on industry and knowledge-intensive services, does not have a spontaneous character, but a deliberate one, that is, the result of decisive political will. However, the one prevailing in Brazil, over the past decades and markedly since 2015, has moved in the opposite direction and contributed to the expansion of inequalities, displacement of industrial products from the export agenda, expansion of the deficit in the trade of high-tech industrial goods and neglect of infrastructure, logistics, and spending on science and technology. Furthermore, it has set in motion a broad process of denationalization and privatization, which tends to disconnect from public control mechanisms and inputs that are essential to Brazilian socioeconomic development. Furthermore, it ostensibly deconstructs the remaining institutional arrangement capable of formulating visions of the future and providing support to the actions intended to pursue them, besides leading to a brutal increase in job insecurity and the impoverishment of large sectors of the population, with visible effects on insecurity and an increase in criminality.

However, history is dynamic and often imposes unexpected imperatives on political and social actors. In the current time, this dynamism becomes evident due to the magnitude of the current health and economic crises, resulting from Covid-19, the first pandemic occurring in a fully globalized world, in which capital is present everywhere and whose productive dynamics have a high degree of specialization or concentration of activities in certain countries.

It is important to put in the foreground, at this final moment, a certainly optimistic perspective, which is: the consequences of the pandemic may perhaps allow the reorganization of part of the globalized productive activities, as a result of the emergence and strengthening of stimuli for certain industries to gradually redirect their production plants to their countries of origin. This hypothetical movement can be justified by virtue of the wide vulnerability verified in the GVCs when, due to Covid-19, the difficulties to import necessary items produced mainly in China began, a process that was aggravated by the devaluation of the exchange rate that started to put pressure on the cost of these imports, especially for the peripheral countries. Besides this, there is a "new normal" impacting the global productive fabric, based on: (i) by fierce geopolitical disputes, from protagonist clashes between the United States and China; (ii) by the acceleration of the destruction of complex regional environments that prevent the population of virulent pathogens from growing, as stated by Wallace et al. (2020); (iii) by the reduction of transmission frictions between animals and between these and humans, due to the profound environmental changes underway, the dynamics of trade, world travel and other fronts of the global circuits of capital.

This may give rise to the possibility of Brazil, *mutatis mutandis,* reorganizing its industrial production chains whose links have been replaced by imports. To this end, it will be necessary to recover the faculty of long-term planning; the capacity for public and private investment, particularly in research, development and innovation (RD&I); and the coordination of existing instruments and public policies. As Cano (2012, p. 832) states: "there is no country in history that has developed without a generalized industrialization and a strong and active role of the National State".

References

Andreoni, Antonio; Chang, Ha-Joon. Bringing production and employment back into development: Alice Amsden's legacy for a new developmentalist agenda. *Cambridge Journal of Regions, Economy and Society*, v. 10, n. 1, mar., 2017.

Bielschowsky, Ricardo. *Investimentos na indústria brasileira, 1995/97. Características e determinantes*. Rio de Janeiro: CNI, 1998.

BRASIL, MDIC, Câmara de Comércio Exterior (CAMEX) (2018). Disponível em: http://www.camex.gov.br/images/PDF/Investimentos/Boletim-Informativo-sobre-Investimento_Edio-Novembro-de-2018-1.pdf. Acesso em: 27/05/2020.

Bresser-Pereira, Luís Carlos. The Dutch disease and its neutralization: A Ricardian approach. *Revista de Economia Política*, v. 28, n. 1, pp. 47–71, Jan./mar., 2008.

Bresser-Pereira, Luís Carlos; Marconi, Nelson. Existe doença holandesa no Brasil? In: Bresser-Pereira, Luís Carlos (Org.). *Doença holandesa e indústria*. Rio de Janeiro: FGV, pp. 207–230, 2010.

Cano, Wilson. A desindustrialização no Brasil. *Economia e Sociedade, Campinas*, v. 21, Número Especial, pp. 831–851, dez. 2012.

Cardim de Carvalho, Fernando. A Influência do FMI na Escolha de Políticas Macroeconômicas. *Revista de Economia Política*, v. 31, n. 4, 2011, 2003.

Carvalho, Laura. *Valsa brasileira. do boom ao caos econômico*. São Paulo: Todavia livros, 2018.
Carvalho, Laura; Kupfer, David. A transição estrutural da indústria brasileira: uma análise dos fatores explicativos pela ótica da demanda. *XXXVI Encontro Nacional de Economia da ANPEC*, 2008.
Chang, Ha-Joon. *Kicking away the ladder: Development strategy in historical perspective*. London: Anthem Press, 2002.
———. *Bad samaritans: Rich countries, poor policies, and the threat to the developing world*. London: Random House, 2007.
Chesnais, François. *A mundialização do capital*. São Paulo: Xamã, 1996.
———. A proeminência da finança no seio do "capital em geral", o capital fictício e o movimento contemporâneo de mundialização do capital. In: *A finança capitalista*. São Paulo: Alameda, pp. 95–182, 2010.
———. *Finance capital today: Corporations and banks in the lasting global slump*. Boston: Brill Academic Pub., 2016.
Ferraz, João Carlos Signatura; Kupfer, David; e Iootty, Mariana. Competitividad industrial en Brasil: 10 años después da la liberalización. *Revista de la CEPAL* 82, abr. 2004.
Furtado, Celso. *Formação econômica do Brasil*. São Paulo: Companhia das Letras. (1959), 2009.
Guttmann, Robert. Uma introdução ao capitalismo dirigido pelas finanças. *Novos estudos*, São Paulo, v. 82, 2008.
Hiratuka, Célio e Sarti, Fernando. Transformações na estrutura produtiva global, desindustrialização e desenvolvimento industrial no Brasil: uma contribuição ao debate Texto para Discussão. IE/Unicamp, Campinas, n. 255, jun. 2015.
IEDI, Carta. Um ponto fora da curva. Edição 940, 2019. Available in: https://iedi.org.br/cartas/carta_iedi_n_940.html. Access at: 15/03/2022.
Kupfer, D. Política Industrial. *Revista Econômica*, Rio de Janeiro, v. 5, n. 2, pp. 91–108, dez. 2003.
Maia, Bento Antunes de Andrade. Economia e Sociedade. *Campinas*, v. 29, n. 2 (69), pp. 549–579, maio-agosto 2020.
Magacho, Guilherme; Mccombie, Jonh; Guilhoto, Joaquim. Impacts of trade liberalization on countries' sectoral structure of production and trade: A structural decomposition analysis, *Structural Change and Economic Dynamics*, v. 46, pp. 70–77, 2018.
Mazzucato, Mariana. *The value of everything: Making and taking in the global economy*. New York: Public Affairs, 2018.
Morais, Lecio; Saad Filho, Alfredo. Da economia política à política econômica: o novo-desenvolvimentismo e o governo Lula. *Revista de Economia Política*, v. 31, n. 4 (124), pp. 507–527, outubro-dezembro, 2011.
Morceiro, Paulo César. Desindustrialização na economia brasileira no período 2000–2011: abordagens e indicadores. São Paulo: Cultura Acadêmica, 2012. (Coleção PROPG Digital – UNESP). ISBN 9788579833717. Disponível em: <http://hdl.handle.net/11449/109252>
Morceiro, Paulo César; Guilhoto, Joaquim. Desindustrialização setorial no Brasil. (2019). Disponível em: https://iedi.org.br/artigos/top/estudos_industria/20190418_desindust rializacao.html. Acesso em: 30/05/2020.
Oliveira, Francisco de. *Crítica à razão dualista/O ornitorrinco*. São Paulo: Boitempo, 2003.
———. *A noiva da revolução/Elegia para uma re(li)gião*. São Paulo: Boitempo, 2008.
Orair, Rodrigo Octávio; Gobetti, Sérgio Wulff. *O gasto público e o ciclo da política fiscal – 1999-2014*. Monografia Prêmio SOF 1° Lugar, Tema 1 – Brasília: Qualidade do Gasto Público, 2015.

Oreiro, José Luís.; Feijó, Carmem. Desindustrialização: conceituação, causas, efeitos e o caso brasileiro. *Revista de Economia Política*, v. 30, n. 2 (118), abr./jun., 2010.

Palma, Gabriel. Four sources of "de-industrialisation" and a new concept of the "dutch disease". In: Ocampo, J. A. (Ed.). *Beyond reforms: Structural dynamics and macroeconomic vulnerability* (pp. 71–116). Palo Alto: Stanford University Press, 2005.

———. De-industrialisation, 'Premature' De-industrialisation and the Dutch-disease, *Revista NECAT*, Ano 3, n. 5 jan.–jun. 2014.

Paulani, Leda Maria. *Brasil delivery*. São Paulo: Boitempo, 2008.

———. A inserção da economia brasileira no cenário mundial: uma reflexão sobre a situação atual à luz da história. *Boletim de Economia e Política Internacional* (IPEA), v. 3, n. 10, 2012.

———. A experiência brasileira entre 2003 e 2014: neodesenvolvimentismo? *Cadernos do Desenvolvimento*, Rio de Janeiro, v. 12, n. 20, jan.–jun. 2017a.

———. Não há saída sem a reversão da financeirização. *Estudos avançados*, v. 31, n. 89, 2017b.

———. O touro dourado e a economia do boi. *A Terra é redonda*, (2021). Disponível em:https://aterraeredonda.com.br/o-touro-dourado-e-a-economia-do-boi/?doing_wp_cron= 1638551846.6440730094909667968750. Acesso em: 30/11/2021.

Reinert, Erik. *Como os países ficaram ricos...e por que os países pobres continuam pobres*. Rio de Janeiro: Contraponto, 2016.

Rodrik, Dani. Unconditional Convergence in Manufacturing. *The Quarterly Journal of Economics*, v. 128, n. 1, pp. 165–204, 2013.

Rowthorn, Robert e Coutts, Ken. De-industrialisation and the balance of payments in advanced economies. *Cambridge Journal of Economics*, v. 28, n. 5, pp. 767–790, 2004.

Rowthorn, Robert e Wells, John. *De-industrialisation and foreign trade*. Cambridge: Cambridge University Press, 1987.

Rowthorn, Robert; Ramaswany, Ramana. *Growth, trade and de-industrialization*. IMF Staff Papers, v. 46, 1999.

Salama, Pierre. Retrocesso na esperança Brasil? 2019. Available in: https://eleuterioprado.blog/2019/05/27/o-brasil-em-retrocesso/.Access at: 05/07/2021.

Sarti, Fernando; Hiratuka, Célio. Desempenho recente da indústria brasileira no contexto de mudanças estruturais domésticas e globais. In: Carneiro, R., Baltar, P., Sarti, Fernando (Orgs.). *Para além da política econômica* (pp. 1–32). São Paulo: Unesp Digital, 2018.

Sicsú, João; Oliveira de Castro, Sidney. Taxa de juros e controle de inflação no Brasil. In: Sicsú, J.; Oreiro, J. L. e P., Luís F. (Orgs.). Agenda *Brasil: políticas econômicas para o crescimento e estabilidade de preços*. Barueri: Manole e Rio de Janeiro: Fundação Konrad Adenauer, 2003.

Singer, Hans. The distribution of gains between investing and borrowing countries. *American Economic Review*, v. 40, n. 2, 1950.Tavares, Maria da Conceição. *Acumulação de capital e industrialização no Brasil*. Campinas: Unicamp, 1985.

———. *Ciclo e crise o movimento recente da industrialização brasileira*. 1998, Campinas: Unicamp, [1978] e 1998.

Timmer, M. P., de Vries, G. J., & de Vries, K. Patterns of structural change in developing countries. In: J. Weiss, & M. Tribe (Eds.), *Routledge handbook of industry and development*. London: Routledge, pp. 65–83, 2015.

Torres, Ricardo Lobato and Cavalieri, Henrique. Uma crítica aos indicadores usuais de desindustrialização no Brasil. *Revista de Economia Política*, v. 35, nº 4 (141), pp. 859–877, outubro-dezembro/2015

Tregenna, Fiona. Characterising deindustrialisation: An analysis of changes in manufacturing employment and output internationally. *Cambridge Journal of Economics*, v. 33, pp. 433–466, 2008.

———. *Manufacturing productivity, deindustrialization and reindustrialization*. United Nations University (UNU)–World Institute for Development Economics Research (WIDER), (Working Paper, n. 2011/57), Sept. 2011.

Wallace, Rob; Liebman, Alex, Chaves Luis Fernando; Wallace, Rodrick. *A Covid-19 e os circuitos do capital*, 2020. Disponível em: https://n-1edicoes.org/026. Acesso em: 11/05/2020.

8

GLOBAL ENVIRONMENTAL CRISIS

Leonardo Freire de Mello, Susana B. Adamo and Sara Aparecida de Paula

In this chapter, we aim to balance different issues connected to sustainable development that are relevant for the environmental crisis since there is a tendency to separate them, with the idea of finding "silo" solutions: social solutions, economical solutions, cultural solutions, and environmental solutions. We are convinced that we need to find a more interdisciplinary and holistic approach for us to think about the way the challenges of the global environmental crisis could be addressed, fully considering that the acceleration of the depletion of the planet's resources does not happen in the same way for each one of us. For example, not all the countries and territories are facing, feeling, and understanding the climate change crisis (a manifestation of global environmental change) in the same way, the Small Island States being the most glaring example.

It is important to highlight the choice to use the global environmental crisis idea instead of climate change. Environment presents itself like a system, while climate is a factor inside this system, and "climate change", a symptom or manifestation of the global environmental crisis. It means that the changes addressed here are a variety of disruptions and transformations on structure, such important examples as: (1) urbanization, its physical structures and the way people live in urban areas, which includes mass consumption and a process of constant individualization; (2) agriculture, food production systems and its characteristics based on monopolistic production model, this model increases vulnerability factors related to climate like the lack of resistance to climate variability (periods of droughts or rain, for example) and related to social dynamics like the exclusion of local producers and race/gender inequalities inside this dynamic; (3) the way people live and consume, like the constant perception of obsolescence and need to have something new, this kind of culture separates Humanity and Nature, creating challenges of how people impact the extra human sides of Environment.

DOI: 10.4324/9781003384366-9

The aforementioned examples show that the environment is a system of relationships among human and extra human actors and factors. For this reason, this chapter presents the necessity of understanding the topic as an interdisciplinary approach to life, which means biogeochemical factors relate to social dynamics, and vice versa. As humans, it is essential to understand both as a complex structure constructed through contradictions.

Contradictions at the global level among countries are mirrored within countries. The center-periphery framework needs to be updated to be applied to different scales and meaning not only territories but also groups within society, looking into different forms of segregation. For instance, people from developed countries tend to have a much bigger environmental footprint than people from developing countries and within the countries there's also numerous differences as well, e.g., the gap between the richer and the poorer ones. The center-periphery started as a global approach between developed and developing countries or they used to be the metropolis and the colonies if preferred, but now there is that same issue within each country when you have the groups that are marginalized, and they live in each of these countries develop and developing and it's the issue now talking about Global North and Global South.

This is also reflected in how these different levels of government are starting to be contradictory with each other. At the local level you have different municipalities with different needs competing with each other, but then you have the state/province level, and other groups of levels, all of them nested in a national level. How are all these different levels going to be harmonizing and coordinating competing needs and competing interests in this global crisis?

When talking about global environmental changes, it is interesting to note the link among scales. There are global changes common to everyone like the changes on the pH of oceans or the frequency and intensity of higher and lower temperatures out of the pattern. Still though, as previously mentioned, people may feel the impacts in different forms. This is the reason why it is so important to comprehend the way territories are organized and who are the communities facing global environmental changes and its local scale forms.

Is there an increased awareness of the emergency, a new sense of urgency? Possibly, and the Covid-19 pandemic could be partially responsible for it because it gave us a sense of what the consequences could be and how present inequalities, the already existing vulnerabilities played out in a crisis environment, a glimpse of what the future could be if certain agreements are not reached in relation to the global environmental crisis (see, for example, Heyd, 2021).

We are bringing Covid-19 to discussion and the new social pacts for transforming the state politics. There is a tendency to not understand Covid-19 also as an environmental issue and to try it completely separated from the rest of the discussion and from the rest of the global environmental crisis scenario. When considering Covid-19 only a health, sanitary, and even hygienic issue leaves out that it is a part of a much more complicated puzzle that we need to assess and understand (e.g., McNeely, 2021). We should be aware and waiting for the next ones because it's not a question of if but of when. Covid-19 affects people in different ways depending on where you live, how rich or poor you are, if you are a man or a woman, if you are black or white or brown. In a way, it could be used as a proxy to understand the global environmental crisis. The Covid-19 pandemic is providing a window into how global disasters could play out, every single inequality, every single vulnerability, every single marker of segregation is playing out, and how connected the spread of the disease has been with the globalization of travel, for example.

Global environmental crisis

The current global environmental crisis is a part of a set of global crises that cast shadow over the viability or feasibility of sustainable development being a reality for all, despite the large advances in combating poverty. The accelerating environmental degradation, which has reached critical levels, inflicts increasing and unequal costs on societies (UNDESA, 2013: 1).

Everyone has experienced environmental changes somehow. Kids learn about the environment and sustainability. All of us every day receive information about disasters all over the planet. In a more specific and explicit way, all of us feel the impacts of extreme heat, cold, rain, or droughts never seen before.

All these changes, somehow, look natural because they are connected to a series of biogeochemical and social dynamics of the planet, related with life itself. However, those issues are becoming more frequent and are causing negative impacts to an increasing number of people daily.

Some time ago, environmental changes used to have a much clearer territorial dimension, being restricted to smaller portions of space. Contemporarily, they are acquiring a broader, frequently global, dimension.

The debate about environmental changes started, effectively, during the 1950s, when several industrial cities – most of them in the Global North – started to feel the impacts of chemical pollution that caused severe respiratory diseases and even some deaths. The main stimulus came from the population of the developed countries itself that started to question pollution, its sources, and its effects over public health. This questioning coming from different societies made environmental changes to become interesting research topics for universities as well for governments and even corporations.

Rachel Carson, published in 1962 "Silent Spring", pointing out that industrial activities and pollution altered the quality of habitats with direct and severe impacts on plants and animals. The deployment of chemical compounds in soil, water, and air was causing diversity loss.

During the 1970s, environmental changes studies – that were until then restricted to the natural sciences – reached human and social sciences, as its critics and debates were embraced by international organizations. In 1972, United Nations Organization (UNO) organized the Conference on the Human Environment, also known as the Stockholm Conference, when, for the first time developed and developing countries gathered to discuss the environment and its connections to human and economic development, pointing out that while developing countries was already the ones suffering more significant impacts of environmental change the developed ones were the most important pollution emitters, mostly of greenhouse effect gasses, the biggest contributors for planet's environmental problems, demanding, this way, the need for a new kind of development that was able to consider the demands of future generations as well focused on reduce inequality levels, given that the environment is strongly associated to a series of human vulnerabilities as poverty, for instance. During this conference, the United Nations Environment Program (UNEP) was founded, creating a discussion arena that brings together Nations and Non-Governmental Organizations. Nevertheless, the focus was kept on biogeochemical issues, leaving social ones to a secondary place. Also in 1972, the first edition of the influential Club of Rome's book "The Limits to Growth" was published.

During the 1980s, a major milestone was the emergence and consolidation of the concept of sustainable development, disseminated by the Brundtland Report (WCED, 1987), although the concept had been in development since the 1970s (see Sachs, 1981), it was with the Report that it became popular in all societies and institutions. The Report stated that sustainable development should "meet the needs of the present without compromising the ability of future generations to meet their own needs" and, in a very realistic and anticipatory way, that "we do not pretend that the process is easy or straightforward. Painful choices have to be made" (WCED, 1987: 16–17).

The greatest contribution that the concept of sustainable development made was to disseminate the idea that development should encompass at least three dimensions: economic, social, and environmental. It brought the focus to the way we produce, consume, and dispose of our waste, individually and collectively. The Global North consumes and disposes of contaminating waste – especially complex chemicals not found in nature and extremely harmful to the maintenance and full functioning of planetary life support systems – much more than the Global South – maybe excluding China, the "great global factory" – and this idea is fundamental for the upcoming discussion. The general idea of a great process – or great processes – of global environmental change began to spread, especially in the Academy, leading scholars to start to elaborate and think about mitigation of and adaptation to these changes.

Some questions were highlighted regarding the role of technology. The rise of technologies was essential for the development of societies, the ability to increase the speed of communication and transport systems. On the other hand, technology also led to two problems: (1) the acceleration of the production model led to the increasing need for inputs, such as fossil fuels; (2) from a sociological perspective, technology is permeated by the discourse of salvation. At this second point, a myth was created that technology can solve any problem, including huge ones such as environmental changes that have largely contributed to reducing the urgency and appearance of the subject – at least for a while – and to bring some peace and quiet to societies, especially the more advanced.

However, with the advancement and improvement of reality capture and analysis systems, this relative peace began to crumble, especially when research results began to highlight that the situation was, in fact, much more complex and serious than had been imagined until then.

During the 1990s, a turning point was the Earth Summit (formally the United Nations Conference on Environment and Development) held in Rio de Janeiro, Brazil, in 1992, in celebration of the 20 years of the Stockholm Conference. One of the main outcomes of the Earth Summit was the Agenda 21 – a call to action and roadmap for integrating and achieve development and environmental goals – and the three conventions on climate change, biodiversity, and desertification.

During the 2000s, the member countries of the United Nations defined the eight Millennium Development Goals (MDGs) that aimed, above all, to eradicate poverty, hunger, increase access to education, reduce social and economic inequalities, define goals, and means of development and ensure environmental sustainability. It is possible to perceive that there is a confluence of objectives, connecting the social, economic, political, and environmental spheres for the joint construction of a better world for all. Although some of these goals were very promising, the challenges continued to exist and to get worse, pointing to the urgent need to expand the agendas.

In this sense, viewing the contemporary context and based on the MDGs, the UN launched, in 2015, the Sustainable Development Goals (SDGs): poverty eradication; zero hunger and sustainable agriculture; health and wellness; quality education; gender equality; clean water and sanitation; clean and affordable energy; decent work and economic growth; industry, innovation, and infrastructure; reduction of inequalities; sustainable cities and communities; responsible consumption and production; action against global climate change; life in the water; terrestrial life; peace, justice, and effective institutions and; partnerships and means of implementation (UN, 2018).

Of the aforementioned SDGs, at least eight have a direct connection with environmental preservation and, when they are all seen in an overview, the idea is clear that the dignified survival of human beings is deeply connected with the preservation of natural resources and the planet in general, through sustainable actions. These objectives are part or response of a scenario taken by sudden changes in different areas, mainly in the environment as a basic element of society. To corroborate this information, it is possible to rely on information from the 2016 United Nations Environment annual report that concluded that 2015 was one of the warmest years, directly affecting ecosystems and the planet's biodiversity, in addition, the environmental changes issues are predominant in the sense of prolonging and driving resource conflicts, for example (United Nations Environment, 2016).

In the same report, researchers also highlighted an international tendency to spend time and economic resources in response to crises. However, a stance of mitigation and adaptation to environmental and climate changes must be adopted to avoid them. Another important fact to be highlighted is that some of the environmental and climatic changes are influenced or driven by human action itself, that is, mainly by the current production, consumption, and disposal patterns. In this way, realizing the need to connect society and the environment, as well as environmental changes in their physical and social aspects, this work aims to promote a discussion on the concepts of Anthropocene and Capitalocene as categories of analysis to broaden the understanding of transformations, how they have occurred, some of their reasons and impacts.

Anthropocene, capitalocene, etc.

In "Thinking the Anthropocene", Hamilton *et al.* (2015: 2–4) suggest that there are three distinctive definitions or viewpoints: a new interval in *geological* history; a shift or change in the Earth system that leaves behind the highly stable Holocene state (Earth system scientists); and the cumulative impact of civilization (from landscape transformation to disruption of the nitrogen cycle). Regardless of the case, the presence of the Anthropocene leads to two corollaries: humans have become a force of nature able to change how the Earth works, and they will suffer (some would say they are already suffering) the consequences of unprecedented global environmental change. Some authors say that the Planet is facing a new geological era, the one that is called the Anthropocene or Humankind era.

The term Anthropocene was coined back in 2000 when, in mid-2002, chemist Paul Crutzen suggested that humanity was forging a new era, different from the Holocene, the last post-glacial geological period (last 10–12 millennia). According to Crutzen, since the Industrial Revolution, human activities, actions, and capability to cause negative impacts on the environment gained momentum, becoming a geological transformation force, confirmed by the increasing concentration levels of carbon dioxide (CO_2) and methane (CH_4) at the atmosphere (Crutzen, 2002, 2006).

As well as the industrial development, the author also brings issues such as population growth, urbanization, and the increased use of natural energy resources into the debate, noting that "in a few generations mankind is exhausting the fossil fuels that were generated over several hundred million years, resulting in large emissions of air pollutants" (Crutzen, 2006: 2).

In a 2007 publication, coauthored by Will Steffen and John R. Mcneil, Crutzen points out that the Anthropocene may have caused Earth to abandon its natural cycle, not least because of the intensification of human activities, which represents not only a deep change in the natural geological cycles but also in the relationship between humans and nature.

Among social sciences and natural sciences researchers, there is a huge debate about when the Anthropocene has truly started. As shown, Crutzen (2006) proposed the Industrial revolution. On the other hand, some authors may argue that this conception shows a Eurocentric history of the world in which industry is a part of a natural process. Then, there is the proposition that colonization is a vital period of this transformation process, as it was essential to industrialization and the consolidation of capitalism as the mainstream economic system. The reason is that segregation between colonies and metropolis was the basis for a new international division of labor in which colonies supplied metropolis necessities (where the soil was environmentally exhausted), and at the meantime it created the basis for the deepening of a monopolistic way of organizing resources, expanding transformations that were local/regional into a global scenario.

The trajectory of the concept shows a deepening of its understanding. It was first discussed in the natural sciences context, mostly considering biogeochemical factors. Though, the discussion about its social sides shows the need to take as a whole structure of physical risks and social/political/economic vulnerabilities. From the Global South perspective, there is a structure of inequalities built upon years, not given/not natural, but constructed to supply other necessities. This assumption does not erase the importance of periods such as industrialization, but it highlights the fact it is not a natural process.

There are a variety of debates to understand Anthropocene's start date. But why is it important in this discussion? Because each one brings some thoughts to better understand the contemporary Global Crisis. For example, the Industrial Revolution shows the deep impact caused using fossil fuels on industrial production, the same for the increase of inequalities (based on racism), vulnerabilities, and a new model of development structured during colonization times.

Of course, those examples are recent compared to the trajectory of human transformations on the environment that took place since the control of fire. Controlling fire allowed humans to adapt the environment resources according to their necessities as they developed the ability to produce food through an organized system like agriculture. In this perspective, the Anthropocene is a long-term process in which Humans left their status as one more species to become "the" species capable of changing the landscape and organizing the extra human factors as they want. These historical marks are the structure of an expanding change during the 20th century.

Adding to the previous periods, authors usually highlight the period from the mid-1800s (not precisely established) to 1945, which is marked by urbanization, industrialization, and the growing and intense use of fossil fuels, such as coal, oil, and gas. As a result, and in conjunction with the use of fertilizers in agriculture and intensive livestock farming, associated with deforestation, greenhouse gasses have increased substantially in the atmosphere, altering rainfall patterns, causing increases in global temperature and an increase – still discrete – of sea levels, among others. These physical changes are followed by or are led by a switch on culture. Industrialization brought a variety of products into the market and as a result, an increase in consumption patterns, which are dominant nowadays. This shows consumption is the intermediate step between humans and their impacts on the environment in a heterogeneous way.

The second contemporary phase, between 1945 and mid-2010s (continuing until the contemporaneity), represents the *Great Acceleration* of the Anthropocene, a period in which the population practically more than doubles, as the birth rate exceeds the death rate, a consequence of development. In addition, there was also significant economic growth with the broad flow of capital and trade in general, the increase in gas and oil consumption, acceleration of the urbanization process and the advent of new and important technologies. A long series of variables also show the same rate of explosive growth pattern, composing what can be called an *environmental crisis*.

Steffen *et al.* (2015) applied a quantitative methodology to analyze some factors such as: population growth, GDP per capita, industrialization levels, use of water, use of fertilizers, transportation, greenhouse gasses emissions, among others. The authors created graphs known as the Great Acceleration graphs meaning that all these variables increased since 1750 and the biggest leap since 1945, the post WWII period.

This information means that the postwar period was marked by the development of innovations and technologies able to surpass the challenges of territorial distance, but it also resulted in an increase in chemical levels and exploitation to meet the challenges imposed by this new context. Another factor is the market flows as international trade has gained great space and shaped the way production and consumption is done on an ever-increasing scale.

The deepening of global trade is important for understanding what is happening today. It is a period marked by the transition to one defined as *business-as-usual* and that has its origins in the 1960s, although it has intensified further in the 21st century, when issues such as the high level of CO_2 emissions and global warming have come to be recognized and debated as consequences driven by human activities. Business-as-usual concerns the fact that economic institutions are still predominant in the world's decision-making processes and that from an economic point of view, the environmental problem is not so big since they are guided by the premise that the market oriented economic system could autonomously deal with environmental changes (Steffen *et al.*, 2007).

Even though the initial date is still not set, and Anthropocene is not yet confirmed as a geological era, it is a fact that the planet is facing frequent and intense disruptions as never seen. The use of concepts helps the analysis to get closer to the general public and to look for answers. During these 20 years, developments have been made on the understanding of the Anthropocene process, i.e., the quantitative method designed on the planetary boundaries.

They were first proposed in 2009 by Johan Rockström from the Stockholm Resilience Centre and Will Steffen from the Australian National University, leading a large group of researchers. It basically states that the planet's ecosystems have nine major limits or operational safe limits that should not be overcome at the cost of environmental imbalances that can bring them to collapse, compromising the capabilities of planetary life support systems and, consequently, the ability of human beings to survive on Earth. At least two of them already reached high risk of collapse levels: biochemical flows (phosphorus and nitrogen flows responsible for the basic survival function of human beings, such as the formation of proteins, for example) and biosphere integrity, which means the loss of biodiversity, affecting all the chain.

The importance of planetary boundaries is in demonstrating the systemic nature of the global environmental crisis. This means that when something is not working, it may be that the other factor is not at the boundary, but it may also be out of balance. For example, land use can affect the availability of water, just as greenhouse gas emissions can change the level of acidification of the oceans. All of this is related to a lack of balance, affecting, in the longer term, the diversity of species and, with it, a natural chain. In addition, it is also necessary to consider those limits in which the capacity for quantification is limited, such as the novel entities, which ignite that they cannot be quantified, but which are very probably affecting many species, such as the impacts of radiation and nanoplastics on the oceans.

More recently, there has been discussions about what is "missing" from the Anthropocene term. Professor Jason Moore has suggested the term Capitalocene to allow for the inclusion of social systems (among them power systems) more explicitly. The author states that the global crisis would not be a result of humans (since one could bring a homogeneous conception of humanity, which is actually based on a structure of inequality), but rather a result of capitalism as an organizer of life, or the web of life.

Jason Moore, sociology professor at Binghamton University, brings in mid-2010s a new perspective, the Capitalocene, criticizing the Anthropocene, considering it a limited idea because, for him, authors linked to the idea of Anthropocene emphasize the Industrial Revolution as the origin of modern flows, focusing mainly on the environmental consequences generated by such processes and hiding the deep relations of capital and power. This way, Moore presents the Capitalocene, or capital era, as a contraposition to the use of Anthropocene (Moore, 2014). Moore explains that in his perspective, the Anthropocene may treat humanity in a homogeneous way, which may imply a lack of critique of the structures of inequality present in capitalism.

One of the essential characteristics to understand the perception of the Capitalocene is to place it as a dynamic and multidisciplinary concept, in which capitalism-in-nature and nature-in-capitalism are part of each other, making capitalism understood as a world-ecology, in which the accumulation of capital, the search for power and the co-production of nature are seen in unity and by different areas, not only physical-ecological, but also historical, geographical, and philosophical.

To explain his theory, he brings the demystification of the Anthropocene, that is, in his words, despite several interpretations, the dominant version says that the modern world has its origins in 19th-century England, when Industrial Revolution was potentiated, above all, by the use of coal and steam. For him, through this vision, it is forgotten to discuss the driving forces behind this process, the relationship between capital, culture, society, limiting itself only to *Anthropos*, that is, humanity as a unit without differences among themselves. Moore thus describes "the Anthropocene makes for an easy story. Easy, because it does not challenge the naturalized inequalities, alienation, and violence inscribed in modernity's strategic relations of power and production" (Moore, 2014: 2). In this sense, Moore points out that one must consider the impacts produced by colonization, which created the possible surplus for industrialization, and also structured the inequalities present between North and South.

Moore also points out that the Anthropocene brings two types of views: (1) atmospheric change and what drives it; (2) the global present as a historical moment resulting from periodization. From this point of view, he highlights the role of the Anthropocene as a simplistic conceptualization, a Cartesian dualism that tends to blame humanity as a single driving force that brings back neo-Malthusian views of the population and forgets to debate the characteristics of groups, their flows and the different relationships that lead to historical, economic, social, and environmental transformations. In this way, believing that the Anthropocene focuses on consequences, the author suggests an interpretation that begins with the origins and conditions of the rapid and fundamental transformations in the planet's biosphere, that is, the decisive changes that occurred in the relations of power and production and, for that, he centers his debate on historical and political issues.

One of his main contributions is the discussion about Cartesian dualism, that is, the discussion that infers a separation between Nature and Humanity, as mentioned. This is why he suggests the concept of world-ecology, which would be the idea of the "whole". This issue is of utmost importance because the environmental discourse is permeated by the idea that humans are at the center of everything and can solve any problem around them, when in reality humans are just another species in a set of relationships and dynamics.

To understand these issues, Moore also describes that capitalism's relationship to and within nature is one of exploitation, in producing abstract social labor, and appropriation, in producing abstract social nature. The fact is that human labor, in addition to becoming a commodity in this system, is a central point in the reproduction of wealth. However, it is important to understand that the system is not defined by this, but by the world market and the necessary conditions for its reproduction, such as the appropriation of the "**four cheap natures**". For him, cheap nature would be unpaid work of an extra-human nature (historical aspects of physical, biological, and geographical activities), separated into four main categories: (1) labor power, (2) food, (3) energy, and (4) raw materials. Thus, capitalism has the "cheap nature" strategy as central, as well as cyclical movements to make nature even cheaper (Moore, 2014).

To complete his idea, he says that the aforementioned transformations are part of a time of transition, not only of change in techniques, but also in mentality, that is, "proliferation of knowledges and symbolic regimes that constructed nature as external, space as flat and geometrical, and time as linear" (Moore, 2014: 22). In short, Moore emphasizes that capitalism must be understood as a world-ecology, in which the accumulation of capital, the search for power and the use of nature must be seen as a whole, making it clear that world-ecology does not mean the "ecology of the world/ecology of nature", but rather "the ecology of the *oikeios*: that creative, generative, and multilayered relation of life-making, of species and environments" (Moore, 2016: 79). He also makes it clear that capitalism is not just a process of accumulation, as it brings with it a whole spectrum of transformation based on cheap nature, that is, on the use of natural resources as if they were unlimited and at a low cost (Moore, 2014, 2016).

Following the idea of cheap nature, in the Capitalocene era there is not only a threat of biological extinction, but it is a process of cultural extinction, since one of the basic premises of capitalism would be to advance through exclusion and inequality. He points out that one of the biggest secrets of capitalism is its exclusive nature, "capitalism was built on excluding most humans from Humanity" (Moore, 2016: 79). Regarding the transformations in the environment, he states that the Capitalocene accelerated changes in a way never seen before, this happened with technologies that facilitated the process but, above all, techniques or "a new repertoire of science, power, and machinery" (Moore, 2016: 98) that allowed broad access to the appropriation of cheap nature. He points out that the capitalist system is in a phase of exhaustion, leading the planet to increasingly intense environmental changes and more devastating economic crises, stating that the planet is not going through an Anthropocene march but is reaching the end of the Anthropocene. Capitalocene as the cheap nature strategy is being exhausted on an ever greater and faster scale.

Despite the existence of intellectual conflicts by the use of concepts, it is noted that each one brings good contributions and also has some flaws, it is possible that the best way is to put the two concepts together. The contribution of the Anthropocene is its presence in the discussions, however, there is still the challenge to be overcome about social analysis, which is sometimes left aside. Anyway, there is no way to understand the contemporary crisis without adopting an interdisciplinary approach in which the physical and social dynamics complement each other, making clear the heterogeneity of societies, and, above all, inequality. In relation to the Capitalocene, it reproduces the importance of historical processes in the consolidation of the current context, however, by placing capitalism as central, there is a sense of naturalization of the economy, when in fact it was created by humans, and the environmental impacts are prior to the consolidation of capitalism, but rather when humans gained greater control over resources, such as food production.

How to measure the global environmental crisis?

The global environmental crisis could be empirically described from several angles. For example, the approaches to the Anthropocene mentioned above have used a set of metrics to attempt to capture the process, among them ecological footprint, identification of planetary boundaries or tipping points, human appropriation of net primary productivity, changes in biodiversity (number of species and their geographical distribution, extinction rates, etc.) (Malhi, 2017).

In addition, temporal and spatial scales are important when considering the empirical evidence. This could be extended to an emerging need to work across scales, (e.g., Keys *et al.*, 2019), and to recognize that challenges are different in each of them, particularly when the scales are associated with levels of government.

At the global scale, a possible way of assessing its magnitude is to take a look at the summary metrics used or proposed by the Rio Conventions: The United Nations Framework Convention on Climate Change (UNFCCC), the Convention on Biological Diversity (CBD), and the United Nations Convention to Combat Desertification (UNCCD).

The state of the planet depicted by the information coming from these conventions is rather grim. The IPCC Sixth Assessment Report (IPCC, 2021: 4) states that "it is unequivocal that human influence has warmed the atmosphere, ocean and land", and that the rate of this warming is the largest in the last 2,500 years. This human-induced warming is already resulting in changes in weather and in an increasing frequency of climate extremes (heatwaves, droughts, tropical storms, etc.). The report also mentions a near-linear relationship between cumulative CO_2 emissions and global warming, for all illustrative scenarios to 2050 (IPCC, 2021: 28). The 2019 report on biodiversity (IPBES, 2019: 11) warns that all ecosystems have been altered because of human drivers (e.g., 75% of the land surface, 66% of the ocean area) and that all the indicators of ecosystem and biodiversity health are displaying rapid decline (e.g., 85% of wetlands is lost, the average abundance of native species has fallen at least 20%). Along similar lines, the UNCCD (2017: 8) report indicates that there is increasing competition and pressures on land (including the agrobusiness model and land grabbing), leading to significant land degradation and threatening society's resilience.

At the country scale or level, several indexes have been developed to summarize the state of the environment and the impact of drivers, using single variable indicators (population size and growth; GDP, poverty, and GDP per capita; emissions and emissions per capita, etc.) or composite indexes at different scales. One of such indexes is the Environmental Performance Index (Wendling *et al.*, 2020; YCELP *et al.*, 2020), which ranks 180 countries (Figure 8.1) according to their environmental health (air quality, sanitation and drinking water, heavy metals, and waste management) and ecosystem vitality (biodiversity and habitats, ecosystem services, fisheries, water resources, climate change, pollution and emissions, and agriculture) using 32 performance indicators across 11 issue categories. As expected, the index is highly correlated with wealth (as measured with the GDP per capita), but there is some variation within income groups (Wendling, 2020).

However, a particular limitation of this index is that it does not consider the effects of trade on the countries' rank, in other words, the impacts of imports and spillovers, which usually penalizes developing countries that are net exporters of commodities. In this respect, De Sherbinin and Mara (2018) show that,

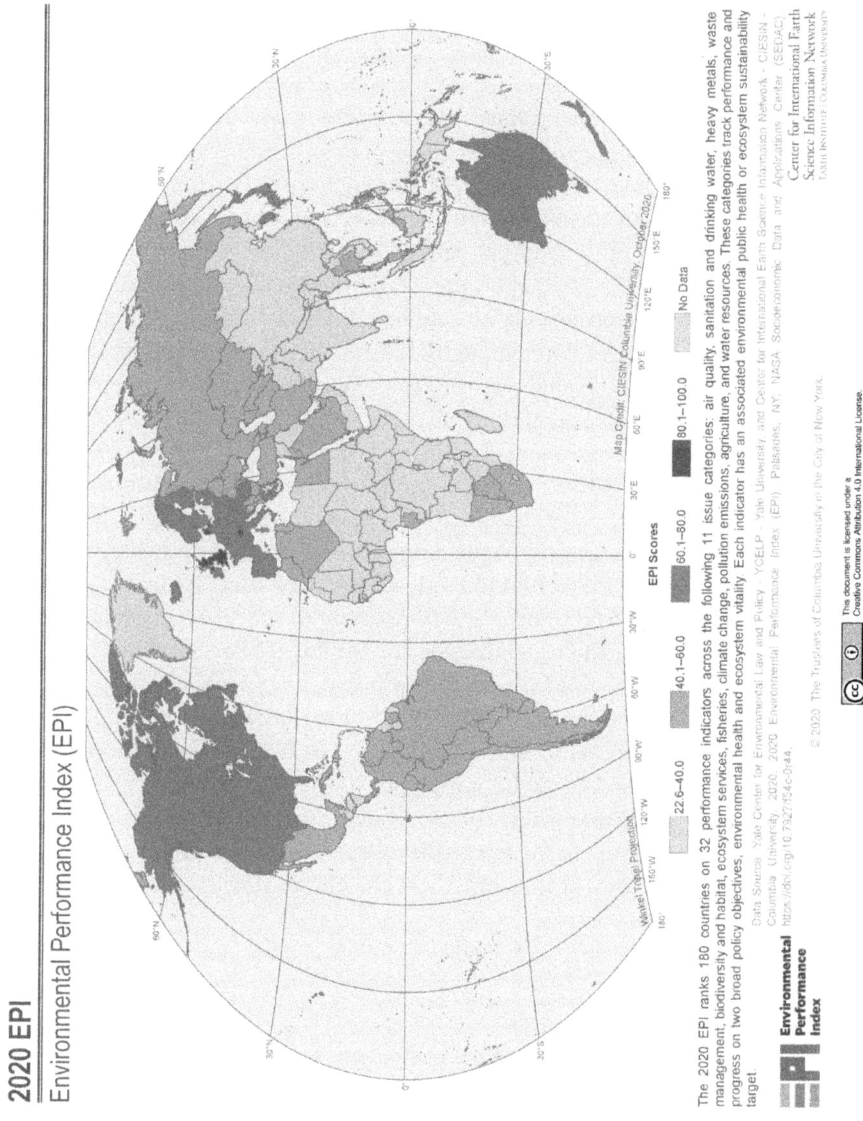

FIGURE 8.1 Environmental Performance Index by Country, 2020.
Source: YCELP *et al.* (2020).

when trade is included in the EPI, some countries' rank changes dramatically. To account for these distortions, the *Environmental Impact Index* aims to be able to track these spillovers and trade effects. A newly developed spillover index made by the Sustainable Development Solutions Network does consider the impacts of one country's action on other countries, and it shows that some countries that rank high in the EPI are also "high spillovers" (SDSN, 2022).

A different approach is focusing on human well-being and development *vis-à-vis* their consequences in the form of deteriorating environments due to, for example, pollution, degradation, and overuse of resources. To address this, the UN Human Development Index 2020 created new human development metrics for the Anthropocene. One of these metrics is the planetary pressures-adjusted human development index (PHDI), which includes environmental and sustainability dimensions (emissions per capita and material footprint per capita). Figure 8.2 graphs the HDI 2019 vs the PHDI 2019. For countries with lower HDI values (up to HDI = 0.7) the impact of the adjustment is small, but it is substantially larger for countries with higher HDI, which could be interpreted as the impact that their development paths have on the planet (UNDP, 2020).

Another scale or level of analysis would be the individual, and here it is possible to focus on people's perceptions of the state of the planet, their opinions regarding the global environmental crisis, or points of view and ideas on these topics. How is the crisis perceived? An example of this is the International Gallup Poll question on perceptions of the threat of climate change, by region, displayed in Figure 8.3, which shows differences among countries that do not necessarily follow a Global North/Global South divide (Rzepa and Ray, 2020).

However, there is a need to further downscaling to the local geographic level (which is different from the individual level mentioned above), which is where the actual problems are/will be found. For example, it is possible to have a global problem in terms of people exposed to flooding or how different populations are exposed to any given environmental hazard, but it is necessary to go to the local level to understand the actual impact, to know what exactly is happening in the territory, in particular places. Beyond the known data issues, this is a challenge, because a problem that is framed in *global terms* requires a *local* solution, policies must be local. But, at the same time, the environmental problems do not

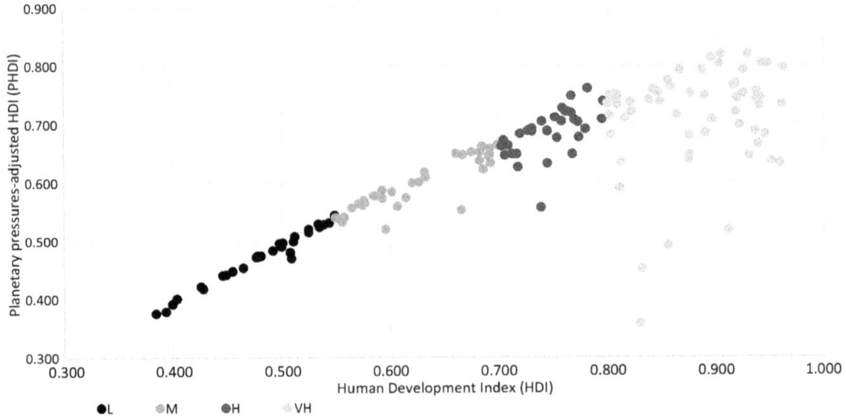

FIGURE 8.2 Planetary Pressures–Adjusted Human Development Index, 2020.
Source: https://report.hdr.undp.org/part-3.html.

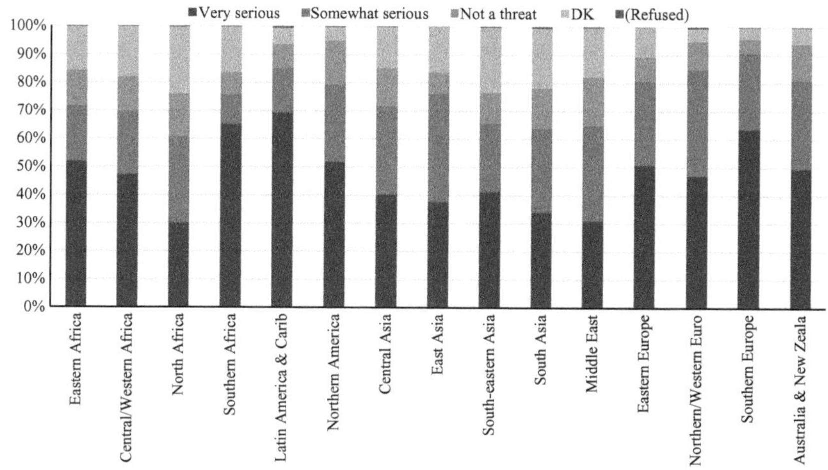

FIGURE 8.3 Perceptions of the Threat of Climate Change.
Source: World Risk Poll https://wrp.lrfoundation.org.uk/data-resources/.

recognize administrative boundaries, which could mean that the definition of "local" may need to be redefined or at least discussed when it is applied to the environmental crisis.

For instance, several cities in the central region of São Paulo state in Brazil have committees to discuss global environmental change but theoretically they will not be very impacted by them – in comparison, for instance, with coastal areas. Considering the expected savannization of the biome and the consequent lack of water supply, people are much more interested in finding ways to secure water from faraway places, or even bearing digging, but in this way, they solve their own problem but create problems for other communities around them.

Overall, the issue of how to provide and secure water for large cities/metropolitan areas (São Paulo, Cape Town, Los Angeles, etc.) could be a good example of the complexities and the many scale issues involved. Similar with transboundary watersheds exposed to droughts, as the case of the Parana basin today.

The case of where large cities are getting their water is a very good example of the complexities of the issues and the competition between different needs and changing availability of resources. In some cases, it is not just scarcity, it is also change and then absolute scarcity. You can replicate what happened in São Paulo with what happened with the city of Los Angeles in the United States that will happen in South Africa in terms of very large water schemes bringing water from very far away from places where they are used. If you have a new reality in terms or resources, you have a different availability of water or distribution, how do those older schemes work? There is a legacy in terms of legal instruments and infrastructure and technological development that may not match what the crisis is uncovering.

This is an increasingly important issue, how to find ways to coordinate the local policies to find a way to take it to the next territorial levels such as supra regional, regional, or even global. Because the causes are global, but actions are usually local, finding a way to find feasible and sustainable solutions is imperative.

Final considerations

This collaboration has characterized and discussed the global environmental crisis in the context of the Anthropocene and Capitalocene, including some selected metrics.

In light of everything that has been presented and discussed so far, the fact that we are experiencing a true global environmental crisis becomes somewhat unquestionable. That said, it is important to try to analyze, even if briefly, what are the causes and agents that promote this crisis, trying to understand and assign responsibilities and seek to find possible solutions to the aforementioned crisis, always in the light of democracy, development, and sustainability.

From the perspective of democracy and justice, it is important to highlight that the crisis, despite being global, does not affect different societies in the same way and that this inequality in impacts and in the ability to resist or adapt to them also varies intensely within the same society, with large groups presenting conditions of much greater vulnerability than others, the result of a robust structure of inequality distribution.

The selection and use of metrics to describe and quantify the environmental crisis is not neutral. These measures select specific aspects to focus on and provide worldwide assessment of the state of the environment, while leaving other aspects out. The scale of the measurements is also relevant, for example, global metrics tend to obscure diversity across countries and social groups. On the other hand, local cases could provide in-depth understanding of the complexities, but make it sometimes difficult to appreciate the extent and/or magnitude of the situation.

If impacts and the ability to resist or adapt to them vary from society to society and within different societies, it is important to bring up the issue of **environmental justice**, given that, in most cases, the generators of the impacts are not necessarily those who will suffer these impacts.

From the perspective of development and sustainability, it is important to critically highlight the role played by international funding agencies that have been systematically encouraging the maintenance and expansion of the hegemonic capitalist mode of production and consumption. The contemporary phase of capitalism, heavily based on the automation of productive activities and the financialization of economies, is extremely harmful to the planet, as it encourages the production, on an industrial scale, of energy, mineral and agricultural commodities, which leads to the increase of extractive activities harmful to the environment and also the deindustrialization of emerging countries and developing countries – especially those from the Global South – aggravating the socioeconomic conditions of workers in these countries, which have a very negative effect on the increase in inequalities and vulnerabilities – including the ones related with the aggravated risks characteristic of the global environmental crisis – of substantial portions of the population global.

References

Carson, R. "Silent Spring". Boston: Houghton Mifflin, 1962.

Crutzen, P. J. Geology of mankind. *Nature*, 415(6867), 23–23, 2002. doi:10.1038/415023a

Crutzen, P. J. The "Anthropocene". In E. Ehlers & T. Krafft (Eds.), *Earth system science in the Anthropocene* (pp. 13–18). Berlin, Heidelberg: Springer Berlin Heidelberg, 2006.

De Sherbinin, A. & Mara, V. *How green are your imports? This index provides an answer.* 2018. https://news.climate.columbia.edu/2018/02/07/green-imports-green-import-index-provides-answer/

Hamilton, C., Bonneuil, C. & Gemenne, F. Thinking the Anthropocene. In C. Hamilton, C. Bonneuil & F. Gemenne, eds. *The Anthropocene and the global environmental crisis: Rethinking modernity in a new epoch.* New York, London: Routledge, pp. 1–13, 2015.

Heyd, T. Covid-19 and climate change in the times of the Anthropocene. *The Anthropocene Review, 8*(1), 21–36, 2021. https://doi.org/10.1177/2053019620961799

IPBES. *Summary for policymakers of the global assessment report on biodiversity and ecosystem services of the Intergovernmental Science-Policy Platform on Biodiversity and Ecosystem Services.* S. Díaz, J. Settele, E. S. Brondízio, H. T. Ngo, M. Guèze, J. Agard, A. Arneth, P. Balvanera, K. A. Brauman, S. H. M. Butchart, K. M. A. Chan, L. A. Garibaldi, K. Ichii, J. Liu, S. M. Subramanian, G. F. Midgley, P. Miloslavich, Z. Molnár, D. Obura, A. Pfaff, S. Polasky, A. Purvis, J. Razzaque, B. Reyers, R. Roy Chowdhury, Y. J. Shin, I. J. Visseren-Hamakers, K. J. Willis, & C. N. Zayas (Eds.). IPBES secretariat, Bonn, Germany, 2019. https://doi.org/10.5281/zenodo.3553579

IPCC. *Summary for policymakers. In: Climate change 2021: The physical science basis. Contribution of working group I to the sixth assessment report of the intergovernmental panel on climate change.* Masson-Delmotte, V., P. Zhai, A. Pirani, S. L. Connors, C. Péan, S. Berger, N. Caud, Y. Chen, L. Goldfarb, M. I. Gomis, M. Huang, K. Leitzell, E. Lonnoy, J. B. R. Matthews, T. K. Maycock, T. Waterfield, O. Yelekçi, R. Yu, and B. Zhou (Eds.), Cambridge and New York: Cambridge University Press, 2021. pp. 3–32. doi:10.1017/9781009157896.001.

Keys, P. W., Galaz, V., Dyer, M., Matthews, N., Folke, C., Nyström, M., & Cornell, S. E. Anthropocene risk. *Nature Sustainability, 2*(8), 667–673, 2019. doi:10.1038/s41893-019-0327-x

Malhi, Y. The concept of the Anthropocene. *Annual Review of Environment and Resources, 42*(1), 77–104, 2017. doi:10.1146/annurev-environ-102016-060854

Mcneely, J. A. Nature and COVID-19: The pandemic, the environment, and the way ahead. *Ambio, 50*, 767–781, 2021. https://doi.org/10.1007/s13280-020-01447-0

Moore, J. W. The end of cheap nature, or: How I learned to stop worrying about 'the' environment and love the crisis of capitalism. In C. Suter and C. Chase-Dunn (Eds.), *Structures of the world political economy and the future of global conflict and cooperation.* 285–314. Berlin: LIT, 2014.

Moore, J. W. *Anthropocene or capitalocene? Nature, history, and the crisis of capitalism.* Oakland: PM Press, 2016.

Rzepa, A. & Ray, J. *World risk poll reveals global threat from climate change.* 2020. Retrieved from: https://news.gallup.com/opinion/gallup/321635/world-risk-poll-reveals-global-threat-climate-change.aspx

Sachs, Ignacy. "Ecodesarrollo: concepto, aplicación, beneficios y riesgos", *Agricultura y Sociedad*, 18, (1981): 9–32.

SDSN. *Tracking bilateral spillover effects.* Sustainable development solutions network. 2022. Available at, last seen in Nov 22nd, 2022: https://spillovers.environmentalimpact.global/#/

Steffen, W., Broadgate, W., Deutsch, L., Gaffney, O., & Ludwig, C. The trajectory of the Anthropocene: The Great Acceleration. The Anthropocene Review, 2(1), 81–98, 2015. https://doi.org/10.1177/2053019614564785

Steffen, W., Crutzen, P. J., & Mcneill, J. R. The Anthropocene: Are humans now overwhelming the great forces of nature? *Ambio, 36*(8), 614–621, 2007. http://www.jstor.org/stable/25547826

UN. The Sustainable Development Goals Report 2018. New York: United Nations, 2018. https://www.un.org/development/desa/publications/the-sustainable-development-goals-report-2018.html

UNCCD. *Global land outlook.* Bonn, UNCCD Secretariat. 2017. https://www.unccd.int/resources/publications/global-land-outlook

UNDESA. *World economic and social survey 2013: Sustainable development challenges.* 2013. http://www.un.org/en/development/desa/policy/wess/wess_current/wess2013/WESS2013.pdf

UNDP. *Human development report 2020. The next frontier: Human development and the Anthropocene.* 2020. https://report.hdr.undp.org/index.html

United Nations Environment. Annual Report 2016. Engaging people to protect the planet. UN Environment, 2016. https://www.unep.org/annualreport/2016/index.php

Wendling, Z. A., Emerson, J. W., De Sherbinin, A., Esty, D. C., et al. *2020 Environmental performance Index.* New Haven, CT: Yale Center for Environmental Law & Policy, 2020. epi.yale.edu

World Commission on Environment and Development-WCED. *Our common future: from one earth to one world. Report of the world commission on environment and development.* 1987. https://www.google.com/url?q=https://sustainabledevelopment.un.org/content/documents/5987our-common-future.pdf&sa=D&source=docs&ust=1647206860760678&usg=AOvVaw2VjrMsipoH262T5bQwYjk1

Yale Center for Environmental Law and Policy - YCELP - Yale University, & Center for International Earth Science Information Network - CIESIN - Columbia University. *2020 Environmental Performance Index (EPI).* Palisades, NY: NASA Socioeconomic Data and Applications Center (SEDAC), 2020. https://doi.org/10.7927/f54c-0r44

9

ARTICULATING LOCAL AND GLOBAL PROCESSES TO ENSURE THE GOVERNANCE OF FOOD SYSTEMS

Arilson Favareto and Patrick Caron

The purpose of this dialogue was to explore some of the interdependencies that exist between the specific issue of agri-food systems and the agenda of democracy, development, and sustainability, which not coincidentally give the name to the core that is at the head of this now published series.

This theme involves a paradoxical situation. On one hand, the agri-food sector is often blamed for a series of world problems. It is one of the main vectors of biodiversity destruction in the world, with the conversion of forest areas into pastures and plantations. It is one of the main responsible for the emission of greenhouse gases associated with climate change, mainly through the changes promoted in land use or with the expansion of livestock activity. And it is also the cause of several problems related to human health. In this regard, one always mention diseases related to the excessive consumption of ultra-processed foods, the global epidemic of obesity also motivated by the type of industrialized foods consumed, with high salt, fat, and sugar contents; but there are also the problems derived from the confinement of animals with high use of antibiotics and risk of disease proliferation.

On the other hand, there are all around us a number of signs that could be considered favorable to a transition to a more sustainable model. There is an increasing expansion of organic production, slow and insufficient, but constant. We have had a reduction in hunger on a global scale, although in recent years this has begun to change. We see an expansion in many regions of the planet of eating habits such as veganism or vegetarianism, or at least a search for fresh and healthy food, which can mean less demand for the consumption of meat and proteins, whose production is associated with environmental destruction, at least in the way it has been happening today. And there are new technologies, some of them very controversial, like lab-grown meat, that also have as a justification to decrease this environmental pressure.

DOI: 10.4324/9781003384366-10

This coexistence of positive and negative vectors is evident when thinking about a more sustainable world. Never has so much good food been eaten in human history, and at the same time, never has so harmful been eaten; nothing could be more paradoxical. Regarding the statement that one is eaten so well, there are many criteria that can be used to support this. Life expectancy is longer, partly because the quality of what we eat has improved over time. The availability of food per person per day has grown steadily worldwide. When we get up in the morning, we have no doubt that there is a variety of food available. This has not always been the case. The risk of food shortages for most of humanity is decreasing. But note that this concerns the majority, because there are still 800 million people who do not eat enough or who have problems accessing food, which is absolutely unbearable, unacceptable, because there is enough production, enough to feed the whole world.

At the same time, environmental problems have been a trigger for some to say that the food system is broken. Perhaps it is incorrect to say this, because we have never eaten so well, the system keeps producing, people keep consuming. But it is certain that this has generated social and political problems, as well as environmental ones, that make the feeling grow that there is a need to change, to evolve.

The UN World Food Systems Summit in 2021 is the best demonstration that something needs to change to reverse the problems that food systems have created over time. But while there is some consensus about the need for change, the same cannot be said about the solutions or the ways to implement that change. We know that a major difference in the transition from the 20th century to the 21st century is that we have gone from a situation where in the 20th century the only priority was to produce more, to increase production through productivity, to a situation, like the present one, in the 21st century, where it is recognized that food is at the heart of a complex system that puts all the dimensions of sustainability together. In other words, changing food is not just something to solve food problems, it is also something to address all the problems of sustainable development: environmental, social, political, and economic. Transforming food is not just about trying to achieve Sustainable Development Goal number 2. It is also looking at poverty problems (SDG 1), health problems (SDG 3), climate problems (SDG 13), biodiversity problems (SDG 15). We could find a relationship with practically all the SDGs. Therefore, food is a gateway to deal with the problems of unsustainability of the planet and of humanity. Being ambitious, it is a way to achieve not only a very limited goal, but it is really about transforming the world through food.

There, in a certain way, the complexity that marks this theme becomes not only much clearer, but also much more complicated. Because it is not only about one criterion, one factor, one transformation. It is also about putting together, at national and international levels, the different paths of transformation of humanity and of the planet. The period in which the objective of agriculture was to produce more, with more technology, investments, capital, was simpler. That is not all that this is about now. It is about facing all of humanity's problems tomorrow.

Are there spaces that deal with issues related to the food summit?

Or, is there space to take this issue as an opportunity to deal with others like climate and biodiversity? Is there this sensitivity among other actors, outside the community directly involved with agri-food issues? In addition to the UN World Summit on Food Systems, two other high-level international meetings on related topics were held in 2021 – the COP on Biodiversity and the COP on Climate Change. But one of the most recurrent criticisms of efforts to improve food systems and generate better impacts involves precisely the fragmentation of agendas. There is difficulty in giving visibility to social issues in the climate agenda or in linking biodiversity protection to the creation of opportunities for the poorest.

There is another paradox here. In these two spaces, dedicated to climate and biodiversity issues, conferences and expert panels have been paying more and more attention to the food issue. The IPCC and the IPBES, which are the two expert panels working on this, have already started to work together, and in this they have addressed the transformation of food systems. No, because the HLPE/CFS is not yet working with the other ones, it is not enough. But, it is possible to expect a more solid intersectoral articulation that aims to produce knowledge in a joint manner. Since there is a certain closeness, there is reason to be happy. On the other hand, the situation is quite complicated. Because every time there is a question at a national or global level, a body is created that works by itself, with little coordination with the others. The food issue is on the table and now some want to create yet another panel of experts or specialists on the food issue, when the most important thing would be to approach these issues in an intersectoral way, for the reasons we have just mentioned.

Besides this, and we can see this very well in the international negotiations, for each sector, each of the countries and nations, there is, at the negotiating table, a posture, a position to defend that today corresponds much more to the defense of their own interests, and not to an attempt to construct a sense of global sustainability. We can see how, for each one of the issues, each national government comes to the table with positions that result much more from the defense of their country's sectors, their country's lobbies, and not with a negotiating posture for the common good of humanity or the planet.

In other words, there are two challenges to move the negotiation tables forward: the first is the fact of working without connections between the different themes and without seeking coherence in public policies at national and international levels; the second is a negotiation posture that responds much more to national development criteria and objectives than to a global vision of the problems to be solved.

This problem verified at the international level is also reproduced at the scale of each country. We could mention the Brazilian case. Many researchers have pointed out the discontinuity of social and environmental policies. But even if we go back a little, in the first decade of this century, when there was a relatively strong institutionality for these themes, a sectorial vision predominated in the agenda of the agri-food sector, with a strong weight of conventional agribusiness. And this, at a time when the Brazilian State was supported by a quite broad and plural coalition of social forces: with business support, yes, but also from workers' organizations and even, to a certain extent, from environmentalists. Well, even this plurality of social forces could not sustain an agenda of transition, of lasting change.

What are the social forces and what coalitions could lead to greater convergence towards a trajectory of change and transition?

At the global scale, is it possible to identify, transnationally, who would be the protagonists of this greater coherence between strategies? Or, will this first have to be resolved at a, shall we say, sub-global, regional, or national scale, so that then the international arenas reflect this kind of arrangement or coherence?

There are two kinds of response to this. The first involves a direction from the local to the global. At the national level those tensions materialize, between sectoral orientations and a global orientation in search of sustainability. The case of Brazil has similarities with that of France. Recently, the neonicotinoid problem, which was arbitrated between the Ministry of Agriculture and the Ministry of Environment, was a very strong example of this. So, in all countries, a question that needs to be put on the table is this: whether the institutions that we produced in past centuries, strongly anchored in sectoral and not transversal dynamics, are today the most adequate to respond to the challenges of the future.

Let's take a simple example: in most countries, even when you have the word food in the title of one of the ministries, there is no "Ministry of Food", the issue is placed in the Ministry of Agriculture, or in the Ministry of Environment, or in the Ministry of Health. The point is that there is a nexus in food as the heart of the interactions between these different sectors, and then it is necessary to make food the object of governance. Little of this institutional construction happens. In other words, we could ask ourselves whether or not the configuration of the ministries, which reflect the governance of a country or a society, really reflects the challenges of the future. When the idea of creating a Ministry of Food was once mentioned in France, immediately there was all the resistance that prevented us from looking a little further ahead.

The second answer is that this problem happens at all levels: from the scale of a specific and localized territory, through the scope of a country, to the international level. And we know very well that to stimulate transformations, it is necessary to reach all these levels. There won't be transformations for sustainability only at the local or territorial level, even if there is an impact for the sustainable development of that territory; it is also necessary to mess with trade, with legislation, with some regulations that happen at different levels. In other words, the challenge today is to manage to articulate transformations at different levels, from local to global, without the predominance of one or the other.

At the same time, it would be totally unrealistic to think that all transformations can happen at the same time at all these levels. You can start at one level and, let's say, contaminate the other levels, by political force, by political pressure. A local initiative can, through example, through the learning capacity, through the political structuring that results from it, stimulate a transformation at another level, at the national level, for example. A particular coalition at a certain moment, and this has already happened in many countries (Brazil, France, others), can stimulate a local transformation, or can be the beginning of a reflection for a regional or global transformation.

In a pragmatic way, we are drawing attention, especially at a time when multilateralism is rather weak, to the challenge of voluntary engagements and commitments, much more than by force of law or regulation. The Paris Agreement on climate, for example, although not binding, can positively contaminate other levels, with governments, companies, and individuals adhering to this narrative and making commitments. A new law can foster the creation of some innovative experiments at the local level. Conversely, local innovative experiences may give visibility to principles that inspire a new law. And so on. Much more than an intellectual challenge, the challenge is practical, in achieving this construction.

A good part of the innovations that we have in the agri-food sector are constituted in niches. They are localized innovations. They are undoubtedly very important, very promising, but without enough strength, at least until now, to counterbalance all those negative effects of the pattern prevailing in the sector today.

How could localized initiatives gain body or have greater repercussion in a perspective of change in the agri-food systems?

If we are thinking about the sustainability of human societies, all solutions have to be adapted to localized contexts, because of ecosystemic and socio-cultural differences. One of the challenges is always to improve the connection and increase the scale and incidence of some of these innovations. But there are more barriers to this. It is hard to imagine that, due to resistance, these changes mentioned above will happen spontaneously or on a determined scale. It takes pressures, experiences, and compromises at other levels for something to happen at a certain level. And this brings us to the issue of "scaling-up".

For those who truly believe in the power of local social innovation, in the importance of the niche, criticizing scaling-up is not about discrediting this dynamic of innovation and experience. On the contrary, it is at the local level that one can reinforce territorial dynamics, social cohesion, consistency, and intersectoral coherence of actions; it is where one can build agreements necessary to achieve sustainability. This is by no means a criticism of the innovation and governance of these experiences.

The limits of scaling-up lie in two easy to understand reasons. First, because these experiences are not reproducible. One of the reasons for this is the specificity of the context, in terms of environment, culture, local capabilities, availability of capital of different types. Moreover, when they include external support, these innovation niches are made in the best conditions, in optimal conditions that are also not reproducible. For example, in the theme of local development there are traditions of investing, in particular, in human resources, with support for initiatives that achieve different degrees of success. But even the most successful cases may not be reproducible, even in close or similar realities, because they are very sensitive and adherent to contextual factors of those territories.

The second reason has already been mentioned above. It is the fact that everything depends on an articulation, on a process that takes place at different levels. It is not only the local dynamics that count, the technology, the form of social organization. It is also legislation, large-scale trade, the spread of diseases and pests, climate change. It is a set of factors, in short, that happen at different scales that make a transformation possible.

For all these reasons, it makes more sense to bet on the ability to learn from these experiences in order to contaminate other scales. Because if we really want to pursue an orientation towards sustainable development, this will have to be done on a global scale. It is not something that can arise from the sum of local processes. The case of climate change is exemplary: there will be no response just by controlling local trajectories.

We can increasingly use the image of the rainbow to illustrate this. That is, the transformations have to be different, responding to different goals and different challenges, relative to each locality, but they have to be consistent as a whole, as a whole at the global level. This requires a process of regulation at different scales to happen. It takes two processes. One process of learning and contamination, discussed earlier, learning from a local experience to build a new national public policy or a new framework for action at the global level and vice versa. Second, we need a process of regulation at different scales, with governance organization that is adapted to the different scales and to each of these different localities. To summarize, perhaps instead of the debate about shifting scales, it makes more sense to look for the interconnection of governance actions at different scales to build a single sustainable development.

To what extent does the post-pandemic context favor the advances considered necessary for a transition towards a more sustainable model of agri-food production, distribution and consumption?

At this moment when we are having this dialogue, there is a great expectation about what the world will be like after the Covid-19 pandemic. We dream of a different world, hoping that the feelings provoked by the pandemic can contribute to this. However, the answer to this question needs to be balanced.

Many things seem to have changed. At least in part of society, it might be correct to say that there is a slightly greater awareness of some issues and problems. Many people speak, for example, of a greater attention to the topic of food, because people have changed some habits during the period of confinement, with the restrictions on movement and the possibility of going to restaurants and eating out. Others talk about a greater attention to environmental issues, because this is also related to the possibility of new pandemics, with the increasing alteration of ecosystems and the greater exposure of humans to pathogenic elements for which we have no natural defenses or even known medicines, as was the case with this virus. And another important change is that the actions of states have returned to the foreground, with the need to cope with the humanitarian crisis, but also economic, generated by the pandemic. It is something quite different from what was seen until recently, under the sign of neoliberalism.

Many see this as an opportunity, a more favorable situation to advance agendas such as sustainability; and within the sustainability agenda, to produce a more inclusive and innovative agri-food agenda. When it comes to groping through which paths this new situation can translate into concrete changes, however, there are differences. Some of the researchers and leaders dedicated to the agri-food issue bet that technologies would be the key variable. According to this argument, the business sector would have the ability to interpret some of these trends and, in the absence of imposing global governance mechanisms, innovations that could spill over to other spheres would come from a kind of business vanguard. Others already place more expectations on consumer behavior, putting pressure on the business sector. And, more recently, there are still many who place a lot of emphasis on the financial segment, as an agent capable of imposing socio-environmental criteria, forcing, therefore, behavioral adjustments to the others, especially the more conservative ones, in the other links of the production chains. These are not mutually exclusive perspectives. They can be seen as complementary. And they occur simultaneously with the advances and impasses we mentioned in the governmental spheres or international multilateral governance.

As for the technological response, it is hard to imagine that it will lead to the needed change. Because we have seen that the last three centuries have been characterized by an unbounded confidence in technology, with the promise of a better world and a tomorrow that enchants. And there is no evidence that this has materialized in that idealized way. The ability to question the relationship between technological development and its impacts has not been called into question with the pandemic. On the contrary, in fact. People still have a lot of faith that the solution will come from technology and from an infinite creativity that will solve everything through technical means. There are no indications that, out there, a solution to the problems we have pointed out can emerge.

On the other hand, it is necessary to recognize that there is an adjustment movement on the part of the business sector, adopting new technologies to somehow dialogue with these new environmental demands. Here too there are paradoxes, a recurring expression in our dialogue. Perhaps it is illustrative to look at what happened in another sector, that of energy production. There have been enormous advances in alternative, less polluting sources of energy, although this has not been enough to get rid of fossil fuels and all the problems of different kinds associated with them. But the possibilities have broadened.

This position is not a denial of the ability of technology to solve problems. On the contrary. It is that there is a disconnect between the capacity of technology and the challenges of sustainable development, because there are no regulatory processes that make innovation guarantee the capacity for sustainability. The private sector alone or civil society alone will not be able to make this adjustment. It is first of all a matter of public governance and public regulation. The capacity for innovation, including the capacity of society, of companies, and also of large companies for reasons of private interests, of reputation, of guaranteeing the future market, all of this is interesting and very likely is the necessary seed for transformation. But it is not enough, especially in the food sector.

Let's remember something that may seem shocking. In the 19th and 20th centuries all the technology that allowed for increased productivity contributed to the production of private goods, and with that to increased production and enrichment, of course, but at the same time it also allowed for the production of public goods, mainly because of the risk of not having enough food to ensure food security. Today this is no longer the case. There is no longer convergence between the production of public goods and private goods. This is the responsibility of the state as the translator of the public thing, the republic, the *res-publica*. It is the state's responsibility to create a regime of action that guarantees the convergence of private goods and the production of public goods. This is the condition for technological innovation to contribute to sustainability. This implies thinking about interdiction, taxation, financial incentives.

It is good to stress that in saying this we are not saying that the role of the private sector or civil society is not important. Because it is not the public sector that will guarantee production. The attempt made in the 20th century by the communist models, in this sense, is quite revealing. We have to invent a new regime of action that allows the state to guarantee the orientation towards sustainability and to mobilize all forces so that innovation – technological, but not only technological – contributes to this.

In other words, if we do not start with this, with these regimes of action, it does not seem plausible to imagine that the post-Covid context can solve the problems of sustainability. This is primarily a political construction, and one that takes place in the spheres of territorial politics, national politics, and international politics. What gives hope in the post-Covid context is the fact that there is not only a greater questioning of environmental issues, but mainly the realization that there is a return of the notion of sovereignty. The idea of sovereignty had been discarded, even in the area of food. Because it was seen as an opposition to the power of the market, and the market was seen as a solution to guarantee the welfare of humanity, without the need for political regulation. Now, a free market is taken as omnipotent in that approach. However, markets have not delivered what was promised. Thus, the pandemic brought back the idea of sovereignty. But, of course, with it also come many risks, including the valorization of identity based on xenophobia, racism, and individualism. This is bad for democracy and for peace. The good side, and this is what needs to be stressed, is that the role of the public actor, the governance of things and of the republic is back at the center of the debate.

The evolution of the world is first of all something that we have to build from a political point of view, through a strong actor that allows us to guarantee the convergence between the different scales and between private and public interests. We managed to do this in the 20th century in the area of food, in the case of diseases and sanitary standards applied to the vegetable and animal production. There are nuances, of course, but world trade rules were created that generated restrictions and reorientations. If we were able to do this with animal and plant disease issues there is no reason why we cannot do this with sustainability criteria, whether social criteria or those linked to the environment.

So, mentioning again the Food Systems Summit, there was a lot of controversy about its realization and results. There was even a whole movement of grassroots organizations and the like denouncing the capture of this space by more traditional interests, with the risk that the future might repeat alternatives and solutions already tried out in the past and that generated the ambiguities or paradoxes that we have mentioned so much, now, for example, extending the productivist model to Africa. Even with these limits, something is moving, albeit very slowly, in these international spaces. The concrete results end up being less ambitious than we need. But the framing of the problems seems to be progressively changing. This is normal, and the opposite would be surprising. This shows that there are interests at stake, that there are issues to negotiate. It is a demonstration that it was a good thing to think about this Summit and that there are challenges ahead. We could regret that there is duality, polarization. But the agricultural sector over the last thirty–forty years has been bipolar: for or against genetically modified organisms; for or against the consumption of animal products; several examples could be given. But this polarization is also one of the factors of transformation. What is striking about spaces like the Summit is that the challenges are so great that, of course, in two years there is no way to reach a consensus. In particular because, as has been said, multilateralism is weakened.

Then, what we can expect from these kinds of spaces is the ability to change agendas, to change the kind of questions that are being put on the table. There is already something of a change when we hold a Summit on Food Systems, and not on agriculture or food. This means implicitly and explicitly admitting the fact that food is not just a matter of production or of feeding people, it is an issue that is at the heart of ambitions for sustainable development.

In doing so, market and trade issues are affected and this is also an important contribution. For example: there is a very big difference between the cost of food and the price of food. The price of food is what the consumer is willing to pay. As for the cost, if all the costs that are externalized were internalized, particularly in the environmental and health areas, the price of food would have to be three or four times higher than it is today. Who pays this differential today? It is paid collectively, because it is socialized, and in a differentiated individual way, because each one of us pays this difference. Putting this on the negotiating table when talking about food systems is already a beginning of questioning the standards of international trade. This is why we must value these spaces and consider their great importance.

Since these are long-term transformations that are measured in decades, not years, what can be said about how the articulations between the demographic and geopolitical dimensions have repercussions on the food issue?

Over the course of this century, we will probably experience a new situation: a possible stabilization of world population growth. This is also a subject about which there is some controversy, but some projections indicate that this should occur in the coming decades. This is something quite different from the sharp demographic growth that we have been experiencing for a long time, and most markedly in the last two centuries. This is important because it shakes one of the bases of a neo-Malthusian discourse, which repeatedly emphasized the need for increased production and the need for productivity growth as ways to cope with a growing world. Even today, there is a discourse that environmental concerns should be mitigated to increase the availability of food, although we know that if there is hunger, it is not for lack of production, but for a problem of access.

On this subject, we can be even more provocative. Contrary to many of the speeches that predominate today, it is worth remembering that we already produce enough on a global level. And we are talking about enough for 10 billion people. We went from 1 billion to 7 billion people in two centuries. And from 7 billion to 9, which is the current movement, the difference will be relatively small. What's more, when you consider that we waste 30% to 40% of production, that many people over-consume, and that because there is, now or in the near future, a tendency to decrease the consumption of animal products, once you consider all of this, then increasing production and productivity is not a priority.

Of course, this does not mean to say that the production dimension should be forgotten, because of problems of soil degradation, of biodiversity degradation. We have to take care of the productive capacity. And we have to recognize that hunger is still one of the main causes of problems in human history, but for different reasons than it was in the past.

Another point: there is a very big difference between Africa and the other continents. Africa is the only continent whose population will grow. We cannot compare it with the rest. Inclusive because there the demographic transition will happen between two and three times faster than in other continents. And if on the other continents this has already been a violent process, in Africa it tends to be even more so. It took 250 years for the world population to multiply by 10, and the African population will multiply by 10 in 100 to 150 years. This is something we have never seen in human history, and it is going to happen now. In a context in which the economic transition is completely different from what happened in the other continents. On the other continents, the demographic transition happened at a time when new job opportunities were created in other sectors. This is not the case in Africa. In other words, the lag between the demographic transition and the other transitions in economic sectors is an unknown factor that will be very difficult to equate.

Specifically, about China, a key question is, how the Chinese consumer will behave in terms of consumption of animal products. Today, the average meat consumption in China is more or less 40 kilos per inhabitant per year – half of the countries that are in the OECD. If the Chinese consumer, on average, consumes twice as much as they do today in terms of animal products on the whole planet, this means enormous pressure on natural resources. Although this is an internal change, it would affect the world markets and, especially, countries like Brazil, whose main product is soybean exports to that country. As the reactions happen in a chain, this would also have repercussions on the forms of land use and on the conservation of sensitive areas such as the Amazon, which is still an area of crop expansion in Brazil.

That is why – treated separately the problem of access to food, and treated separately the issue of Africa – the biggest challenge in demographic terms involves the transformation of the consumption pattern driven by urbanization, rather than population growth, per se.

And, continuing with China, it seems that we are facing more of a problem of organization of consumption chains than a global problem. Let's take an example: 80% of the consumption of palm oil is happening in Asia, and between China and Southeast Asia. If tomorrow the Europeans put regulations in place to prohibit the use of oil that is being produced under environmental conditions or under social conditions unacceptable to them, China will reorient the regional market. It won't need the Europeans or international trade rules to rethink a trade architecture.

But China is being attracted or motivated by two distinct paths: one is the fall of sustainability due to internal and external causes – internal, for example, the quality of water resources, and external, climate change, which it recognizes and integrates in its policies; and, on the other hand, the hegemonic position, from the point of view of trade, due to economic and demographic reasons. Between these two guidelines the future is not written and China will certainly be one of the protagonists of this future, taking into account that Chinese direct investments in Africa have increased a lot.

There is great expectation about how the Chinese position will be in international negotiations from now on. In Brazil, it is very common to hear from more conservative business leaders the following argument: if the Europeans are very careful with environmental variables, China is not; and since we export more and more to China and not to Europe, we won't have a problem. But everything indicates that this is a limited vision. Precisely because of its ambition to be an important international *player*, China will be able to get closer to international demands in themes and agreements related to climate or trade negotiations, in which agriculture and food will be central.

Moving the emphasis now to scientific approaches to the topic, how has the treatment of the challenges to transition in food systems been considered here?

There are a significant number of very influential approaches in the current landscape. The dietary literature emphasizes more dominant patterns, while here we have given more emphasis to diversity and the coexistence between patterns in the contemporary world. Another much emphasized approach is that of neo-Schumpeterian influence, which bets on scaling from the niches of localized innovations. Here, we refer more to adaptability and multiscale articulations. The look that has been attempted in these pages opens many dialogues with systemic approaches, with complexity theories, and with the idea of polycentric governance. This may be a frontier capable of providing good interpretative and analytical tools for the processes of transition. This is where our recent research is positioned.

10

EMBODIED POLITICAL ECOLOGIES OF WATER, GENDER, AND URBAN SPACE IN INDIA AND BRAZIL

Vanessa Empinotti and Yaffa Truelove

This chapter is an opportunity to discuss the geographies of water access, gender, and inequality in urban settings, topics that we have developed in our research in the last ten years. It is a dialogue between north and south institutions and researchers, reflecting on urban water crises and problems through the analysis of cities in different regions of the global South, from Latin America and Asia and, more specifically, from Brazil and India, finding not only some similarities but also differences and challenges to overcome water inequities and insecurity.

We start our conversation reflecting from the new paradigm of the Industry 4.0 that impacts work relations and production practices. Even though the concept is still under dispute, Industry 4.0 is defined as the integration of people, machines, objects, and information and communication technologies (ICT) systems to forecast, control and plan better business and social outcomes (Bauer et al., 2015; Qin et al., 2016). It is assumed that, for example, the use of smart machines to deal with large amounts of data will lead to a new future that is more efficient and less wasteful. As consequence robots, artificial intelligence, machine learning, the internet of things and the cloud will take production systems and decision-making to another level, impacting not just the labor force but how we organize, make choices, and develop new production practices.

In the context of water, and more specifically, urban water supplies, the Industry 4.0 approach promotes a reflection on how to improve efficiency and the rational water use. The assumption is that water problems are mainly technological problems such as water losses and inefficiency in water supply systems (Soares et al., 2019). Therefore, innovation in promoting new ways of controlling and monitoring water flows through big data analyses should create opportunities to solve water problems related to water distribution and access (Kosolapova et al., 2021).

DOI: 10.4324/9781003384366-11

The solutions based on the Industry 4.0 tools to the water sector are aligned to the neoliberal approaches in which privatization of water services, the use of market tools to mediate water access and private financing will create opportunities to solve this problem (Leigland et al., 2016; World Bank Group and UNICEF, 2017). Water inequality is framed as a technology problem, in which innovation combined with the private sector management skills and economic tools such as water pricing should be the best option to solve it.

In order to reflect on the assumptions presented above, we organized our conversation in four main questions that allowed us to reframe water inequalities based on the critical perspective of political ecology and feminist approaches and how they dialogue and challenge the Industry 4.0 paradigm. Below, you can find our thoughts and reflections based on the reality and research we have been developing in two major cities in the Global South: New Dehli in India and São Paulo in Brazil.

What are the main productive technological and financial transformations in process?

What would be the main productive technological and financial transformations in process in the case of water supply and distribution in urban settings?

If we bring this discussion to the macro level, we could look at processes of privatization and financialization of water supply systems and how they impact water governance practices and decision-making processes. In this context, how do we make decisions towards water? And who gets access to water or priority for water access? Proponents of privatization, for example, speak to the need for investment on data collecting and monitoring and data analyses become key for guaranteeing water supply and push towards private finance. Such concerns and strategies are aligned with water management studies under the hydraulic mission which is based on practices of controlling nature through the construction of large-scale infrastructure managed by hydraulic bureaucracies responsible for addressing issues of flooding, energy generation, irrigation, and urban water supply at a regional scale (Molle et al., 2009). According to this framework, water access should be solved by means of technology, governance, and infrastructure planning.

However, it is important to recognize that new approaches to solve water inequality problems take place in a context of historic and contemporary forms of inequality that are already in place and thus not new. For cities of the global South, historic inequality is rooted in the colonial period in a way that power structures are reproduced and sustained through time. Such structures of inequality have a direct impact on who should have access to water and what is acceptable or not. For example, the colonial legacy of some people having no access to water in terms of quantity and quality is normalized, accepted, and recognized as part of life. However, the 4.0 industry paradigm understands that water problems are rooted in inefficient water systems and the solution, for example, should operate through technology such as the monitoring of water quality as well as data storage and management (Soares et al., 2019). Such technological transformation would be part of a new financial model where water supply companies would be able to rely on private financing and be more independent from public resources (World Bank and UNICEF, 2017).

For the Indian context, particularly the cities that we study, it is a combination of colonial legacies and the entrenchment of inequalities through the postcolonial state that has substantially contributed to high levels of water inequality and inequity in cities like Delhi. For example, historical water inequality started at least as early as the colonial period, and probably in less systemic ways before that. Cities like Delhi deliberately planned by the British as "dual cities" that would first and foremost extend new large-scale piped infrastructure to areas occupied by the colonists, while leaving off the grid the majority of the local population. This occurred while British cities themselves, like Manchester and London, were for the first time getting something close to what looked like a universal water supply, with pipes extending to neighborhoods across the city. Thus, what we see in India's colonial cities like Delhi is the beginning of a very bifurcated city in terms of socio-spatial divisions and infrastructure. Thus, water infrastructure became a tool of the colonial state to reinforce spatial divisions, social hierarchies and control, beginning the legacy of a system of pipes that serviced elite areas of the city while excluding the "walled city" of Old Delhi where most of the Indian population lived (Sharan, 2006).

Of course, this is true for many colonial cities in and beyond Asia at the time, and is not really unique to India itself. But this nonetheless created a legacy in which the materials of infrastructure, in this case pipes, that the British put in place have a lasting legacy of servicing certain urban areas and not others. We see this legacy in the current postcolonial period because even when India became independent, it had both inherited this material legacy of a bifurcated water supply that excluded areas of the city where indigenous populations were living, and also had a difficult time rectifying these systemic exclusions. In the case of Delhi, the postcolonial state called in American planners to consult on how to address the growing slums and uneven infrastructures that were only being exacerbated through partition and sudden arrival of displaced people. Ford Foundation planners advised that the city should not extend universal infrastructures which would be a substantial and costly undertaking, but should rather keep people at different and even substandard levels of infrastructure in hopes that as residents move up the socio-economic ladder, they could later move in to more standardized housing with better services within areas of the planned city (Sharan, 2006).

Through this history of both the colonial and postcolonial state, we start to see the roots of unequal water and services being tied to the uneven socio-spatial geographies of the city, with universal access never given priority by either government. In contemporary times, what we now see in terms of the infrastructural landscape in Indian cities is extremely fragmented. While there are all kinds of different water sources, technologies, and practices of urbanites to

How to alleviate distributive asymmetries, based on popular solutions and state action?

To alleviate asymmetries through popular solutions and state actions in the post-pandemic and post-tragic political, economic, social, and environmental scenario represented by the rise of the extreme right in several central and peripheral capitalist countries, it will be necessary to develop actions to rebuild devastated nations. The preservation of the environment must overcome the infantilizing campaigns of certain NGOs and communication companies, which present individual, voluntaristic solutions and exempt states and large companies from responsibility. It is necessary to start from the realization that the historic inequalities of classes and between poor and rich nations have been maximized due to the dismantling of the incipient policies to promote racial and gender equality that have been developed over the last two decades, in the pursuit of the "welfare state" and the compensatory policies carried out by countries that, for a time, were led by political groups of leftist or popular origin.

We must face a post-war scenario in traumatized countries, living the hangover from the wave of fear, emerging from the tsunami of hatred and ignorance spread by denialists, white supremacists, religious fundamentalists, proponents of armamentism, and thousands of political groups with a Nazi-fascist orientation. There is no way to depoliticize the post-Covid period, since this pandemic was criminally politicized and the anti-science discourse, responsible for hundreds of deaths and incalculable suffering, became a political argument, splitting society and stigmatizing the defenders of life, pointed out as enemies and carriers of harmful ideologies. In the economy, for these countries to survive, within the framework of capitalism or by implementing a left-wing program, a kind of New Deal or New Plan will be necessary. In the economy, for these countries to survive, within the framework of capitalism or if a leftist program is implemented, a kind of *New Deal* or *Marshall Plan will be* necessary, since the social result of the tragedy is of unprecedented proportions, requiring solutions that are also unprecedented.

The data available today from all research institutes tell us that the virus is not "democratic", as some media outlets would have us believe. We know that the virus was more lethal and had a particular impact on vulnerable groups, and also that these groups are characterized by color, race, gender, age, and inhabit certain geographical spaces. This is a contingent that cannot afford social detachment due to the precariousness of their housing, was unable to practice *home office due to the* nature of their work, and had no access to emergency aid or received derisory amounts, insufficient for people to stay in their homes and avoid using public transportation, one of main vectors of virus transmission.

Thus, any economic and public policy initiative that will be implemented in the post-Covid period will only be successful if the racial, generational, and gender dimensions are considered. On the other hand, the State will not be able to face a catastrophe of these dimensions without the active participation procure water on any given day, there is scant state data on how heterogeneous infrastructures really are. In Delhi specifically, the state water board (called the Delhi Jal Board) is not required to provide in-house access to the centralized water supply for any house that "is in contravention to any law," which includes residents living in informal settlements (who constitute approximately 50% of the city) (DJB, 1998).

This means that a majority of urbanites are systemically excluded from household access to the city's pipes. However, even if a household is connected to the central water supply, its residents may not have adequate water access. For example, many households have to rely on a number of regular and often time-consuming water practices to access and store water, since the city's water supply typically only runs one-two hours per day and is characterized by low pressure. Many residents utilize pumps and motors to increase pressure that are illegal, and water needs to be siphoned into overhead storage tanks so it can be accessed throughout the day. And on days when water is insufficient, private purchases are often relied upon. Residents thus use a host of everyday and often gendered practices of pumping and storing water, as well as other small technologies that usually are not part of the story and dominant narratives of how water circulates in Delhi.

In our work, we have given explicit attention to the gendered and bodily practices of accessing water on a daily basis, whether in the planned or unplanned spaces of the city to understand the rippling effects of water fragmentation and insecurity. Whether it is the gendered labor of waiting for and hauling water, or negotiations with neighbors, politicians, and engineers, residents rely on a host of differing practices and negotiations for water that produce disproportionate hardships for particular social groups, including working class women, non-dominant caste groups, and Muslims.

It is worthwhile to observe that the technical solutions proposed by the 4.0 Industry paradigm that are aligned with new financial practices are thus not necessarily in a position to solve these sorts of problems. For example, the privatization of the water sector was not able to reverse water inequality conditions and actually often reinforced them (Goldman, 2005). There is thus a disconnect between solutions oriented towards the formal water supply system and the part of the population that lives under informal conditions for housing and water access, for example, does not stand to gain. Technological shifts, absent of social, cultural, and political shifts, would not be able to change the flows of water and power already in place.

In the case of many cities, particular aspects of the water supply have been privatized, like water treatment plants, etc. This is more of a public-private partnership. We do not really see a change on the ground, because when you have a public water supply that is not equitably serving half of the population at a minimum and it is not getting distributed to them, then privatization is not likely to fix that, either. Obviously, it is costly to try to install pipes to places. It does not really make sense through a cost-benefit analysis to service some of these urban areas and yet the public supply is also failing. So, there have to be solutions in which we think beyond the public-private divide, and instead think about the reality of how can more water equity come in. Maybe this means different ways of thinking about small scale interventions and we are going to talk about that later. But, we definitely see public and private both causing significant issues and thus it is not really about some universal prescriptive model, such as "if we just stick with public everyone will get coverage" or "privatization is just going to fix this automatically".

How do interstate disputes and environmental challenges manifest?

In the past few years, we have been working on issues of drought and water shortage in cities such as São Paulo in Brazil and New Delhi and Shimla in India. We look at how the interaction among different institutional levels, governance and day by day practices with water produce realities of water inequality in the context of droughts, crises and other events that co-produce water shortages (Empinotti et al., 2019; Truelove, 2019). The issue of water scarcity and drought is also permeated by infrastructure interventions such as water diversions and the reorientation of water in artificial ways to guarantee access to water to some areas and not to others (Empinotti et al., 2018; Truelove, 2018). On top of that, climate change, through the occurrence of extreme events potentialized the problems already in place and reinforces conditions of vulnerability to the poorest in urban areas (Young, 2022).

We both work on water insecurity and inequality through hydrosocial relations, and this framework is important for understanding the construction and uneven consequences of water scarcity or cities that are deemed waterless during periods when pipes run dry (whether from drought, infrastructural crisis, or inter-state water disputes). Shimla, India provides a unique example of periods of time in which this tourist destination in the Himalayan foothills has been deemed "waterless." While climate change driven drought has been blamed in the media and by government officials for the city's water problems, a closer look at the hydrosocial cycle funneling water from the hinterland into and through the city shows how cultural, political, and economic processes alongside socio-spatial divisions in the city also substantially contribute to constructions of water scarcity. Even in times when water is "restored" to the city, some social groups experience chronic water problems.

Shimla is only one case study, and probably less well-known than cities like Cape Town and São Paulo in which there was international media coverage and public countdowns for cities running out of water. While the media might indicate that it is just these specific moments in which cities like Cape Town and São Paulo are in water crisis or going "waterless", understanding waterless cities requires investigating whether chronic forms of waterlessness and everyday crisis exist for marginalized social groups on an ongoing basis, instead of in these spectacular moments that receive increased media and government attention. We do not hear those stories because water inequality for the urban poor, who often lack centralized water access and experience a fragmented and unreliable supply, has been normalized and is part of the status quo. On the other hand, when you have middle-class residents in cities like Cape Town suddenly standing in long lines to access water from a spigot, a practice usually associated with socio-economically disadvantaged groups living in townships, a crisis is declared. While significant numbers of urban-dwellers across the globe South are actually living in something akin to a waterless city on a daily basis even if the city has flowing water on a daily basis, this everyday emergency is made normative and thus does not surface in mainstream narratives concerning which cities are experiencing waterlessness. The hydrosocial model gives us the tools to analyze how socio-political as well as environmental systems shape the flow of water, including where water is going, whom is it serving, and who is in control of it. As political, cultural, and economic systems fuel socio-spatial divisions in the city and uneven access to resources, severe scarcity and struggles for water exist in many cities of the global South during times of both crisis and abundance.

In most Indian cities, you see this lack of water and constructed scarcity, even when there's heavy rains and water sources feeding cities are relatively stable. In other words, we are getting people that are not getting water no matter how large the aggregate quantity of water is. Vice versa, on the other side, even if water is very scarce, when half of a city's pipes have been temporarily stopped providing water, there are still people that are able to get water. Middle-class and elite social groups often have the political and financial capital to be able to buy water, install back-up wells that are often illegal, and/or know the right person who might be able to deliver tanker water to them. Thinking through hydro-social relations brings the opportunity for us to unveil the layers of social power that combine with other political, economic, and environmental factors to shape where water flows in times of relative scarcity and abundance.

In the case of Sao Paulo there are some parts of the city, the more informal and marginalized invisible parts of the city, when there is water supply and it's unstable, intermittent and it does not respond to household demands. So, people need to organize their lives around the presence or not of water. On the other hand, the middle- and upper-class neighborhoods, mainly after the drought that took place in 2014/2015, started to realize that there was this fluctuation of water availability in their households too. In cities of Brazil, like in India, the water supply system does not offer 24 hours, 7 days a week continuous water flow. The water is distributed in different periods of the day. Because of that, every household and building should have a "caixa d'água" or water tanks to storage water to make it available any time. People that live in upscale neighborhoods started to notice such water supply intermittence during the drought. It was not part of their conversation or part of their day-by-day activities, but they realized that under the drought, the water supply company decreased the amount of distributed water that led to less water storage and impacted the water availability for these households. This reality shows that the instability of the water supply is a component of the water system. The water supply system in place does not guarantee water for all, under drought or normal conditions.

However, the issue of water access is much more complex. Usually, people relate the problem to water storage so we should guarantee infrastructure to store this water and to distribute the water to solve the problem. But from our standpoint this is not the only problem. We learn and understand the water inequality issues from the household and bodily scale, how flows of water take place at these scales and impact peoples' day-to-day lives. That is why getting to more of a bodily scale can be really important to see these meso-processes. Some of them are environmental. There is a drought going on, for example, or there is an interstate dispute, and there are water diversions or water gets prioritized to certain places. In Delhi, diverting water to the city from neighboring dams is part of what is called "an urban bias". Delhi as the capital city gets water priority, so water is diverted from rural areas and people may suffer in those rural areas as a result. What makes the situation more compounded is that, although sufficient water to service the city enters at the macro scale, 50% of the population or more is still struggling sometimes just for basic amounts of water. In this case, you get rural people having less access to water that gets prioritized for Delhi, and even people in the city are not seeing sufficient amounts of that water.

To understand this phenomenon, you have to scale down to the body in order to analyze why particular bodies in the city experience high levels of water scarcity and insecurity despite sufficient water, more than 200 liters per person per day, entering the city at the macro scale. Here, we see how particular social groups, that include women, non-dominant caste groups, and those in a lower socio-economic stratum that live in informal settlements, experience disproportionate hardships in finding and managing water, and rely on a host of off-grid sources. At the bodily scale, you can see how particular social groups experience processes at the neighborhood, city, region, and national scale that shape their uneven access and power over water flows. Such reflection takes us to the next topic of our conversation in relation to distributional consequences from an intersectional standpoint.

What are the distributional consequences, including from an intersectional standpoint?

In some of the research in Delhi, I've been trying to think through intersectional water inequalities through the idea of bodies acting as infrastructure (Truelove & Ruszczyk, 2022). Because the urban majority in Delhi struggle with accessing sufficient, safe, and reliable water, and often must rely on off-grid sources, bodies often have to do the labor that compensates for a lack of functioning infrastructure. However, due to prevailing gender relations and social hierarchies, it is often the female, non-dominant caste, and/or Muslim working-class body that has to substitute for absent pipes. This includes waiting for and transporting water so that it reaches homes. For example, women in informal settlements often wait for the arrival of tanker water from the state, sometimes losing hours of their work day, and then fill and transport cumbersome plastic containers of water back to their homes for their family's use. If a tanker does not come that day, women must find water from additional sources such as private purchases, neighbors, or even employers.

Patriarchal gender relations designate managing water as the gendered work of women and girls and women who haul water also distribute it the house, first to kids or their husbands, often sacrificing their own water use for bathing and washing. They also separate clean water from re-usable dirty water that can be recycled multiple times to rinse dishes and cutlery, and find ways to minimize and conserve what little water the family must survive on (Truelove, 2021). Thinking of bodies as acting as (absent) urban infrastructure starts to speak to the kind of intersectional (gender, caste, class, race) inequalities you see in the everyday that surround both the production of infrastructure and the distribution of water. It helps to reveal the invisible story of how urban-dwellers get water in everyday practice at a very high price. It is not just the monetary price of water, but it is also the highly unequal physical, embodied, and social costs of having to do all of that labor and go through all of those hardships at the expense of other life opportunities.

As we have discussed, when we bring layers of gender and race to understand about how power relations and socio-spatial divisions operate across scales of the region, city, neighborhood, and household, we can particularly observe these relations and uneven subjectivities on bodies. I think one point that is important to highlight too is that depending on the perspective, scale, and framework from which you look at the problem, you are able to unveil or not how differing dimensions of inequality take place. Oftentimes, the problem of water access is understood through a technological framework that takes into account quantity and quality available, and price, and a municipality's ability and capacity to distribute water at city-regional scale to a household. If a family has tap water at home, the problem is purportedly solved. But when we look from the national, city-region, neighborhood, and bodily scale, we start to look at new questions and dimensions of everyday forms of inequality and the ways they are produced.

When your body becomes part of the infrastructure, when the infrastructure is not in place, you become the one that carries the water, distributes water, that defines who is going to have the priority access to it. So, you bring these layers of gender, class, and race relations that we know combine to further situate and produce the different experiences that each individual feels in their lives and their everyday practices and how it impacts them. If we looked from the engineering infrastructure perspective, we don't see any of such layers, but if we look from the body's perspective, it is a totally different constellation of relations and components that transform how we look at the problem.

There is a political imperative, for researchers to analyze these scales and practices because they reveal an invisible kind of violence, what we call "situated infrastructural violence" (Truelove & O'reilly, 2021) that is happening to different groups of people. Historically, particular social groups have been denied access to the planned city and housing based on class and caste. They are structurally in this position to not get adequate water for a variety of reasons and at the intra household scale we can also clearly see the long-standing patriarchal structures that place women with a bigger burden for problem solving particular aspects of getting water. If we bring visibility as researchers to this, then we can see in the case of cities like Delhi, gendered labor is completely subsidizing the flow of water, and that the government would not be getting water to people if women didn't do that labor. That includes even middle-class women that are connected to the grid, as water only flows a few hours a day if that, and these women still have to turn on a motor at 4am in the morning oftentimes to channel city water into overhead tanks. They still have to problem-solve for the days when water doesn't come as it is intermittent.

Then, bringing visibility to this actually completely changes the narrative of how and from where water circulates in the city. When we kind of look at a policy, these practices must be taken into account to recognize the absence of material infrastructure and the ways bodies unfairly and uneven must become part of the infrastructure. Policies must consider whose labor and the structures of power, gender, class, and caste asymmetries, that are already in place that become even further solidified when it is only particular social groups that have to do this kind of labor or that disproportionately suffer from inadequate water. This kind of analysis could really change the way we talk about water both in a policy and a research realm.

Such discussion also shows us that it is not just a matter of water on its own, but its connection to socio-political, cultural, and economic relations and power geometries in cities. Water cannot be understood in isolation, rather water problems and their rippling effects are related to socio-spatial divisions, housing access, job opportunities, and access to education and so many other things. It is thus difficult to separate and to solve the problem of water as a sectorial problem, without looking at all these other components that are related to it (Empinotti et al., 2021). Therefore, the hydrosocial relational approach is so critical for understanding water security and insecurity along the lines of all those different ways, including the right to water, social power relations, and how water is experienced at the bodily scale along with other scales. This is critical if we want to get to any kind of social and environmental equity.

In relation to Brazil, the access to water in Brazilian urban areas is closely related to housing conditions. If you live in places that are not formally designated as housing areas, it is much harder and sometimes impossible to have access to water through the water supply system service. So, people are keen to pay for the service; they do not want water free of charge. They believe that once they are considered as consumers, they will be able to get a better service and become citizens since they are visible to the state (Ranganathan, 2014). They became part of the city through becoming clients of the water system supply companies.

So, absolutely the situation in Brazil is very similar to what we have studied in Indian cities. That if an urban resident lives in one or another form of what the state considers formal housing, the waterscape is differently experienced, particularly the right and ability to access water from the centralized supply in homes. Accessing water, the unplanned city becomes an issue of citizenship and the right to the city and who has rights to urban space in general. We can see that playing out in macro ways with competition over who has rights to use urban space and for what purposes, and micro ways with how people are claiming space and providing their own infrastructure. Those who live in the unplanned city often both petition the state for various types of resources, and also find workarounds with informal actors and middlemen. These residents do all kinds of things, like showing receipts that they paid state water (even the water never came to their house) or they're getting a bill even if they're in my case people in some informal settlements get bills to show the state they not only have a right to water, put to also claim citizenship and belonging in the city. This can help build their capacity to stay in the city, even when they are under threat of demolition and displacement.

How to alleviate distributive asymmetries, based on popular solutions and state action?

We have already discussed how people often try to solve their problems without relying on the state, in conditions where there is no infrastructure in place (Aguilar et al., 2021; Drew et al., 2021; Empinotti et al., 2021; Roque et al., 2021). They become responsible for building their own infrastructure to guarantee water to their households, sometimes as a temporary solution, expecting that in the future they will be supplied by the water distribution system. Such strategy opens the discussion to the realm of strategies and solutions to guarantee water access and that reflect specific contexts.

As there is so much to consider when planning and implementing solutions, it is important to dialogue between different sites as we are between India and Brazil we have to think through context-specific solutions. We have to make sure that communities, and their diverse social groups, are having their, say, in policy-oriented solutions and their implementation, and that their knowledge and way of understanding the problem and potential solutions are brought to the forefront. As we have discussed, even conceive the right to water that a community may want differs from place to place. The creative solutions that could come in may also differ so perhaps in some communities, connecting to the centralized water supply does not have to be the solution or the only solution and there could be other solutions driven by community members and their lived experiences. In the case of Delhi, and in our research specifically, I have not seen off-grid sources solving overall water problems for the urban poor, particularly because of the micropolitics that surround tube wells and how they are managed and controlled in communities and by NGOs.

For example, water from tube wells has been contaminated, and often key leaders or strongmen in the community are in charge of operating the well, sometimes over-charging, pocketing extra money, or unevenly distributing the water. This is only scratching the surface of the complexities of some of these different solutions, but it demonstrates that it is very hard to think of an umbrella solution that could work in all of these places. Rather, we have to hear from communities and differing sub-groups and marginalized persons within communities about their experiences, needs, and aspirations for improved water systems. What I've heard from the communities that I study overall is that they want the water right to water on paper, and in practice they want centralized and treated piped water to their house. They want it to be clean and they want it to solidify further rights to the city itself. So, in this urban context they see it as very interconnected to other rights. First and foremost, they want to solve the fact, particularly for women, that they are losing work hours to find water, and they do not want their whole lives turned upside down, or to face harassment because they have to go around to other neighborhoods and encounter men and other people that are harassing them to get water. They have to go to politicians' offices, they have to go to employers, they have to go to neighbors. It is a full-time exhausting, stressful, physically taxing, and emotionally draining unpaid job that they are doing in the worst-case scenario. Certainly, for them, the solution is that the city recognizes that as human beings in the city they have a right like anyone else to safe, clean, affordable, and accessible water that does not require women to constantly negotiate and use their labor to problem solve water. From the lived experiences and voices of women about these hardships, you get to hear about their vision of how water could be a lot of different.

On the one hand, people expect the state to solve their problems with regard water access. The state should invest and implement water pipes system so the community members could pay for water services and at the same time, be recognized and treated like citizens. It is not a matter of just having water access, but it is the meaning of it. To pay a water bill, for example, you need to have an address and it formalizes people's existence and how they belong to the city. However, there is not necessarily a push or mobilization to build their own water system supply in urban areas, independent from the state. The main call is to be seen by the state and have their rights to the city recognized and respected. Being part of the city, it means to have access to state services, jobs, education, and everything else that comprises the city. At the same time, when we look at rural settings, water access could be seen as ways to create dependency and control, mainly in semiarid regions such as the Brazilian Northeast (Carvalho, 1988).

In this context, access to water represents access to power. Many times, the individuals would not have access to water if they did not belong to networks permeated by control and exploitation, historically constructed since the beginning of the colonial period (Domingos, 2004; Pang, 1979). Up to the 1990s, water access was trade with vote, political support, and dependence. However, in the end of 1990s, a network called ASA – Semi Arid Articulation, composed by social movements, NGOs and grassroot movements created a program that later became a government program during Lula's Presidency in Brazil (2003–2011) and was called One Million Cisterns, where the goal was to build cisterns in the northeast rural areas (Empinotti, 2011). The program was not just distributing infrastructure, but it was empowering the local population to become water independent from local politicians.

First of all, in order to choose who would get access to the infrastructure there was a local community committee in place, composed by local leaderships, having a significant presence of women as members. Such a committee would choose who would be the families under the worst condition that should have access to water as soon as possible. For example, elderly people, single mothers, and people with special needs. The most vulnerable ones were identified by the community as having priority to receive the cisterns in their properties. To build the cisterns, members of the community would learn how to build and how to maintain such infrastructure. The goal was to collect water during the rainy season so they would have access to water in the household during the dry season, and they wouldn't need to rely on local politicians to have access to water through water trucks, for example. They didn't need to compromise their vote to get access to water, they could make their own decisions, and they didn't depend on others to have access to water, they controlled the access to water. Therefore, such a program was so emblematic, so powerful because it was one of the first times that an intervention really changed or started to disrupt the power structures in place. However, the program is not perfect, there are problems with regard to water quality control, for example. But this shift in water access really changed power relations in that specific context.

This is a powerful example why we need much more of a holistic hydrosocial approach to understand what are the effects of water interventions, how they work in practice, and whether that are correcting some of these asymmetries or experiences related water but not limited to water. The issue of water access is much more complex than just offering a solution based on efficiency, investment, or transforming water into a commodity and using the economical tools to mediate water distribution and access. Or even transforming water into an asset, as something to invest in.

During our conversation, we have discussed the complexities of water inequality and how to begin addressing them. Infrastructure and new technologies can contribute to the solution to such a problem, but they do not solve the problem by themselves. The use of the Industry 4.0 framework to solve water inequality will not be enough if we disregard the problem's causes and multiple dimensions. Our research and our experience on international development, together with many other academics and practitioners, indicates that looking at water inequality just from a technological and economical perspective will not help us to solve the problem as a whole.

For example, Delhi already has enough water and technological know-how for everyone to have about 200 liters per person per day. If it was just a matter of pumping water across the city, the technology and engineering solutions already exist. If it was just a matter of pricing water, almost everyone is willing to pay, and evidence suggests the poor pay far more in the city for water than the middle-class and elite. However, because water funneled through politics, we see we have to think about how the city is planned, socio-spatial divisions and inequities, and all types of governance and social power relations. Accessing water is tied to what kind of city Delhi aspires to be, and who belongs in the city, who has space and the right to space in the city. Thus, one really has to approach water problems from a different standpoint because unfortunately the technological solutions actually exist but they're not solutions to these kinds of problems. We know how to pump water but it does not mean it is going to get to where it needs to go.

Final considerations

This chapter emerges from an informal discussion between the authors, and reflected on different ways of understanding and addressing water inequality and insecurity in this contemporary context. We even did not touch on the issues of the Covid-19 pandemic, which brings another layer and actually makes visible even more of the inequities that we are talking about. The pandemic brings to light another layer of what an emergency starts to disclose, but everyone we study was already in an emergency before when it comes to water access. In the Covid-19 context, suddenly there is a momentum that we need this water for human health such as a pandemic but that is a whole other can of worms.

It's been really fun and really enriching to hear and think through comparatively what is going on in Brazilian cities, and what is going on in Indian cities. So many of the same processes are at play, although very historically and contextually different. There is a lot to learn between these cases and how to approach thinking through these problems.

References

Aguilar, B. H., Lerner, A. M., Manuel-Navarrete, D. and Siqueiros-García, J. M. Persisting narratives undermine potential water scarcity solutions for informal areas of Mexico City: The case of two settlements in Xochimilco. *Water International*, v. 46, n. 6, p. 919–937, 2021.

Bauer, W., Hämmerle, M. Schlund, S. and Vocke, C. Transforming to a hyper-connected society and economy—towards an 'industry 4.0. *Procedia Manufacturing*, v. 3, p. 417–424, Jan. 2015.

Carvalho, O. D. *A Economia Política do Nordeste: Secas, Irrigação e Desenvolvimento*. Rio de Janeiro: Editora Campus, 1988.

Delhi Jal Board Act. 1998. Section 9 (1) (A).

Domingos, M. The powerful in the outback of the Brazilian Northeast. *Latin America Perspectives*, v. 31, n. 135, p. 94–111, 2004.
Drew, G., Deepika, M. G., Jyotishi, and Suripeddi, S. Water insecurity and patchwork adaptability in Bangalore's low-income neighbourhoods. *Water International*, v. 46, n. 6, p. 900–918, 2021.
Empinotti, V. L. E se eu não quiser participar? O caso da não participação nas eleições do comitê de bacia do rio São Francisco. *Ambiente e Sociedade* (Campinas), v. 14, p. 195–211, 2011.
Empinotti, V. L. Gontijo, W. C. and De Oliveira, V. E. Federalism, water, and (de)centralization in Brazil: The case of the São Francisco River water diversion. *Regional Environmental Change*, v. 18, p. 1655–1666, 2018.
Empinotti, V. L., Budds, J. and Aversa, M. Governance and water security: The role of the water institutional framework in the 2013–15 water crisis in São Paulo, Brazil. *Geoforum*, v. 98, p. 46–54, 2019.
Empinotti, V., Jepson, W., Budds, J., Millington, N., et al. Advancing urban water security: The urbanization of water-society relations and entry-points for political engagement. *Water International*, v. 46, p. 1–13, 2021.
Goldman, M. *Imperial Nature: The World Bank and Struggles for Social Justice in the Age of Globalization*. CT: Yale University Press, p. 384, 2005.
Kosolapova, N. A., Matveeva, L. G., Nikitaeva, A. Y. and Molapisi, L. The rational use of water resources in the strategy of industry 4.0. *Water Resources Management*, v. 35, p. 3023–3041, 2021.
Leigland, J., Trémolet, S. and Ikeda, J. Achieving universal access to water and sanitation by 2030. The role of blended finance. *Water Global Practice*: Discussion Paper. World Bank: Washington, pp. 1–20, 2016.
Molle F., Mollinga P. P. and Wester P. Hydraulic bureaucracies and the hydraulic mission: Flows of water, flows of power. *Water Alternatives*, v. 2, p. 328–349, 2009.
Pang, E.-S. *Bahia in the First Brazilian Republic: Coronelismo and Oligarchies, 1889-1934*. Gainesville: University Presses of Florida, 1979.
Ranganathan, M. Paying for pipes, claiming citizenship: Political agency and water reforms at the urban periphery. *International Journal of Urban and Regional Research*, v. 38, n. 2, p. 590–608, 2014.
Qin J., Liu Y. and Grosvenor R. A categorical framework of manufacturing for industry 4.0 and beyond. *Science Direct Procedia* CIRP, v. 52, p. 173–178, 2016.
Roque, A., Wutich, A., Brewis, A., Beresford, M., García-Quijano, C., Lloréns, H. and Jepson, W. Autogestión and water sharing networks in Puerto Rico after Hurricane María. *Water International*, v. 46, n. 6, p. 938–955, 2021.
Sharan, A. In the city, out of place: Environment and modernity, Delhi 1860s to 1960s. *Economic and Political Weekly*, v. 41, n. 47, p. 4905–4911, 2006.
Soares J., Leite, P., Teixeira P., Lopes N. and Silva J. P. Data warehouse for the monitoring and analysis of water supply and consumption. In: Ramos I., Quaresma R., Silva P., and Oliveira T. (eds) *Information Systems for Industry 4.0. Lecture Notes in Information Systems and Organisation*, v. 31, 1–12. Springer Nature, Cham, 2019.
Truelove, Y. Negotiating states of water: Producing illegibility, bureaucratic arbitrariness, and distributive injustices in Delhi. *Environment and Planning D: Society and Space*, v. 36, n. 5, p. 949–967, 2018.
Truelove, Y. Gray zones: The everyday practices and governance of water beyond the network. *Annals of the American Association of Geographers*, v. 109, n. 6, p. 1758–1774, 2019.

Truelove, Y. Gendered infrastructure and liminal space in Delhi's unauthorized colonies. *Environment and Planning D: Society and Space*, v. 39, n. 6, p. 1009–1025, 2021.
Truelove, Y. and O'Reilly, K. Making India's cleanest city: Sanitation, intersectionality, and infrastructural violence. *Environment and Planning E: Nature and Space*, v. 4, n. 3, p. 718–735, 2021.
Truelove, Y. and Ruszczyk, H. A. Bodies as urban infrastructure: Gender, intimate infrastructures and slow infrastructural violence. *Political Geography*, v. 92, p. 1–10, 2022.
World Bank Group and UNICEF. *Sanitation and Water for All: How Can the Financing Gap Be Filled? A Discussion Paper.* Washington DC: World Bank, 2017.
Young, A. F. From federal transfer and local investments to a potential convergence of COVID-19 and climate change: The case study of São Paulo city. *Sustainable Cities and Society*, v. 76, p. 1–15, 2022.

11

PRODUCTIVE TRANSFORMATIONS, INTERSTATE CONFLICTS, AND ENVIRONMENTAL DEGRADATION

The non-white youth and asymmetries in the Global South

Ramatis Jacino

From a perspective of the "global south", but focused on Brazil, this article will seek to problematize the impacts of productive, technological and financial transformations, as well as interstate disputes and environmental challenges, in the pre- and post-pandemic period for workers in countries on the periphery of capitalism. We will also present some ideas on how to alleviate distributional asymmetries through popular solutions and state actions, with a preferential focus on youth.

What are the main productive, technological and financial transformations in process?

We live in a time of profound scientific and financial transformations that affect production and the world population. To the detriment of the vast majority of the world's population and approximately 180 nations, which do not benefit from them, the extraordinary technological advances of the 20th and 21st centuries – the result of scientific development and the genius of human beings – have been appropriated and are at the service of a small number of individuals who own capital and a little more than a dozen countries. This appropriation is not unprecedented. The usurpation of the cultural and scientific legacy of the vanquished nations by the victor nations has been a constant throughout history. The privatization of culture and science by the dominant classes and the state that serves them, and its use as an instrument of control and domination of the rest of the population, has also been a rule throughout human development. The uniqueness of our time is the fact that the concentration of wealth, of political power, and the use of science and technology in the service of the few to the detriment of the majority have reached such an extraordinary level.

DOI: 10.4324/9781003384366-12

Technological transformations and their use solely to obtain profit led to an exponential increase in productivity which, nevertheless, did not represent benefits for the workers; on the contrary, it allowed for an increase in the exploitation of labor and the ability to exploit it anywhere on the planet, as exemplified by the migration of North American and European companies to Asian, Latin American, and African countries, even using labor analogous to slavery. Thus, the perennial violence in labor relations also manifests itself in the explicit and spectacular violence perpetrated by companies and the State, usually classified as episodic outbreaks, but which, in fact, are part of the method and logic of the overexploitation of labor. It is not an exception that in Bangladesh one of the 4 million inhabitants of the capital, Dhaka, work making clothes for the foreign market, making the country the second largest garment exporter in the world, with a volume of US$ 28 billion in transactions. The immense profitability of this business is the result of the overexploitation of a labor force composed of 85% women, with wages of less than 3 dollars a day.

And this country is just one among several others to which large global companies have transferred their production in search of cheaper labor. This reality is illustrated by the fact that in the 1960s, about 95% of the clothes sold in the United States were manufactured in American territory, a percentage that in 2014/2015 was no more than 3%, and the largest apparel trade is located in China, with $173.4 billion in exports, followed by Bangladesh, Vietnam, Cambodia, and Ethiopia. Nike Inc., a North American giant that has been making footwear, clothing, and accessories since 1972, has been systematically denounced for using child labor in its factories in Asia, where part of the 80 billion pieces of clothing sold around the world come from.

With more than 6.6 thousand stores operating in 88 countries and revenues of approximately US$ 15 billion, the Spanish company Zara, created in 1975, has become notorious for repeated allegations of the use of slave-like labor in its supplier network. Not by chance, its founder and main shareholder, Amancio Ortega, accumulates a fortune of US$ 69.2 billion and is considered by Forbes the fourth richest man in the world. The search for cost reduction, which has made large corporations decentralize and pulverize their production since the 1980s, moving to countries where labor legislation is more lenient and where there is no tradition of union organization, has led to absolutely predictable and avoidable tragedies such as the one that occurred in April 2013, when the Rana Plaza, an eight-story building in the outskirts of the capital of Bangladesh that housed five garment factories, collapsed killing 1,133 people.

In an irrefutable example that this tragedy was the result of the exploitation network established by the big international conglomerates: the investigations concluded that the five factories housed in that building, employing more than two thousand workers working 10-hour days, six days a week and earning less than 67 dollars a month, produced items for the colossal American department store Walmart Inc. This company shared space with Ireland's Primark Stores

Limited, which has 68,000 direct employees and profited 6 billion euros in 2016. A situation denounced by the famous The True Cost, a 2015 documentary directed by the American Andrew Morgan, which demonstrates the existence of a network of exploitation and precarious work by the fashion industry and its tragic consequences.

Separated by almost a decade and occurring more than 15,000 kilometers away from each other, three notorious examples, are closely linked, because they make up the same web that leads to the overexploitation of workers and necessitates extreme violence, racism, misogyny, and xenophobia, ideologies disseminated and maintained by the owners of economic power. In January 2014, in Cambodia's capital, Phnom Pehn, textile workers who were peacefully demonstrating to raise their wages to $160 a month were attacked by police, who shot and killed 3 workers. In the year 2016 in Bangladesh, Shima Akhter, a 23-year-old textile worker, was leading a movement for better wages and working conditions when she was the victim of an ambush armed by her bosses and assaulted, along with her comrades, with chairs, pieces of sticks, and scissors. In Rio de Janeiro, in the first month of 2022, the Congolese Moïse Kabagambe, 24 years old, was beaten to death in a commercial stall located in a famous tourist beach when he tried to collect the money he was owed for his overly precarious job.

The discourse insistently conveyed by the large communication conglomerates, that the global tragedy represented by the coronavirus pandemic has affected the rich and the poor equally, is nothing more than an instrument to justify and legitimize the increase in inequalities, the result of the optimization of exploitation mechanisms. The financialization of the economy and the concentration of income were increased in the period thanks to the deepening of the already brutal exploitation; making labor relations even more precarious, suppressing rights, increasing the working day, laying off massively, and reducing salaries. The most recent Oxfam report, from January 2022, informs that since March 2020, therefore during the pandemic crisis, the ten richest people (or families) in the world doubled their fortunes, reaching 1.5 billion dollars, the same period in which 160 million people were pushed into poverty and extreme poverty.

How do interstate disputes and environmental challenges manifest?

As far as the impact of the pandemic and its overcoming is concerned, Oxfam forecasts that by the end of 2023 the rich countries will resume the pre-pandemic economic growth trend, while during the same period the countries on the periphery of capitalism should experience a drop of around 4%. The extreme inequality, however, was already a widely known reality, and the indicators that measure health care, access to food, and the way the environment has been treated are the most significant. The World Health Organization estimates that each year 5.6 million people in poor countries die from lack of access to health care, and that hunger kills more than 2.1 million people annually.

Climate change, resulting from the predatory way in which some states and large multinationals treat the environment, has increased inequality and caused poverty to worsen in the first two decades of the 21st century. Using data from the World Bank, Oxfam states that environmental decontrol could push 132 million people into extreme poverty by 2030. The pandemic, therefore, has contributed to make explicit and maximize inequalities and highlight how the central countries of capitalism and the large economic conglomerates treat the rest of humanity. The transformation of the vaccines against Covid-19 in a profitable commodity and the sacralization of the profit of the big laboratories, which sold (and sell) to those who can pay more, led to the fact that, according to WHO data, by February 02, 2022 little more than 11% of people in African countries had received a dose of the vaccine and while in rich countries 75% of the inhabitants had already been immunized.

Brazil is the most significant example of the negative impacts of the radical appropriation of science and technology by economic power, especially due to the ethnic and gender component of its population. Inequalities of race and gender were dramatically deepened in this country in the pre-Covid period and throughout the pandemic, in addition to having been maximized the centuries-old inequities resulting from a nation built by slave labor, which imposed ethnic marginalization in the transition to wage labor (Jacino, 2008) and historically managed in a patriarchal way (Saffioti, 1976). It is a fact that there were social and economic advances in this country between 2003 and 2016, which reduced race and gender inequalities, bringing the unemployment rate to 3%, as opposed to 13% in the previous period, resulting from the creation of more than 20 million jobs and raising the minimum wage from 70 to 320 dollars. However, these advances were insufficient to stop the growing precariousness of the labor market, especially with the labor deregulation imposed from 2016 onwards. The reality experienced today by the millions of young people who work as delivery drivers by apps is one of the most significant and dramatic examples. These young men and women with low education levels, from poor families and performing hyper precarious jobs, use rented motorcycles or bicycles, have no formalized labor relationship, have no social security or insurance, have no right to medical care, and work enormous workloads. They are paid by delivery, which forces them to develop high speeds and disrespect traffic laws, becoming champions of accidents that result in disease, mutilation, and death. Added to this is the dismantling of the Unified Health System and of Social Security, which results in a legion of injured people unassisted by the State. Certainly, most of the victims of these accidents are young blacks, since in May 2020 they were the majority of those employed as drivers, motorcycle couriers, and delivery men.

Systemic in Brazil and in other countries with historical and demographic similarities (such as the United States), violence and racial and gender discrimination are here promoted by the State, which allies itself with capital by disregarding the principles of decent work, and that contributes to the maintenance of inequities by not guaranteeing access to education, health, and social security.

The pandemic, therefore, hits whites and blacks, young people and adults, men and women, rich and poor, citizens of rich countries and of countries in the periphery of capitalism, in a differentiated way. It is known that the new coronavirus can be fatal for those who have diabetes, asthma, or hypertension, diseases with a higher incidence in the black population. In Brazil, this pandemic affects in a dramatic way the most vulnerable workers; deliverers of food and various objects, porters, self-employed and informal workers, in cleaning, security, and employees of public health services. In addition, of course, to the inhabitants of precarious housing and people living on the streets, all of them mostly black. According to information from the Ministry of Health, published on the United Nations Brazil website on 05/12/2017, almost 80% of SUS users are black and, although this is still one of the best health systems in the world, the notorious lack of resources, management problems and the systematic dismantling it has been suffering since the 2016 coup led to the fact that, in times of pandemic, its shortcomings are worsening, once again to the detriment of the poor population.

Interstate conflicts generally result from disputes between factions of the world ruling class, to which national states are subordinate. They also concern geopolitics and the search for advantageous positions in global chess. The bipolar world of the Cold War period was rehearsed for multipolarity, with the rise of the European and Asian countries in the aftermath of that conflict. With the extraordinary economic growth of China and the maintenance of the power of post-Soviet Russia, the planet was moving towards a new bipolarity, with one side led by these two superpowers, supported by Brazil, India, and South Africa, organized in the BRICS, and on the other side by the United States and its traditional partners. This trajectory, however, was interrupted by the rise of right-wing nationalism in 2014 in India with Narendra Modi; the coup d'état in Brazil in 2016, aggravated by the rise of the far-right led by Jair Bolsonaro in 2018, and the resignation of Jacob Zuma from the presidency of South Africa in the same year.

It is also important to understand that the United States offensive against the attempt to establish a new world order has been paved with coups and actions aimed at weakening non-aligned political leaderships in economically less significant countries that, in some way, contributed to the pluripolarity, or at least to the new bipolarity. The constant aggressions and pressures, using the mainstream media, the Armed Forces and the Judiciary, in addition to explicit coups d'état, re-edit in the 21st century the belligerent actions of the 1960s and 1970s. Sponsored directly by the White House or outsourced to large companies and local groups, the attacks on democracy in Latin America serve US interests. The coup d'état in Honduras in 2009, the attempt to take power by force in Ecuador in 2010, the *impeachment of* the president of Paraguay in 2012, the bloody insurrection led by religious and military fundamentalists involved in organized crime in Bolivia in 2019 are notorious examples of the attempt by Washington and international financial capital to interdict any policy of poor countries minimally committed to its population. The constant aggressions against Venezuela, reissuing the hostilities of more than 5 decades to Cuba, including an attempted coup carried out from the kidnapping of President Hugo Chaves in 2002, is another example of the attacks against the self-determination of those peoples and even of disrespect to electoral processes that occurred in the frameworks of bourgeois democracy.

The so-called Lava Jato operation in Brazil, which imprisoned former President Lula, Brazilian political leaders and businessmen, paving the way for the coup against President Dilma Rousseff in 2016, with obvious involvement of the CIA and international financial capital, is perhaps the most notorious example of the actions of a global power that hovers above most national states. However, China and Russia (and their respective satellites), not necessarily with coinciding positions and interests, maintain the tension and prevent the unipolarity sought by the United States, whether that represented by the extreme right led by Donald Trump, or by the classic imperialism practiced in the Joe Biden administration. The crisis in early 2022, generated by NATO's expansion into Eastern Europe and Russia's reaction with China's support, made it clear to Europeans that their peace and stability is fragile and the possibility of armed conflict is not a threat that hovers only over other continents. It is a situation that once again highlights the need to confront the power of the United States, the nation that nowadays represents the greatest danger to the survival of humanity.

The environment is one of the components of these conflicts and its preservation is constantly threatened, since, in order to meet the interests of the large corporations that benefit from and are the protagonists of the conflicts, it is necessary to make available mineral, vegetable, land, and river resources, promote deep and predatory changes in demography, expelling populations from certain territories, forcing them to seek precarious housing on the outskirts of large cities, which do not offer basic sanitation and allow irregular occupation of areas that should be preserved. The cause-and-effect relationship between climate change and the social and economic reality that we have discussed above is analyzed by Plowman, who informs that the increase in textile factories in Bangladesh is the result of floods in the plantations and soil degradation that led to the mass migration of peasants to Dhaka, where they found the only way to survive in submission to overexploitation in the textile industry.

Thus, it demonstrates the perfect conjugation between aggression against the environment and the emergence of new and more efficient forms of exploitation of workers, reconciling the predatory interests of agribusiness, mining, and lumber companies with the most modern forms of industry and commerce. The permission for predatory exploitation of natural and mineral wealth and the brutal concentration of profits from this exploitation has been one of the reasons for the overthrow of leftist political leaderships, or even minimally nationalist political leaderships, that in their programs sought the defense, even if incipient, of the mineral wealth of their nations.

Today, once again, Brazil is an example of submission to the large international capital that predates the environment, as it has become a protagonist in the escalating destruction of the planet in favor of these interests. With the explicit support of the federal government, even altering legislation and prevaricating by not complying with the legislation in force, the most diverse groups have greedily set out in search of the riches that the Brazilian soil and subsoil offer, promoting unprecedented destruction. Organized crime, be it the classic traffickers and smugglers or the self-styled militias, who pose as loggers and miners, invade preservation areas, attack indigenous, quilombola, and riverbank communities, poison the waters with mercury, cut down hundred-year-old trees, set fire to the forest, expel the local population, or subject them to labor analogous to slavery.

Widely covered by the media, the fires of 2020 and 2021 in the Amazon and Pantanal regions, and the illegal mining in several rivers of the northern region, represent environmental tragedies resulting from the pro-business policy implemented by a government that serves their interests, to the detriment of the Nation and its people. The result, on a global level, are the violent climate changes that make us face devastating droughts, temperatures never before experienced, hurricanes, and tsunamis, signs of a serious environmental imbalance that threatens humanity and, once again, victimizes the poor and the miserable, who are often coerced into inserting themselves in a subordinate manner to the projects of global capitalism.

What are the distributional consequences, including from an intersectional point of view?

In order to discuss how environmental aggressions and productive transformations reverberate, from an intersectional point of view, interstate disputes, it is necessary to consider the history and demographic composition of the nations of the global south. Colonialism and slavery left traces in these countries that have not been overcome (on the contrary, they have been perpetuated) with the transition from slave or forced labor to wage labor, with the substitution of archaic forms of obtaining wealth and the overcoming of colonialism by European and American imperialisms. Indigenous and black youth are the social segment that suffers most from the perennial violence of the states on the periphery of capitalism, which seek to perpetuate the privileges of the white minority. Pushed into alternative forms of survival, some of them illicit, these youth are persecuted by the State for trying to survive in an informal manner, regardless of whether they practice illegal acts or not.

Brazil, which – due to its geographic and population dimensions, history and economic importance – can be presented as one of the great examples of how non-white youth are treated, both in central countries and in nations on the periphery of capitalism, where necropolitics reigns supreme. According to the Anuário Brasileiro de Segurança Pública 2018, published by the Brazilian Public Security Forum, for every four people murdered by the police in Brazil, three were black, and in the year 2016 we had 65,517 homicides, with a rate of 30.3 deaths per 100,000 inhabitants, 30 times higher than that seen in Europe. From

2005 to 2015, the number of blacks murdered grew by 18.2% and the number of non-blacks fell by 12.2%. The Portrait of Gender and Race Inequalities (2017), produced by IPEA in partnership with UN Women and the results of the 2017 Map of Violence report that the mortality of non-black women had a reduction of 7.4% between 2005 and 2015, reaching 3.1 deaths per 100,000.

In contrast, the mortality of black women had an increase of 22% in the same period, reaching the rate of 5.2 deaths per 100 thousand, representing 65.3% of murdered women in Brazil. With regard to the prison situation, 37,380 women were imprisoned between 2006 and 2014. In this period the female population in prisons increased by 567%, while the average increase in the male population was 220%. Fifty percent of incarcerated women are between the ages of 18 and 29, and 67% are black. Twenty-six percent of the male prison population is incarcerated for trafficking, while among women, 62% are incarcerated for this type of crime. The National Survey of Penitentiary Information (INFOPEN), of 2016 reports that Brazil has the third largest prison population in the world, adding 726,712 people, 64% black and 55% young. According to that map, in the early 1980s, the peak of the homicide rate was at age 25, currently this rate is around 21. According to data from the Ministry of Health, between 2005 and 2015, there was a 17.2% increase in the homicide rate of individuals between the ages of 15 and 29. In other words, incarceration remains black and young, it is becoming feminized, and people are being killed younger and younger.

The true genocide to which non-white youth are subjected in Brazil, the ultimate example of this discriminatory violence, is not the most lethal form of oppression that befalls this population segment. The economic and social marginalization to which the entire black and indigenous population has been subjected throughout the history of colonized nations is the main factor responsible for their physical elimination. According to the National Household Sample Survey (PNAD-IBGE), the third quarter of 2018 recorded that the unemployment rate among brown people was 13.8%, among black people 14.6%, and among white people 9.9%.

In research focused on the following quarter, it was found that people who declared themselves white had an average monthly income of R$5,416 while brown people reached R$2,467, and black people R$1,746. In 2015, the total female unemployment rate was 11.6% and the male rate was 7.8%. The rate for black men was 8.5% and for black women, 13.3%. If affirmative policies are maintained at the pace achieved before the 2016 coup, Brazil would need 70 years to achieve economic and social equality between blacks and whites. The forecast for the achievement of gender equality, which would be reached in 99 years, was changed to almost 136 years, as a result of the end of affirmative policies, aggravated by the effects of the pandemic.

The social exclusion and the miserable condition of the poor population in general, composed of a majority of blacks, has increased significantly with the growth of unemployment, underemployment, and the dismantling of social protection programs since the coup d'état of 2016. One of the most dramatic indicators is the increase in the number of homeless people. According to an article published by Yahoo Notícias, on September 15, 2019, the National Movement of the Homeless Population (MNPR) denounced that between mid-2016 and September 2019, about 40,000 people lived on the streets of the city of São Paulo, more than double the number recorded by the Economic Research Foundation (FIPE) in 2015, which reported there were 15,905 people living in these conditions.

Based on Mbembe's (2016) elaboration, we can infer that, for capitalism in its current stage, a significant part of the reserve army of labor is dispensable, and it is necessary that it perishes for the model to be successful. If once it was part of the logic of capitalism to keep a large group of people at the margins of the system, today it is in the nature of capitalism to kill off part of this group, which has grown vertiginously as a result of the concentration of income and technological advances. They are the "leftovers", for whom there is no work or access to the consumer market, who only "hinder" the system and can no longer be served by the compensatory policies foreseen in the original neoliberalism. In times of financialization, today's "hard" neoliberalism needs to practice necroeconomics. If, as Lenin affirmed in 1917 imperialism is the top stage of capitalism, the politics of death means the maximization of the kind of society that this globalist capitalism has forged.

Evidently, death is selective, and those who must perish are the undesirables, the non-consumers, the non-acculturated, the "inferiors". In the crisis of the new coronavirus, the street demonstrations by businessmen and members of the upper middle class (whites, in totality) defending that their employees (blacks and indigenous, in majority) go back to work – facing the certain contamination in a public transportation where it is impossible to maintain social distance – represent the visible part of necropolitics/necroeconomics. Consciously or unconsciously, those individuals are the vanguard in the radical application of the economics and politics of death. They thus allow the real operators of such orientations to remain in the background, comfortable in their learned, hygienic, and polished peroration, masking the genocidal character of the system. The caricatured protesters against the social distancing measures, with their insane conspiracy theories, bad language, denialism, and attacks on democratic institutions, are not substantially different from the balanced and rational business and political leaders who advocated a return to work at the peak of the pandemic.

These two groups have in common the certainty that the death of the producers of (their) wealth should be naturalized. They are convinced that they are disposable individuals, easily replaceable by some other desperate unemployed, willing to submit themselves to precarious working conditions, without rights and at risk of contracting this or another disease. The pandemic, therefore, maximizes the secular tragedy of the excluded, as well as makes crystal clear the behavior of the elites, benefited by this tragedy, which is not only a result of the coronavirus pandemic. It is historical, perennial, and decreases or increases depending on the economic reality and on how the State is managed.

of organized civil society, especially the legitimate representatives of those most vulnerable: unions, social movements of black, indigenous, and women, neighborhood organizations, religious communities, and youth groups of culture and leisure in the peripheries. Once the tragedy is over, the political groups that take over the State will only succeed in rebuilding the nations if they consider the uniqueness of their demographic picture. Therefore, any economic and social intervention aimed at development must necessarily focus on the age-old inequalities of income, gender, and race, which have deepened as a result of the economic choices of recent years and the way the pandemic was fought by these states. It will require the deepening and broadening of several policies, as well as the implementation of new and bold programs to reduce historic social and racial inequality.

Because of its size, population size, history, economic importance, and the levels reached by the pandemic, Brazil can once again be presented as a great example. Even with the reduction of asymmetries resulting from public policies implemented in this country since 2003, gender inequalities add to racial inequalities, perpetuating black women at the bottom of the social pyramid, a result of the end of affirmative policies, aggravated by the effects of the pandemic. Thus, the relief of asymmetries, more than in any other period, depends on popular solutions by the State, which will only succeed with broad social participation through organizations representing segments whose historical marginalization was aggravated by the pandemic and by the concentration of income that occurred in the period and by the dismantling of policies to promote equality and reduce inequalities.

The resumption of policies to promote racial, gender, and generational equality needs to be the structuring axis for the development of cross-cutting policies, spearheaded by all areas of the Executive, with support from the Judiciary, the Legislature, and the involvement of organized civil society, especially popular organization entities. However, beyond the political decision, a "road map" must be followed, with decisions that materialize the implementation of such policies in a concrete and objective way. The starting point is the availability of resources, since public policies cannot be made without the allocation of considerable amounts of money. Therefore, the legal and bureaucratic obstacles resulting from the imposition of neoliberal rules, which advocate the reduction of the State, need to be removed. It is fundamental to democratize and open the state apparatus to the participation of organized civil society, with priority to popular organizations, and it is also necessary to reinvent this participation by opening up space for social organizations of traditional peoples and historically discriminated ethnic groups, of women, and of youth.

In every country on the planet, women remain the main victims of inequalities, whether from an economic point of view, or due to discrimination that impedes their access to decision-making and power, or due to systemic violence. In the countries of the global south this condition is aggravated by poverty and by societies that have developed based on patriarchalism. Gender issues, therefore, are a problem of societies as a whole. Thus, policies that aim to correct gender inequalities and discrimination need to be at the center of the debates, of the popular demands led by feminist movements, and of state initiatives.

It is necessary to overcome the idea that health is a commodity, the damage caused to human beings by its commercialization was more than evident during the pandemic, a period in which the big laboratories got rich in a scandalous way and millions of people died because their countries could not compete in the true auction promoted by these laboratories, making the vaccine a privilege of the rich countries. Moreover, the privatization of most health systems even in rich countries and the high costs of medicines, have made health an expensive and restricted commodity. It is necessary to invest in the creation of state and universal health systems, along the lines of the Brazilian SUS, which, despite the disinvestment and continued attacks by the current government, is still one of the most efficient in the world. Drug addiction, as well as alcoholism and smoking, which affect a significant part of the youth, also need to be considered public health problems, with the decriminalization of drugs and the creation of physical, psychological, and harm reduction programs resulting from the abuse of licit and illicit drugs. It is also necessary that, in health promotion, the ancestral knowledge of the original and diasporic peoples be taken into consideration, understanding the singularities of the health of women, youth, the elderly, and the diverse ethnic groups with their acquired or hereditary physical characteristics.

The rise of the extreme right in the world had as one of its most important instruments Christian fundamentalism, which uses religious racism to persecute vulnerable groups, exacerbate historical prejudices, and try to impose a unilateral world view. Besides this, neo-Pentecostalism has given rise to business-churches, owners of radio and television channels that disseminate the "prosperity theology", distorting the humanitarian character of Christianity, which, although it disseminates patriarchalism, originally preaches peace, detachment from material goods, and universal brotherhood. These businessmen, many of them with strong connections to organized crime and the misappropriation of public funds, have conquered great political power and put forward reactionary demands, defend their financial interests and ally themselves with the extreme right, threatening the secular state. Donald Trump in the United States, Bolsonaro in Brazil, and the coup plotters in Bolivia are among the most visible cases of the dangerous union between fundamentalism and anti-democratic political proposals, and demonstrate the necessity and urgency of defending the secularity of the State. It is essential to conduct institutional campaigns against religious racism and to punish the media that promotes hatred towards other religious confessions, as well as to legitimize the priests and priestesses of the traditional religions of colonized and enslaved peoples and promote their legal recognition, so that they can have dialogue with the State on the same level as other religious leaders.

Black and indigenous youth are not a problem, they are the solution for the development of nations that experienced colonization and slavery. This part of the population has been the main victim of persecution by the states, of generational prejudice, of structural violence, of institutional and systemic racism, in poor countries and also in the United States and European countries, where xenophobia and anti-immigration have become flags of the extreme right. The killing of youth by the forces of repression, the hyper-incarceration, the lack of opportunities for work and education, and the capture by organized crime have taken the lives of millions of young people who could be producing material and intellectual wealth, both in the central and peripheral nations. Besides this waste, the way in which these youth are treated compromises the future of these nations, because it is creating a legion of workers on the margins of the system, with low intellectual formation, without professional qualifications, unmotivated for the exercise of citizenship, and discouraged.

They are, therefore, potential active or passive sociopaths, incapable of contributing to the maintenance of society, let alone of organizing themselves to make it more just. Besides compromising the future of the country itself and increasing the economic and social vulnerability of their families, the treatment given to youth by the states generates costs to human integrity and dignity, as it triggers a succession of tragedies. Older women, who for historical and cultural reasons are usually the epicenter of those families, even if not directly involved in the violence or loss of freedom, are affected emotionally and acquire or have aggravated physical and mental illnesses. Younger women are condemned to raise children alone who, due to the same lack of opportunities as their fathers and mothers, will follow similar paths, demonstrating that systemic violence against non-white youth extends to their entire family, passes from one generation to the next, and will be perpetuated if there is no change in the orientation of the State.

Final considerations

In a new post-pandemic order and after the reactionary wave is over, the states and organized civil society need to address the impacts of productive transformations on non-white youth, considering the effects of environmental degradation on the world of work and the quality of life of the poorest. The asymmetries of the global south will only be overcome if there is priority for this segment of the population that is especially vulnerable, but also owner of an extraordinary potential for generating intellectual and material wealth. In this sense, one of the paths to be taken would be the establishment of large national pacts in defense of young people, aiming to promote their economic and social inclusion, with the participation of the Executive, Legislative, and Judiciary branches, of the Public Ministry, and of the organized civil society, especially the popular organizations and the representatives of black, indigenous, and peripheral young people. The starting point would be the elaboration of projects on de-imprisonment, drug decriminalization, and reduction of police lethality.

This pact however cannot be only reactive nor reduced to defensive actions. It needs to be offensive, attacking the causes from two major axes: work and education. For this, it is necessary to have a vigorous state investment aiming at the generation of well-paid and quality jobs through a large public works project, necessary and urgent in any of the countries in the periphery of capitalism, absorbing and, at the same time, training and qualifying this labor force. The educational system also needs to be universalized and its great capillarity used to offer free and quality education, also promoting the active search for those who have dropped out or are not enrolled at school age.

The concession of scholarships in amounts that guarantee survival, disputing these young people with the precarious labor market and organized crime, should be one of the bases of a project of this nature. The school environment would also need to become the epicenter of cultural, sports, environmental, and sociability projects, opening itself to cultural and leisure manifestations, contemplating, in fact, the proclaimed juvenile protagonism, defended but not practiced by many educators. The unfolding of this pact and its concretion need to happen from those two great axes, materialized in governmental programs and public policies. This pact in defense of non-white and peripheral youth may represent a path to overcome the serious inequalities in the countries of the global south, to save the lives of millions of young people and transform them into central elements in the (re)construction of countries whose wealth will benefit their own population, with greater social justice and equality of gender and race, therefore more democratic and with happier populations.

References

Jacino, Ramatis. *O Branqueamento do Trabalho*. São Paulo: Nefertiti, 2008.
Mbembe, Achille. Necropolítica. *Revista da UFRJ*, n. 32, 2016. https://revistas.ufrj.br/index.php/ae/article/view/8993/7169. Access em 07/04/2021
Saffioti, Heleieth Iara Bongiovani. *A mulher na sociedade de classe: mito e realidade*. São Paulo: Vozes, 1976.

FINAL REMARKS

Cristina Fróes de Borja Reis, Tatiana Berringer and Rodolfo Aguiar

After what seemed to be an unprecedented time of uncertainty due to the pandemic of Covid-19, we now have more convictions – and renewed doubts – about this emerging reality of the present moment. To accomplish the dialogues on Development, Democracy, and Sustainability, as well as to provide material for those who are looking for alternatives and new paths to achieve a critical understanding of the global transformation in motion – reasoned from a truly interdisciplinary and non-Eurocentric perspective – this is a remarkable step in a shared journey. One might claim this is an overstatement, but we hope we can clarify the relevance of the work provided by the authors in this book.

In the introduction, we said that the book had two primary aims. First, to better understand democracy, development, and sustainability interconnections, critically assessing the Agenda 2030. Second, to propose a methodological contribution for the research on International Political Economy (IPE) evolving towards a World Political Economy (WPE), grounded in plural perspectives from different approaches and disciplines, perspectives from different approaches and disciplines.

Regarding the first objective, our conceptualization of democracy, development, and sustainability adopts a balanced perspective, which does not dismiss the SDGs, but does not shy away from pointing out that in the normalization of the discourse on development and sustainability, there are structural aspects lost or minimized. From a critical perspective, development is a process of structural and institutional changes related to performing economic activities and tasks of value chains that enhance employment and income levels and qualities, reducing functional, intersectional, and personal inequalities while allowing for living standards in accordance with people's cultural values and environmental preservation. In opposition, the SDGs do not tackle the roots and the dynamics of inequalities besides disregarding idiosyncrasies of each country's development

DOI: 10.4324/9781003384366-13

path (Lubbock, 2018). We recognize that the 2030 Agenda is a remarkable and necessary advance in how environment, inequality, and several issues are dealt with in international governance. Nevertheless, it is an insufficient advance, full of limitations. In this sense, our ambition was to improve the knowledge available for reaching SDGs, both to the scientific world and the decision-makers, about sustainable and inclusive development.

As discussed in Chapters 5 and 6, the first studies on developmentalism and neocolonialism emerged in Latin America and Africa during the post-war period as a counterpoint to the modern mainstream thoughts (Reis, Barbosa and Cardoso, 2019). The development agenda was embedded in the UN's regional branches, such as ECLAC, and in some influential research groups from universities in Latin America, Africa, and Asia. Its key concern was how to promote industrialization, but soon many streams of thought, from more conservative to radical ones, started criticizing its impacts on nature and its capacity to reduce inequalities. Alias, in these regions, the State development policies rarely were based on sustainable and democratic mechanisms. After a couple of decades, with very few exceptions, such as Japan, China, and the Asian tigers (Wade, 1993), the uneven industrialization processes could reduce the technological and financial differences between the center and periphery.

However, when international structural crises led to a strong balance of payments constraints and or to other macroeconomic vulnerabilities, as well as to further political and social degradation in the Global South, they intensified internal and external distributive struggles that put the associated dependency models (Cardoso and Faletto, 1981) in check. In these cases, as Furtado (2004) has affirmed, more democratization was urged via structural reforms such as agrarian, educational, administrative, urban, etc. However, the elites are so conservative that they have been interrupting these movements with military dictatorships or other authoritarian political regimes.

The faster and deeper financial and productive internationalization during neoliberalism after the 80s, structured by the US economic and political-ideological domain (Panitch and Gindin, 2012), as explained in Chapter 2, increased the centralization and concentration of technology innovation and capital accumulation in the richest states and TNCs of the world-system. During the neoliberal phase, the dependent relationships between center and periphery assumed a new status, called by Fiori (1995), Amin (2002) and Saes (2007) as "extremely new dependence". Then and there, the financialization processes underpinning the material structure of social, economic, and political reproduction in neoliberalism (Fine and Saad-Filho, 2016) drove the deindustrialization and denationalization of the South economies, resulting in unemployment and poverty.

Additionally, the attacks against the unions and labor rights and the privatization of public services increased the social inequalities. Meanwhile, the neo-extractivism was revamped, furthering environmental degradation. Both in the metropolitan cities and rural areas, social clashes, violence, hunger, and misery increased and even accelerated with Covid-19. All these losses and setbacks once more evidence how development, democracy, and sustainability are inseparable triads of the same process of capital accumulation and inter-state disputes.

According to O'Donnell (2010), the ideal of democracy promoted by the countries of the Global North has severe limitations when we look at the different realities and complexities in the South. There would not be a simple evolutionary process of civil, political, and social rights as formulated by classical thinkers. Contemporary democracy would be an institutionalized, universalist, and inclusive bet. Thus, in addition to thinking about universal suffrage and electoral competition, it is necessary to build a public space in which the citizen is not just a bearer of rights but has a legal personality. In this sense, the citizen is the agent whose power of action is the transformation. This transformation has a dialogical sense of change. It faces the contradictions generated by capitalism, especially the dependent capitalism. This includes cultural and national differences, constitutions of plurinational states, and the advancement of public policies and rights globally.

In our view, dependencies link the international arena, the domestic structure (social and economic spheres), and the political and ideological insertion of a peripheral state. In this vein, inequalities refer not just to distributive conflicts between classes but to the intersectional conflicts between class, gender, and race spheres – as in the Brazilian case shown by Jacinto in Chapter 11. In neoliberal and authoritarian times, those conflicts are increasingly shaped by internet networks and social media. As both are structuring the new phase of world politics, the left-wing and progressive social movements have to improve their analyses of this topic and present alternatives, such as done by Penteado and Campos-Dominguez in Chapter 3 and by Saad and Berringer in Chapter 2.

In parallel, global warming became the hottest research field in global studies. Covid-19 crises reinforced the urgent need for sustainability actions as another imbalance in nature provoked during the Anthropocene or Capitalocene. As argued in Chapter 8, it is better seriously look at the environmental crisis in the world system rather than only talk about climate change. That includes several complex impacts of the new international division of labor imposed by the financialization, such as the urbanization discussed in Chapter 4, the agri-food systems in Chapter 9, and the water and sanitation issues in Chapter 10. That is why it became inexorable to rethink the idea of development based on the intertwining of democracy, development, and sustainability.

It means not just to stop the environmental crisis, but to preserve native peoples' traditions and cultures and guarantee common goods and collective and popular-formulated policies. The definitions of rights and duties impacting power and wealth distribution have been crucial for the South people. Then, the idea of looking into the economics of care, including not just to rethink the women's reproductive function, but also their structural relationships with land and water, technological and financial resources, that define productive and trade patterns so much that nowadays international investment agreements consider gender issues in their negotiations.

Sustainable development is usually assumed in line with the Brundtland (1987) definition that addresses the needs of the present without compromising the ability of future generations to address their own needs, while affirming that this is a new era of vigorous growth that is both socially and environmentally sustainable. In fact, this mainstream definition does not include several aspects relevant to challenging social and environmental inequalities. The basic to assume is that sustainability is a process that provides orientation through a holistic vision relating three dimensions: ecological, economic, and social justice (Grober, 2015).

Therefore, the concept of environmental justice discussed by Heynen and Travassos in Chapter 4 is more than welcome. It articulates democracy, development, and sustainability through many other relevant issues that are dear to South cultures, such as transition, ecology and *buen vivir.* Environmental justice requires energy and technological transition patterns, new agricultural and food systems, mobility, and transport new infrastructure for smart-cities that carefully consider the relationships among urban and rural areas of developing countries – what is much more complex than the sustainability dimensions of the Agenda 2030.

Moreover, though public policies for renewable and clean energy such as solar, wind, or water-based energy sources are extremely important, we cannot be so naïve when looking at the geopolitical dimensions of WPE. As underlined in Chapter 1 (and can be exemplified by the war in Ukraine), military and inter-state disputes are still based on the geopolitics of oil and gas, even if the actual greatest powers USA and China are heavily investing in innovation to boost carbon-free economies along the next three decades.

According to Fraser and Jaeggi (2020), there is a paradox in center-periphery relations: on the one hand, the Global North aspires to a post-material world but remains dependent on energy from coal, oil, and gas; on the other hand, the Global South experiences a process of despoliation of its natural resources such as ore, oil, and export-oriented agriculture. Thus, the environmental movements are divided between the defenders of "green capitalism" in one side and "environmental justice" in the other side, which was internationalized from in the Global South after improving its networks and political and financial external support (Fraser and Jaeggi, 2020, p. 120). The international agreements regarding the carbon emission neutralization goal in the Agenda 2030, for example, must be accompanied by funding for technological access, implementation, and monitoring mechanisms. Right now, the SDG could represent more a new market share than a shared responsibility to the world, as discussed in Chapters 1, 4, and 6.

So, the non-exhaustive examples of interconnections between democracy, development, and sustainability presented in this book demonstrate once again the importance of strengthening popular forces in the South in order to alleviate inequalities. In opposition, the SDGs are not integrated into a common and robust political and economic approach, besides several implementation difficulties. Thus, we propose to move forward by working with democracy, development, and sustainability goals in the same analytical unit capable of better explaining and proposing solutions to global challenges.

In this sense, regarding the second proposition, we believe that the chapters of this book gave us several relevant elements for preparing a research agenda of WPE in the 21st century. Let's appoint the fundamental epistemological boundaries of this agenda: (i) imperialism, dependence, class/race and gender struggles, and environment linkages; (ii) leveraging South studies; and (iii) interdisciplinary approach (through economics, sociology, philosophy, politics, ecology, and even natural sciences).

Regarding the first boundary (i), through all the chapters of this book, it was possible to assimilate the crossing between those subjects and challenges to comprehend contemporary interrelated *problématiques*, avoiding out-of-context and superficial interpretations. For example, Marxist thought has pointed to the theory of imperialism and colonialism through dependents and colonial social formations that would only see resoluteness as Russian and China revolutions and the national liberation movements have risen in Central América, Africa, and Asia. Nowadays, as emphasized by Schutte and Prashad in Chapter 1, imperialism studies bring analyses about economics, society, politics, and culture trying to get a proper investigation of its dynamics to understand unipolarity and multipolarity in the current global transformation. Regarding the idea of the inter-states rivalries as a starting point, the question about China imperialism or the hegemony transition is the central point for these studies, and for the political strategies in the whole world.

Besides, contemporary analysis regarding dependence issues should not only focus on the economic arena, as it doesn't mean only a matter of super-exploitation of labor (Marini, 1973; Smith, 2016). It is not only caused by external elements, but it is also the link between local fractions, foreign capital, and imperialist interests (Cardoso and Faletto, 1977) – which nowadays are facing new contexts of political subordination and domination. In this sense, instead of the thesis that sustained the end or the transformation of the national-States, let's investigate the role and the characteristics of the Dependent States. How does it work to reproduce the new forms of dependency (Granato, 2021; Souza, 2021).

Dependence is divided in phases as imperialism and affects the states with new forms of privatization, devastation, and financialization. As Amin [2010] stated, there are new forms of dependence, and now we are facing Dependence 4.0 (Paulani, 2021). Many efforts have also been made to comprehend environmental imbalances and inequalities as historical problems derived. However, as discussed by Reis and Kvangraven in this book, to properly answer the challenge of bringing in intersectional inequalities into the theory – as within the dependency theory – we shall need to do more than just incorporate as it is necessary to conceive an epistemological standpoint. From this perspective, how should we begin this process of renewed epistemological configuration?

Resorting to the shaping process of thinking in South studies seems like a reasonable effort. That brings us to the second boundary (ii). The thesis of the shaping of peripheral rationality in the Global South amidst processes of invasion or colonization stands in the peripheral disjunctive, i.e., the intellectual dynamic that moves through the conundrum of "being like the core" versus "being like ourselves" (Devés-Valdés, 2008, 2012), and retracing the historicity of this formation enables an unprecedented improvement of our research programs. Fortunately, we can refer to significant contributions that already have explained how even the industrial civilization and its processes had been implemented in peripheral societies (Furtado, 1978).

To comprehend what happened with decolonial strategies of South Economies, as analyzed through comparison in African countries (Adedeji, 2010), is part of conforming a holistic perspective of the shaping of interrelation in contemporary processes, such as the new forms of dependence cited previously. One topic of concern is that eventually, leading proponents of the decolonial perspective do not expose an understanding of what or which is the power dynamics of contemporary capitalism (Fischer, 2015). That flaw can occur if we just do not consider historic contributions in our research fields that have already addressed these concerns in their times but now are misread or even put aside directly.

One could think at this point that we have already delimited sufficiently an epistemological scope for an agenda of WPE in the 21st century. However, if the endorsement of an interdisciplinary approach, our third boundary (iii), was in the past a major differential to provide answers for research questions – mainly in social sciences – now the concrete reality is one with tipping points on the upcoming prospects that bring the following question: What is the role of researchers in the scientific community is and in the whole society? This question acquires a crucial sense for our interest in conforming a research agenda for WPE, which is the need to make co-joint theoretical and empirical research.

Many studies and handbooks of the IPE from the Eurocentric tradition focused on the theoretical associations between transnational corporations and national states, particularly while analyzing US hegemony. Though these are also key matters for the WPE, it is important to define relevant research objects from the world periphery perspective. Then, making a critique of democracy, development, and sustainability, both theoretically and empirically, must be one of the main commitments of the research agenda of WPE. As argued by Cardoso and Alves in this book, to change the knowledge edification process through decolonizing foundational frameworks is a form to drive an alternative development process. An example is illustrated in a review of literature regarding unpaid work issues in macroeconomic analysis, which contains conclusions about the risk if policies do not to take account of the extensive load of unpaid work performed by woman: an adverse effect to the well-being of women and, consequently, to the whole community involved (Ilkkaracan, 2017). This is similarly remarked regarding when the effect of developing and democratizing new technological infrastructure away from neoliberal core ideas – privatization, rejection of social justice as a driver-mechanism, entrepreneurialism – could be helpful to edification of cities oriented through community interests (Morozov and Bria, 2018).

Regarding the arrangements in global subjects – fundamental to convene political delimitations and to determine distributions of knowledge outputs in scientific research – global governance was conceived in line with the idea of international regimes (Rosenau, 1992) but has been playing a role less centered in the State' dimension, which means a form of acting in many spheres in society based on ideas as deregulation through market-driven mechanisms and policies (Paterson, 2000). The standardization of technocratic frameworks expressed in this current notion of governance remains as an important barrier for establishing new paradigms capable of bringing conceptual diversity in process of interest, for example, as argued by Mello, Adamo and de Paula in this book and other authors that stands for taking account of the societal boundaries in world of climate crisis beyond the planetary boundaries (Brand *et al.*, 2021).

As this is not a trivial task, we should reflect from our research fields what does it mean to assimilate decoloniality, just to illustrate, as an epistemological injunction and a mark for allyship. As a good example, in reply to the argument that degrowth is a topic of concern of middle-class sectors in the Global North, it was argued that in fact, the concept is rooted in anti-colonial principles for recognizing that economic growth in the North relies on patterns of colonization through appropriation of Southern resources and labor (Hickel, 2021).

To wrap-up, we believe the agenda of WPE in the 21st century based on those three boundaries, and on theoretical and empirical commitments, might be also potent to explain the growing interconnections and contradictions arising between democracy, development, and sustainability in times of renewed dependence and imperialism's disputes between states, capitals, classes, and gender and race intersections.

References

Adedeji, Adebayo. Estratégias comparadas da descolonização econômica. *História geral da África, VIII: África desde 1935*. Brasília: UNESCO, pp. 471–516, 2010.

Amin, Samir. *Oltre il capilatismo senile*. Milão: Punto Rosso, 2002.

Amin, Samir. *Eurocentrism*. New York: Monthly Review Press, 2010.

Brand, Ulrich *et al.* From planetary to societal boundaries : an argument for collectively defined self-limitation. *Sustainability: Science, Practice and Policy*, v. 17, n. 1, p. 265–292, 2021. Disponível em: https://doi.org/10.1080/15487733.2021.1940754.

Brundtland Commission. *World commission on environment and development: Our common future*. Oxford: Oxford University Press, 1987.

Cardoso, Fernando H. & Faletto, Enzo. *Dependência e desenvolvimento na América Latina: Ensaio de interpretação sociológica*. Quarta Edição. Rio de Janeiro: Zahar Editores, 1977.
Cardoso, Fernando H. & Faletto, Enzo. *Dependência e desenvolvimento na América Latina: ensaio de interpretação sociológica*. 6ª edição. Rio de Janeiro: Zahar Editores, 1981.
Devés-Valdés, Eduardo. *O Pensamento Africano Subsaariano: Conexões e Paralelos com o Pensamento Latino-Americano e o Asiático (um Esquema)*. Rio de Janeiro: CLACSO/ EDUCAM, 2008.
Devés-Valdés, Eduardo. *Pensamiento Periférico: Una tesis interpretativa global*. Santiago: Ariadna Ediciones, 2012.
Fraser, Nancy & Jaeggi, Rahel. *Capitalismo em debate: uma conversa na teoria critica*. São Paulo: Editora Boitempo, 2020.
Fine, Ben & Saad-Filho, Alfredo. Thirteen things you need to know about neoliberalism. *Critical Sociology*, v. 43, n. 4–5, p. 685–706, 2016.
Fiori, José Luis. *A globalização e a novíssima dependência. Em busca do dissenso perdido: ensaios críticos sobre a festejada crítica do Estado*. Rio de Janeiro: Insight, 1995.
Fischer, Andrew M. The end of peripheries? On the enduring relevance of structuralism for understanding contemporary global development. *Development and Change*, v. 46, n. 4, p. 700–732, Jul. 2015.
Furtado, Celso. *Criatividade e dependência na civilização industrial*. Rio de Janeiro: Paz e Terra, 1978.
Furtado, Celso. Para onde caminhamos. *Jornal do Brasil*, v. 10, 2004.
Granato, Leonardo. *O Estado latino-americano: teoria e história*. São Paulo: Editora Expressão Popular, 2021.
Grober, Ulrich. The discovery of sustainability: the genealogy of a term. In: Enders, J. C. and Remig, M. (eds). *Theories of Sustainable Development*. New York: Routledge, pp. 6–15, 2014.
Hickel, Jason. The anti-colonial politics of degrowth. *Political Geography*, v. 88, p. 102404, Jun. 2021.
Ilkkaracan, İpek. Unpaid Work in Macroeconomics: A stocktaking exercise. In: Connely, Rachel & Kongar, Ebru (Org.). *Gender and time use in a global context*. New York: Palgrave Macmillan US, p. 29–50, 2017.
Lubbock, Rowan. Development and imperialism. In: Munck, Ronaldo & Fagan, Honor (eds.), *Handbook on development and social change* (p. 44–68), Massachusetts: Edward Elgar, 2018.
Marini, Ruy Mauro. *Dialética da Dependência*. Primeira edição: Ensaio datado de, 1973.
Morozov, Evgeny & BRIA, Francesca. Rethinking the smart city - Democratizing Urban technology. *Rosa Luxemburg Stiftung*, City Cities #5, 2018. https://www.rosalux.de/fileadmin/rls_uploads/pdfs/sonst_publikationen/rethinking_the_smart_city.pdf
O'Donnell, Guilhermo. *Democracia, agência e estado; teoria como invenção comparativa*. São Paulo: Paz e Terra, 2011.
Panitch, Leo & Gindin Sam. *The making of global capitalism: The political economy of American Empire*. London: Verso, 2012.
Paterson, Matthew. *Understanding global environmental politics: Domination, accumulation, resistance*. London: Macmillan Press LTD, 2000.
Paulani, Leda Maria. Dependency 4.0: Theoretical considerations and the Brazilian case. *Latin American Perspectives*, v. 42, n. 2, p. 24–38, 2021.
Reis, Cristina Fróes de Borja; Barbosa, Muryatan Santana & Cardoso, Fernanda Graziella. The South's thoughts on development: Links between Latin America and Africa. *Revista de Economía Mundial*, n. 52, p. 191–216, 2019.

Rosenau, James N. Governance, order, and change in world politics. In: Rosenau, James N., Czempiel, Ernst-Otto, & Smith, Steve (eds.), *Governance without Government: order and change in world politics.* Cambridge: Cambridge University Press, p. 1–29, 1992.

Saes, Décio. Modelos políticos latino-americanos na nova fase de dependência. In: Francis, Nogueira, & Rizzoto, Maria (eds.), Políticas sociais e desenvolvimento: América Latina e Brasil. 1ªedição. São Paulo: Editora Xamã, Vol 1, pp. 155–172, 2007.

Smith, John. *Imperialism in the twenty-first century: Globalization, super-exploitation, and capitalism's final crisis.* Reno: Grassroots Books, 2016.

Souza, Angelita Matos. *Dependência e governos do PT.* Curitiba: Editora Appris, 2021.

Wade, Robert. "The visible hand: The state and East Asia's economic growth." *Current History*, v. 92, no. 578, p. 431, 1993.

INDEX

For Product Safety Concerns and Information please contact our EU
representative GPSR@taylorandfrancis.com
Taylor & Francis Verlag GmbH, Kaufingerstraße 24, 80331 München, Germany

www.ingramcontent.com/pod-product-compliance
Ingram Content Group UK Ltd.
Pitfield, Milton Keynes, MK11 3LW, UK
UKHW020004200926
475702UK00015B/2462
9781032470436